International Law in Silver Perspective: Challenges Ahead

Nijhoff Law Specials

VOLUME 90

The titles published in this series are listed at *brill.com/nlsp*

International Law in Silver Perspective: Challenges Ahead

Edited by

Karel Wellens

BRILL
NIJHOFF

LEIDEN | BOSTON

Library of Congress Control Number: 2015949533

This publication has been typeset in the multilingual "Brill" typeface. With over 5,100 characters covering Latin, IPA, Greek, and Cyrillic, this typeface is especially suitable for use in the humanities.
For more information, please see www.brill.com/brill-typeface.

ISBN 978-90-04-27167-8 (paperback)
ISBN 978-90-04-27168-5 (e-book)

This book is printed on acid-free paper.

Contents

Preface

In the autumn of 2013, at breakfast on the morning after a valedictory conference, the idea was born to invite the slowly but steadily growing number of emeriti professors of international law – in Flanders and the Netherlands – to embark upon a joint endeavour and to have a closer look at (some) of the challenges international law will have to face in the years to come.

In my letter of invitation I mentioned that our lifetime dedication to public international law did not come to an abrupt end on the day of our retirement, quite to the contrary.

And yes indeed, soon after their initial enthusiastic response, quite a number of colleagues came to realize that they already seemed to have taken on too many other professional and/or research commitments.

Much to their regret other colleagues had to decline the invitation for reasons of a personal nature.

Hence the present volume, while maintaining the original concept, contains a more limited selection of essays than originally envisaged.

Being informed about the project, Alan Stephens, in his unrivalled creative spirit, provided us with an appropriate title for this volume: International Law in Silver Perspective.

We are grateful that Brill-Nijhoff kindly agreed to publish this volume.

This publication would not have been possible without the well-known continuous, wholehearted and professional support of Lindy Melman and her team.

I am of course more than grateful to my colleagues who have indeed identified and discussed challenges ahead in their favourite field of expertise.

Karel Wellens
25 May 2015

CHAPTER 1

International Law Mastering the Future: Global Governance Millennium Development Goal

*Paul de Waart**

1 International Law in Development

By comparison with the Encyclopedia of Public International Law (EPIL) published between 1991 and 2001 under the direction of Rudolf Bernhardt, the 2012 Max Planck Encyclopedia of Public International Law [hereinafter MPEPIL][1] under the direction of Rüdiger Wolfrum includes quite a number of new subjects, such as community interest, democracy, global administrative law, governance, responsibility to protect (r2p), rule of law and universality. Moreover, the number of entries on terrorism increased substantially.[2] In so doing, the MPEPIL shows convincingly the increasing significance of international law both at national and regional levels. It gives ample evidence of merging international law with international human rights law. This merger affects the principles the United Nations [hereinafter UN] and its members have to take into account, while acting in pursuit of the purposes of the Organization.[3]

The present chapter examines the relevance of international law for achieving the Millennium Development Goals (MDGs) in and beyond 2015. To that end it gives first of all a rough sketch of the present place of international law in the development agenda in respect of managing the

---

* Emeritus Professor of International Law, VU University of Amsterdam.

1 RÚDIGER WOLFRUM (ed.), The Max Planck Encyclopedia of Public International Law (2012) [hereinafter MPEPIL]. The Encyclopedia appeared in print and online. The tenfold printed version of roughly 1100 pages each contains around 1700 essays of over 800 authors from more than 80 countries. Illustrative for its extent is the additional Index and Tables Volume of over 1100 pages.

2 The half of MPEPIL's size four-part EPIL contains 1300 essays of roughly 450 authors from 35 countries. The additional Lists-Indices Volume runs to 275 pages.

3 U.N. Charter, Article 2; BRUNO SIMMA ET AL., THE CHARTER OF THE UNITED NATIONS: A COMMENTARY 123 paras. 4 and 5 (3d ed. 2012) [hereinafter SIMMA].

Karel Wellens (ed.), International Law in Silver Perspective: Challenges Ahead.
 ISBN 978-90-04-27167-8. pp. 1-30.

unpredictable and mastering the probable, both in a general way and as emerging international law of sustainable development. The latter provokes questions as to the reality of international law.

2 International Law in the Development Agenda

By analogy with a 1979 study of the Organisation for Economic Co-Operation and Development (OECD), the present paragraph focusses on managing the unpredictable of future international law and on its mastering the probable through computing development and the identification of MDGs. In that context the emergence of international development law as a regime or school of thought will be discussed. In doing so, fragmentation of international law and its impact on the global legal system pass in review, albeit in a bird's-eye view.

2.1 *Managing the Unpredictable*

America's then President Franklin D. Roosevelt excited the world in 1941 with his Four Freedoms[4] as "a definitive basis for a kind of world attainable in our own time and generation".[5] The present international community faces, more than ever before, the challenge to adapt international law in such a way that the global market as self-regulated system secures freedom from want everywhere in the world as a condition for the realisation of the remaining three essential freedoms. This challenge was already implicit in the 1960 U.N. Declaration on the Granting of Independence to Colonial Countries and Peoples[6] and explicit in the 1974 Declaration on the Establishment of a New International Economic

---

4 State of the Union to the U.S. Congress of January 6, 1941. The four freedoms of every person everywhere are the freedom of speech and expression; the freedom to worship God in his own way; the freedom from want; and the freedom from fear.

5 WILLEM VAN GENUGTEN ET AL., THE UNITED NATIONS OF THE Future: Globalization with a Human Face 23-24 (2006).

6 G.A. Res. 1514 (XV) of December 14, 1960.

Order [hereinafter NIEO Declaration][7] and the Charter of Economic Rights and Duties of States [hereinafter CERDS].[8]

The NIEO-controversy and the 1972 report of the Club of Rome[9] *The Limits to Growth* induced OECD to start in 1976 a three-year research-project, referred to as INTERFUTURES. Its report *Facing the Future: Mastering the Probable and Managing the Unpredictable* analysed prospects, constraints and issues in the longer-term perspective in respect of, amongst others, possible physical limits to growth related to energy, raw materials or the environment on future development.[10] The prospective analysis concluded that the following might occur beyond the year 2000: breakdowns in energy supplies, socio-political instability in the Third World, a decline of democracy or weakening of the State in the developed countries and a spreading of protectionism.[11] At present, one can only be impressed by this masterly example of facing the future by managing the unpredictable and mastering the probable.

2.2 *Mastering the Probable*

After the examples of the Club of Rome and the OECD, international organizations started to compute development and that on an annual basis. The World Bank submitted in 1978 its first World Development Report [hereinafter WDR] to help clarify prospects for accelerating growth and alleviating poverty.[12] The U.N. Conference on Trade and Development (UNCTAD) submitted in 1981 to that end its first Trade and Development Report. As lost decade for development, the 1980s brought no

---

7 G.A. Res. 3201 (S-VI) and 3202 (S-VI) of May 1, 1974; GIORGIO SACERDOTI, *New International Economic Order (NIEO)* in MPEPIL Volume VII 661-662 paras. 11-14 and 666, para. 32.

8 G.A. Res 3281 (XXIX) of December 12, 1974, adopted by 120 votes in favour, 6 against (Belgium, Denmark, the Federal Republic of Germany, Luxemburg, the United Kingdom and the US) and 10 abstentions (Austria, Canada, France, Ireland, Israel, Italy, Japan, the Netherlands, Norway, Sweden and Turkey); KRISTEN BOON, *Charter of Economic Rights and Duties of States (1974)* in MPEPIL Volume II 89 paras. 12-14.

9 The Club of Rome is an informal association of independent leading personalities from politics, business and science. See www.clubofrome.org/?p=324.

10 OECD iv, 2, 9 and 409 (1979), available at www.oecd.org/futures/35393713.pdf.

11 *Id.* at 397-398.

12 WDR 1978, PROSPECTS FOR GROWTH AND ALLEVIATING POVERTY, Chapter 1, Introduction, available at www.wdronline.worldbank.org/worldbank/a/c.html/world_development_report_1978/.

initiatives of other international organizations as to that.[13] The fall of the Berlin Wall in November 1989 got things going again. The U.N. Development Programme (UNDP) launched in 1990 its first Human Development Report [hereinafter HDR]. In those days the focus was on reducing the number of people in (extreme) poverty as the central objective of development strategies in the 1990s by 2000.[14] Despite the progress made, this is still the prime MDG until this very day.[15] These and other efforts to compute development were not clearly invoked in the speculation of heads of State and Government on the twenty-first century at the dawn of the new millennium.

The U.N. Millennium Declaration was in essence a political statement in respect of shared responsibility for managing word-wide economic and social development.[16] The same applies to the Outcome of the World Summit, convened in 2005 in order to remove doubts that the outbreak of the 'War on Terror' on September 11, 2001 had pushed the Millennium Declaration into the background. The Millennium Declaration limited the role of international law to the peaceful settlement of disputes and the strengthening of the UN. Moreover, it left aside whether international law includes human rights law.[17] The World Summit Outcome was more explicit, albeit specifically in respect of the fight against terrorism as a new MDG. States ensured that "any measures taken to combat terrorism comply with their obligation under international law, particularly human rights law, refugee law and international humanitarian law."[18]

Otherwise, both documents did not identify international law as a key objective to be translated into action with regard to achieving development and poverty eradication. The pertinent provisions of the Millennium Declaration did not consider the realization of its aims as an obligation under international law and human rights law.[19] The same holds true for the 2005 World Summit Outcome. It underscored the shared responsibility and interest of heads of State and Government to provide

13 WDR 1990, POVERTY 7.

14 HDR 1990 61, available at www.hdr.undp.org/sites/default/files/reports/219/hdr1990en.

15 HDR 2013 THE RISE OF THE SOUTH: HUMAN PROGRESS IN A DIVERSE WORLD iv, 28, available at www.hdr.undp.org/en/2013-report.

16 A/RES/55/2 of September 18, 2000 para. 6; Gunter Pleuger, *United Nations, Millennium Declaration*, in MPEPIL X 400 para. 4.

17 A/RES/55/2 paras. 4 and 30.

18 A/RES/60/1 para. 85.

19 A/RES/55/2 Chapter III *Development and poverty eradication.*

multilateral solutions to the problem-areas, identified in the Millennium Declaration: development, peace and collective security, human rights and the rule of law and strengthening of the UN.[20] However, the 17 pages dealing with development include only one reference to international law[21] and one to international human rights law.[22] Small wonder that the elaboration of the key objectives into MDGs by international organizations (IGOs) did not differ substantially in that respect. UNDP, World Bank, the OECD and other IGOs specified the eight MDGs[23] by subdividing them into 18 targets and by developing 48 indicators for assessing the progress[24] without a single reference to international law. The latter absence has given rise to an intense and profound discussion on the normative and practical relationship between MDGs and human rights and their impact on a post-2015 development agenda.

The conclusion of a recent extensive study of many authors – scholars and practitioners from the fields of economics, law, politics, medicine and architecture – is that the place of human rights should be more central in the current and future development agenda, but with widely varying views on what exactly that means: priority to the MDGs, priority to human rights, or align the two on equal footing.[25] It is striking that the study does not examine the integration of international law, international human rights law and international humanitarian law. For the fragmentation of international law impedes the realization of community interest such as the protection and creation of common goods and

20 A/RES/60/1 paras. 15 and 16.

21 *Id.* para. 56 (o) concerning the freedom of the navigation and the cessation of the transport of radioactive materials through the regions of small island developing States.

22 *Id.* para. 58 (f) concerning the protection of civilians during and after armed conflict.

23 www.undp.org/content/undp/en/home/mdgoverview/. The eight MDGs are: Eradication of extreme poverty and hunger; achievement of universal primary education; promotion of gender equality and empowerment of women; reduction of child mortality; improvement of maternity health; combatting of HIV/aids and other diseases; ensuring environmental sustainability; and development of a global partnership for development.

24 Pleuger, *supra* note 16, at 400-401 para. 6.

25 Malcolm Langford et al. *Back to the Future: Reconciling Paradigms or Development as Usual?* in THE MILLENNIUM DEVELOPMENT GOALS AND HUMAN RIGHTS: PAST, PRESENT AND FUTURE 545, 552-556. (Malcom Langform et al. eds., 2013).

common values as well as redistributive and intergenerational justice.[26] Moreover, it prevents that law from being identified as a millennium development goal or target or as an indication for assessing the progress.

2.3 *International Development Law*

2.3.1 Fragmentation of International Law

In 2006 a Study Group of the International Law Commission (ILC) published a report on *Fragmentation of International Law: Difficulties Arising from the Diversification and Expansion of International Law*, finalized by Martti Koskenniemi, chairman of the group.[27] According to the author[28]

> [T]he fragmentation of the substance of international law (...) does not pose any very serious danger to legal practice. It is as normal a part of legal reasoning to link rules and rule-systems to each other, as it is to separate them and to establish relations of priority and hierarchy among them. The emergence of new branches of the law, novel types of treaties or clusters of treaties is a feature of the social complexity of a globalizing world. If lawyers feel unable to deal with this complexity, this is not a reflection of problems in their "tool-box" but in their imagination about how to use it.

The challenge to mainstream theories and doctrines by new theories and novel doctrines provides international law "the intellectual tools not only to interpret the world but to change it."[29] The real risk of fragmentation undermining the universality of international law lies in the ambition that international law is an instrument to change the world. For that ambition runs the risk that the means justify the end because of a missing common vision on a global legal system. This holds true the more since Koskenniemi is of the view that law is what international

26 Isabel Feichtner, *Community Interest*, in MPEPIL II, 479-481 paras. 13-35 and 485 para. 57.

27 As chairman of the group, the author was supported by many members, but the content of the report remained his sole responsibility. See A/CN.4/L.682 of April 13, 2006 1, footnote.

28 *Id.* 115 para. 222.

29 Martti Koskenniemi, *International Legal Theory and Doctrine*, in MPEPIL III 982 para. 33.

lawyers do and how they think.[30] Moreover, he passes the message that international law is an argumentative practice to persuade targeted audiences such as courts, colleagues, politicians, and readers of legal texts about the correctness of the position one defends.[31]

2.3.2 Global Legal System

The editor of the MPEL, Rüdiger Wolfrum, surprises the reader somewhat by starting his answer to the question whether international law is really law with the provocative view of the American international lawyer and former Ambassador to the UN John R. Bolton in 2000.[32] In a then published article Bolton concluded: "International law is not law; it is a series of political and moral arrangements that stand or fall on their own merits, and anything else is simply theology and superstition masquerading as law."[33] In his own answer to the above question Wolfrum concludes that the particular implementation and enforcement mechanisms of international law reflect its nature "as a legal system based on co-ordination and co-operation among equals."[34] According to Wolfrum, it is general accepted that "international is of a horizontal character, meaning it is developed between its subjects, compared to the vertical nature of national law which is developed by institutions empowered with this task."[35] However, the differences between national and international law are not so much the creation of law but the interpretation and implementation of law.

Just like to citizens and their organizations at the national level, applies to States and their organizations at the international level, that between dreams and actions are laws and practical objections. The fact that a State has approved international law either explicitly – treaties and other binding decisions – or implicitly through its conduct – customary law – does not imply that it may prevent enforcement by invoking its sovereignty. In other words, the horizontal character of (inter) national Law concerns law-creation, not law-implementation. The vol-

---

30 Martti Koskenniemi, The Politics of International Law, 293 (2011).

31 Martti Koskenniemi, *Methodology of International Law*, in MPEPIL VII 124-125 para. 1.

32 Rüdiger Wolfrum, *International Law*, in MPEPIL V 822 para. 11.

33 John Robert Bolton, *Is There Really International "Law" in International Affairs?* 10 TransntIL&ContempProbs 48 (2000).

34 Wolfrum, *supra* note 32, at 824 para. 21.

35 *Id.* at 823 para. 20.

untary jurisdiction of the International Court of Justice (ICJ) does not alter that fact. For judicial settlement is only one of the means to fulfil the duty to settle disputes which may endanger the maintenance of peace and security peacefully. Doubts about the suitability of international law as global legal system does not so much regard law-making as law-maintaining. As appears from the preamble of its Charter, the UN concentrates on the establishment of "conditions under which justice and respect for the obligations arising from treaties and other sources of international law can be maintained." [36] Admittedly, the impact of the Preamble upon U.N. decision-making is minimal. It is striking , however, that precisely the millennium reports of U.N. Secretary-General Kofi Annan refer to it.[37]

2.3.3 Regime or School of Thought

Special regimes are meant to bridge the gap between law-making and law-implementation, to facilitate compliance with commitment.[38] The need for establishing such regimes makes itself felt particularly in the transitional period of progressive development of international law. The first use of the expression international law of development or international development law has been ascribed to a former French minister of economic affairs and finance, the economist André Philip. He launched it in 1964 on the eve of the first meeting of the U.N. Conference on Trade and Development in Geneva. The idea was immediately accepted with open arms by the French professor of international law Michel Virally, who became the spiritual father of the concept, albeit not as an autonomous branch of international law.[39] Indeed, the U.N. development strategy provoked the discussion whether this strategy should give rise to international development law as a school of thought or as an autonomous new discipline of law. The latter view found little support out of fear that it would be confined to the poor world.[40] Virally became the

---

36 U.N. Charter, Preamble para. 3.

37 SIMMA, *supra* note 3, at 105 para 13.

38 Any Bradford, *Regime Theory, in* MPEPIL VIII 737 para. 1 and 739 para. 15.

39 Ahmed Mahiou, *Development, International Law of*, in MPEPIL III 78, para. 1; Paul de Waart, *Participants and their Role in the Development of International Development Law,* in UNESCO ENCYCLOPEDIA OF LIFE SUPPORT SYSTEMS (EOLSS) I *International Sustainable Development Law 1* at www.eolss.net/sample-chapters/c13/E6-67-01-04.pdf.

40 Mahiou, *supra* note 39, at 80 para. 7-9.

proponent of the idea that international law of development should permeate through international law as a whole. For then international law could (re)gain its position as a common basis in the heated discussions on a (the) NIEO. The need for that only increased in the 1990s, when the global market obtained as it were the exclusive right to distribute wealth among states and peoples.

In the global market the leading actors are not so much States as non-State actors, viz. multinational or transnational corporations (MNCs). States and non-State actors established non-regulatory instruments such as the U.N. Global Compact initiative of 1999 or special legal regimes for issue areas as, for example, investments and sustainable development. In doing so, the actors involved supplemented or, if more feasibly, circumvented the State-centred character of international law. Particularly in the latter case international law was exposed to the risk of a harmful fragmentation, either because of doubts about the universality of international law as a global system for co-operation or, what's more, the negation that international law is really law.

Anyhow, neither the Millennium Declaration nor the World Summit Outcome refer to the international law of development. This is partly due to the ambiguous legal status of the right to development.[41] The NIEO controversy in the UN had provoked the question whether the right to development belonged to States – particularly poor States – or (also) to human beings, individually and/or collectively (peoples).

3 Good Governance Development Goal

The present paragraph reviews the relation of good governance with the right to sustainable development as both a human right and a principle of public international law; and the impact of globalization and good governance on the principles of international law concerning friendly relations and cooperation among states. Finally, the scope and content of good governance, and efforts to define and assess good governance are examined.

41 Alhagi Meron, *Development, Right to, International Protection*, in MPEPIL III 88, para. 23.

3.1 *Right to Sustainable Development*

3.1.1 Relation to International Economic Order

The intense debate on international economic order in the 1970s spurred the French Society for International Law to organize a number of colloquia, one if which was devoted to the topic of developing countries and the transformation of international law. Its agenda included economic inequality and evolution of international law; institutional framework and techniques for the elaboration of international law; and the fundamental principles in the international law of development.[42] In conclusion of the colloquium, Virally divided his findings in three main themes which will remain topical in the foreseeable future: (I) The jurist and international law of development; (2) Is the international law of development an exceptional law?; (3) The dialectics between sovereignty and cooperation.

As for the first theme, jurists are more than ever involved in the historic adventure of development, while the key to turn the project is deposited with economics, politics, sociology and culture.[43] For that reason, – theme 2 – the origin of international development law is not so much the need for an autonomous new branch of international law as for a particular approach of international law as a whole.[44] Finally, theme 3 replacing peace through law by development through law is too arrogant.[45] In his summary Virally underlined that not values – justice, equality and independence – dictate the call for international development but facts, viz. the facilitation of a balanced development of the international society and a development of the States themselves.[46] Precisely in that originates the opposition of industrialized countries, headed by the United States [hereinafter US), against international development law and the right to development as a right of States.

3.1.2 Development a Human Right

In 1981 the U.N. Economic and Social Council (ECOSOC) approved the establishment by the U.N. Commission on Human Rights (CHR) of a

42 SOCIETE FRANÇAISE POUR LE DROIT INTERNATIONAL, COLLOQUE d'AIX-EN-PROVENCE, PAYS EN VOIE DE DÉVELOPPEMENT ET TRANSFORMATION DU DROIT INTERNATIONAL (1974) [hereinafter COLLOQUE].

43 *Id.* 308-309.

44 *Id.* 310.

45 *Id.* 311.

46 *Id.* 308.

Working Group on the right to development consisting of 15 governmental experts from all corners of the world to be appointed by the chair of the Commission.[47] From the very beginning, the work of the experts[48] was dominated by considerable differences of opinion on the nature of the right to development and the relationship between that right and the NIEO. As for the nature of the right, the main point at issue was whether States could have human rights, or whether the adjective human should be reserved to individuals only, or also to groups of individuals, i.e. minorities and peoples. States should not be included, since their position has been clearly defined in international law. Against this it was argued that the latter might be true for old States but not for new States. For that reason developing countries should have a right to development to enhance their capability for promoting and protecting the human rights of their subjects, particularly the economic, social and cultural rights.

As for the relation to the discussion on international economic order in the seventies, the Working Group was not able to reach a consensus. It is true that the NIEO Declaration was adopted by consensus, but that result had been nullified by the subsequent dissension on the CERDS between developed and developing countries.[49] The experts from France and the Netherlands tried in vain to reach a consensus on a UN Declaration on the Right to Development [hereinafter UNDRD]. In their common draft proposal for such a Declaration, they did not refer to NIEO instruments but to international instruments which reflect a consensus among States with different economic, social and political systems.[50] The Working Group, however, could not agree on a common text for a draft UNDRD.[51] For that reason, the CHR took over the draft of a Decla-

47 ECOSOC Decision 1981/149 of May 8, 1981; CHR Resolution 36 (XXXVII) of March 11 1981. The present writer was a member of that group until 1986. See *infra* at note 50.

48 The members came from Algeria, Cuba, Ethiopia, France, India, Iraq, Netherlands, Panama, Peru, Poland, Senegal, Syrian Arab Republic, US, USSR and Yugoslavia. The expert from Poland was later replaced by one from Bulgaria.

49 Boon, *supra* note 8, at 87, para. 2 1 and 89, para. 12.

50 www.ohchr.org/EN/Issues/Development/Pages/Documents.aspx: E/CN.4/1985/11 of January 24, 1985, Report of the Working Group of Governmental Experts on the Right to Development, Rapporteur Georges Gautier (France), Annex III, Article 10.

51 To the report were annexed a draft Declaration of the experts from the non-aligned countries (Annex II), a Technical Consolidated Text (Annex IV), draft Articles of the expert from the USSR (Annex V); Compilation of proposals sub-

ration on the basis of a Yugoslavian proposal that had browsed through all annexes, particularly the drafts from the non-aligned countries and the France/Netherlands text. Anyhow, the U.N. General Assembly [hereinafter UNGA] could thus approve in 1986 with a substantial majority the Declaration on the Right to Development as a human right and as a right of States, including even a reference to the promotion of a new international economic order.[52] Since then the Working Group focussed on points to be included in a questionnaire as a basis for periodic reports by States on the implementation of the Right to Development. An illustrative list of points was submitted in the final report of the Working Group in 1989.[53]

That the right to development has taken root in the international society has been amply illustrated in the recent voluminous collection of essays on the realization of the right to development, published by the Office of the High Commissioner for Human Rights (OHCHR), to commemorate the 25th anniversary of the Declaration in 2011. In her essay on the UNDRD in the context of U.N. standard-setting, Ms. Tamara Kunanayakam (Sri Lanka), as of 2011 Chairperson-Rapporteur of the annual sessions of the Open-Ended Working Group on the Right to Development, rightly underlined that the UNDRD is founded first and foremost on the U.N. Charter.[54] She even concluded that the Declaration has obtained a normative character, although it is not a multilateral

---

mitted to the seventh session of the Working Group (Annex VI); Compilation of proposals at the eighth session (Annex VII), Compilation of Proposals at the ninth session (Annex VIII); Texts of the Draft Declaration on which general agreement in principle has already been reached at the seventh and nine session.

52 G.A. Res. 41/128 of December 4, 1986, adopted by 146 votes in favour (including France and the Netherlands), 1 against (the US) and 8 abstentions (Denmark, Finland, the Federal Republic of Germany, Iceland, Israel, Japan, Sweden and the United Kingdom), Articles 1, 2.3, 3.3 and 9.

53 www.ohchr.org/EN/Issues/Development/Pages/Documents.aspx:E/CN.4/1989/10 of February 13, 1989, Report of the Open-Ended Working Group of Governmental Experts on the Right to Development, Annex I.

54 Tamara Kunanayakam, *The Declaration on the Right to Development in the context of UN standard-setting,* in REALIZING THE RIGHT TO DEVELOPMENT, ESSAYS IN COMMEMORATION OF 25 YEARS OF THE UNITED NATIONS DECLARATION ON THE RIGHT TO DEVELOPMENT [hereinafter Essays], (OHCHR 2013) 46, available at www.ohchr.org/EN/PublicationsResources/Pages/Publications.aspx.

treaty.[55] In this connection it is conspicuous that the most authoritative commentary on the U.N. Charter unlike the French one has no thought for it at all![56] This might explain the comment of the present High Commissioner for Human Rights (HCHR), Navi Pillay, that the debate in the UN on the UNDRD since its adoption in 1986 "while generating plenty of academic interest and stimulating political theatre" has done little 'to free the right to development from the conceptual mud and political quicksand in which it has been mired all these years."[57] This somewhat pessimistic observation might also be prompted by the focus of the OHCHR publication on development as a right only. However, all human beings, individually and collectively, have a responsibility for development as well.[58] They should therefore promote and protect an appropriate political, social and economic order for development, particularly for the benefit of people living in absolute poverty. [59] A just and fair distribution of wealth to secure freedom from want and freedom from war for everyone requires that the right to development is firmly based not only in international human rights law, but also in public international law. To link the human right to development only to duties of States ignores that in fulfilling their duties States are dependent on the support of their citizens, anyhow in a democratic society.

3.1.3 Development Principle of Public International Law

The Declaration on Legal Aspects of a New International Economic Order, adopted by Sixty-Second Conference of the International Law Association (ILA) at Seoul in August 1986 [hereinafter Seoul Declaration], laid down that the right to development is a principle of international law in general and human rights law in particular.[60] The Seoul Declaration reflects to great extent the results of an extensive Dutch legal research project in the 1970s on the changing structure of interna-

55 *Id.* at 48.

56 *Supra* note 3; JEAN-PIERRE COT ET AL. La Charte des Nations Unies Commentaire article par article (3e éd. 2005) 364-370.

57 Narvi Pillay, (HCHR) *Foreword, in* Essays iii.

58 G.A. Res. 41/128, Article 2.2.

59 U.N. Doc. A/HRC/21/39 of July 18, 2012, *Final Draft of the Guiding Principles on Extreme Poverty and Human Rights*, para. 9.

60 ILA, REPORT TO THE SIXTY-SECOND CONFERENCE HELD AT SEOUL AUGUST 24th to 30th, 1986 1-19, *Declaration on the Progressive Development of Principles of Public International Law Relating to a New International Economic Order* at 7: The right to Development.

tional economic law. For a main conclusion of the research has been that more radical reforms are needed for a NIEO than those proposed in the CERDS: "What is not possible is the combination of a just and efficient new international economic order with states aiming only at their own objectives, on the basis of absolute internal and external sovereignty".[61]

The consensus in the ILA in August 1986 at Seoul heralded in winds of change resulting in the adoption of the UNDRD. According to the 1992 U.N. Rio Declaration the right to development must be fulfilled so as to equitably meet developmental and environmental needs of present and future generations.[62] The ILA Committee on Legal Aspects of Sustainable Development, that had succeeded the same year the NIEO Committee,[63] amended the Seoul Declaration accordingly in its fifth and final report, submitted to the ILA in 2002. The New Delhi Declaration of Principles of International Law relating to Sustainable Development put the right to development in the context of the principle of equity and the eradication of poverty[64] and of the duty to co-operate for sustainable development and the attainment of equity in the development opportunities of developed and developing countries.[65] In doing

61 Pieter VerLoren van Themaat, The Changing Structure of International Economic Law: A Contribution of Legal History, of Comparative Law and of General Legal Theory to the Debate on a New International Economic Order 375 (1981). VerLoren van Themaat was the Dutch member of the ILA Committee on Legal Aspects of a New International Economic Order (NIEO Committee). The present writer was his alternate.

62 A/CONF.151/26 (Vol. I), REPORT OF THE UNITED NATIONS CONFERENCE ON ENVIRONMENT AND DEVELOPMENT (Rio de Janeiro, 3-14 June 1992) Annex I, Principles 3 and 4.

63 ILA, REPORT OF THE SIXTY-FIFTH CONFERENCE, HELD AT CAIRO APRIL 21 TO 26, 1992, Resolution 12, 12-13. Chairman was again Dr Kamal Hossain from Bangladesh. Nico Schrijver was rapporteur. See also Pieter VerLoren van Themaat, *Ten Years after the ILA Declaration of Seoul, in* ERIC DENTERS AND NICO SCHRIJVER (EDS.), REFLECTIONS ON INTERNATIONAL LAW OF THE LAW COUNTRIES IN HONOUR OF PAUL DE WAART 21-23 (1998).

64 ILA, REPORT OF THE SEVENTIETH CONFERENCE, HELD IN NEW DELHI APRIL 2-6, 2002 Res. 3/2002 22-30, at 26 para. 2.3.

65 The other principles relating to sustainable development are: the Duty of States to ensure sustainable use of natural resources; common but differentiated responsibilities; the precautionary approach to human health, natural resources and ecosystems; public participation and access to information and justice; integration and interrelationship, in particular in relation to human rights and social, economic and environmental objectives.

so, the ILA New Delhi Declaration supplemented also the U.N. Rio Declaration.

Ten years later, the final report of the ILA Committee on International Law of Sustainable Development, submitted to the ILA Conference at Sofia, described in broad outline the significance of International Courts and Tribunals as well as quasi-judicial bodies in elaborating sustainable development as laid down in the New Delhi Declaration.[66] The ILA approved Guiding Statements for the interpretation of the New Delhi Principles, derived from international jurisprudence.[67] As for good governance, that principle had remained largely outside the jurisprudence of the International Court of Justice (ICJ). However, elements were seen in activities of other judicial bodies, such as the International Tribunal of the Law of the Sea as well as quasi-judicial bodies.[68]

3.2 *Friendly Relations and Cooperation among States*

3.2.1 Impact of Globalization

Although the untouchability of States is under pressure,[69] the U.N. Declaration on Principles of International Law concerning Friendly Relations and Co-operation among States in accordance with the Charter of the United Nation [hereinafter Friendly Relations Declaration] still sets the tone in interstate relations as a document of, and an instrument in, the struggle of conflicting interests at the peak of both the Cold War between East and West and the NIEO-discussion between North and South.[70] The struggle is still there but its setting has changed radically under the influence of globalization. Precisely after the fall of the Berlin Wall, globalization changed international law substantially in respect of subjects, objects and nature.[71] However, globalization may have shaken

66 ILA, Report on the Seventy-Fifth Conference, held in Sofia August 2012 825-837. The ILA established the Committee in 2003 to study the legal status and legal implementation of sustainable development with particular reference to the ILA New Delhi Declaration. Professor Nico Schrijver (The Netherlands) succeeded Dr. Kamal Hossain (Bangladesh) as chairman of the new committee.

67 *Id.* 49-52: Res. No. 7/2012 Annex 2012 Sofia Guiding Statements on the Judicial Elaboration of the 2002 New Delhi Declaration of Principles of International Law Relating to Sustainable Development.

68 ILA Report, *supra* note 66 at 861-863.

69 Daniel Thürer and Thomans Burri, *Secession*, in MPEPIL IX 64 para. 42.

70 Helen Keller, *Friendly Relations Declaration* (1970), in MPEPIL IV, 259 para. 42.

71 Frédéric Mégret, *Globalization*, in MPEPIL IV, 496 501, paras. 20-23 (subjects); 23-30 (objects); and 30-43 (nature).

the foundations of international law as a law of friendly relations and co-operation among states, international law has also taken up the challenge of directing it to global distributive justice through developing principles relating to actual topics such as NIEO, rule of law, sustainable development and good governance.[72]

The Friendly Relations Declaration must be interpreted and applied in the context of the U.N. Charter. That context is neither static nor immutable but dynamic, open as it is to the scattered interpretation resulting from the own responsibility of each of the U.N. political organs and the ICJ as the principal judicial organ.[73] UNGA interpretations of the Friendly Relations Declaration are not binding, decisions of the U.N. Security Council (UNSC) on the other hand are. It is evident that the UNSC may not act *ultra vires.* However, States and non-State actors have no possibility to oppose UNSC decisions on that account.[74] A way out might occur when the implementation of a UNSC decision would preclude a court from reviewing complaints that a State or supranational organization had other ways and means to harmonize the intent of the pertinent decision with its duties under national or supranational law:[75]

> [T]he Community judicature must, in accordance with the powers conferred on it by the EC Treaty, ensure the review, in principle the full review, of the lawfulness of all Community acts in the light of the fundamental rights forming an integral part of the general principles of Community law, including review of Community measures which, like the contested regulation, are designed to give effect to the resolutions adopted by the Security Council under Chapter VII of the Charter of the UN.

---

72 *Id.*, at 5011-502 paras. 43-47.

73 Jean-Pierre Cot, *United Nations Charter*, in MEPIL X, 249, para. 78 and 250, para. 87.

74 SIMMA, *supra* note 3, at 98-99 para. 73.

75 Joined Cases C-402/05 P and C-415/05 P, Yassin Abdullah Kadi and Al Barakaat International Foundation v. Council of the EU and Commission of the European Communities, Judgment of the European Court of Justice (Grand Chamber) [hereinafter ECJ], September 3, 2008, para. 326. In Joined Cases C 584/10 P, C 593/10 P and C 595/10 P, Kadi, Judgment of the European Court of Justice (Grand Chamber), July 18, 2013 the ECJ dismissed appeals of the European Commission, European Council, and numerous individual EU members against the former judgment.

The decision has been commended for confirming human rights protection in the EU and for pressing the UNSC to do the same in the UN.[76] With the exception of aggression (principle 1.2), violation of fundamental human rights in a state of necessity[77] (principle 5.2) and oppression of peoples (principle 5.7), the Friendly Relations Declaration does not contain *jus cogens*.[78] For the rest, this Declaration may be understood in the context of new principles of international law such as good governance.

3.2.2 Impact of Good Governance

Almost all States are members of the UN. The present exceptions are Vatican City and Palestine, having been officially recognized by the UN as Non-member States.[79] Other countries claiming to be a State and having been recognized as such by member-States are Taiwan[80] and Kosovo.[81] U.N. members do not derive their sovereign equality from the U.N. Charter but from international law.[82] This implies that the principle of sovereign equality of States is the basis of the international legal order as a whole. The Friendly Relations Declaration let there be no mistake that all States enjoy sovereign equality.[83] The legal significance is that each State has the right freely to choose and develop its political, social, economic and cultural systems but also the duty to comply fully and in good faith with its international obligations and to live in peace with other States.[84]

The sovereign equality of members does not imply that States may shirk back at their own discretion from obligations entered into or being part of customary international law.[85] It may well be so that good governance is not an obligation explicitly contained in the U.N. Charter or

76 Clemens Feinäugle, *Kadi Case*, in MPEPIL VI, 562 para. 26.

77 David Kretzmer, *Emergency, State of*, in MPEPIL III, 396-397 paras. 23-29.

78 Jochen A. Frowein, *Ius cogens*, in MPEPIL VI, 444 para. 8.

79 www.un.org/en/members/nonmembers.shtml.

80 JAMES CRAWFORD, THE CREATION OF STATES IN INTERNATIONAL LAW 219 (2d ed. 2006).

81 Stephan Oeter, *Yugoslavia Dissolution of*, in MPEPIL X 1086-1088 paras. 82-87.

82 SIMMA, *supra* note 3, at 157; Juliana Kokott, *States, Sovereign Equality*, in MPEPIL IX 571 para. 3.

83 G.A. Res. 2625 (XXV) of October 24, 1970, Principle VI para. 1.

84 *Id.* paras. 2 sub e and f.

85 *Supra* text at notes 39-40.

a tradition of the organization,[86] but the concept of governance has become the subject of investigation in legal theory since the rise of plural legal orders.[87] The concept of good governance may have deep historical roots;[88] its present connotation is from recent times. The normative modern implications of the adjective good are still under discussion. A consensus on their scope and content is taking shape, although a legal definition of good governance still fails.[89]

3.3 *Good Governance Principle of International Law*

3.3.1 Scope and Content of Good Governance

The scope and content of good governance are closely connected with the idea of a sacred trust from civilized nations appointed as mandatories towards mandated territories – League of Nations Covenant – or as trustees towards trusted territories: U.N. Charter.[90] But it were not the advanced States, entrusted with such tutelage, but the Bretton Wood financial institutions that introduced the concept of good governance in their relations with developing countries.[91] Beyond the scope of dependency relationships, the sovereignty of States has prevented a consensus on a legal definition of good governance. Nevertheless, international law stimulates good governance to some extent albeit to protect the territorial integrity of sovereign and independent States against secession[92]

> Conducting themselves in compliance with the principle of equal rights and self-determination of peoples and thus possessed of a government representing the whole people belonging to the territory without distinction as to race, creed or colour.

International practice shows that the international community outside the colonial context is quite eager to maintain the prohibition of secession also when there are serious doubts on the representativeness of the

86 SIMMA, *supra* note 3, at 48 para. 21.

87 Karl-Heinz Ladeur, *Governance, Theory of*, in MEPIL IV, 551 paras. 33-35.

88 Edith Brown Weiss and Ahila Sornarajah [hereinafter Weiss & Sornarajah], *Good Governance*, in MEPIL IV, 516 para. 2.

89 *Id.* at 516 para. 3 and 526 para. 73: www.ohchr.org/en/Issues/Development/GoodGovernance/.

90 Covenant of the League of Nations, April 28, 1919 Article 22; U.N. Charter, Article 73.

91 Weiss & Sornarajah, *supra* note 88 at 516 para. 1.

92 G.A. Res. 2625 (XXV), Principle V para. 7.

government concerned.[93] Even when there was some willingness of the international community to recognize a seceded State because of bad governance in the dismembered State, international law was not the deciding factor. All in all, normative implications of good governance have been so far mainly defined by donors with regard their recipients. This may explain that the MDGs do not include good governance as yet.[94] Good governance is only included as one of the commitments towards Goal 8: the development of a global partnership for development.[95] However, the situation has somewhat changed after the fall of the Berlin Wall in the World Bank, the European Union [hereinafter EU] and the UN.[96]

3.3.2 Defining and Assessing Good Governance

An overview of good governance from 1999 focusses on accountability, transparency, participation and the rule of law.[97] The U.N. Millennium Declaration did not define good governance, but only mentioned it under the headings "Development and poverty eradication" and "Human rights, democracy and good governance". The 2005 World Summit Outcome dealt with that, neither. The ACP-EU Cotonou Partnership Agreement considered as good governance[98]

> The transparent and accountable management of human, natural, economic and financial resources for the purposes of equitable and sustainable development. It entails clear decision-making

---

93 Thürer & Burri, supra note 74 at 57 para. 17; JAMES CRAWFORD, BROWNLIE'S PRINCIPLES OF PUBLIC INTERNATIONAL LAW 141-142 (8th ed. 2012).

94 *Supra* note 23.

95 www.unstats.un.org/unsd/mdg/Host.aspx?Content=Indicators/OfficialList.htm: Target 8A the further development of an open-rule-based, predictable, non-discriminatory trading and financial system.

96 Weiss & Sornarajah, *supra* note 88 at 521-524 *Approaches of International Institutions to Good Governance within States.*

97 EB 99/67/INF.4 of August 26, 1999. www.ifad.org/gbdocs/eb/67/e/EB-99-67-INF-4.pdf.

98 Partnership Agreement between the Members of the African, Caribbean and Pacific Group of States of the One Part, and the European Community and its Member States of the Other Part, signed in Cotonou on June 23, 2000, revised in Luxembourg on 25 June 25, 2005 and in Ouagadougou on June 22, 2010, art. 9.3. D.A. DAM-DE JONG, INTERNATIONAL LAW AND GOVERNANCE OF NATURAL RESOURCES IN CONFLICT AND POST-CONFLICT AREAS, 21-22 (2013).

> procedures at the level of public authorities, transparent and accountable institutions, the primacy of law in the management and distribution of resources and capacity building for elaborating and implementing measures aiming in particular at preventing and combating corruption.

With the exception of the above ILA New Delhi Declaration, good governance is not yet seen as a principle of international law but as a condition for sustainable development just like democracy, participation, transparency and the rule of law are. According to the ILA, the principle of good governance is essential to the progressive development and codification of international law relating to sustainable development and commits States and IGOs to[99]

> (a) Adopt democratic and transparent decision-making procedures and financial accountability;
> (b) Take effective measures to combat official or other corruption;
> (c) Respect the principle of due process in their procedures and to observe the rule of law and human rights; and
> (d Implement a public procurement approach according to the WTO Code on Public Procurement.

The Declaration also underlines that good governance calls for corporate social responsibility and socially responsible investments as conditions for the existence of a global market aimed at a fair distribution of wealth among and within nations.[100] The seeds for this definition of good governance were sown at a conference on legal principles of sustainable development and good government at the University of Graz in 1994, convened by the then newly established ILA Committee on Legal Aspects of Sustainable Development.[101] In assessing the quality of governance in national and international constitutional orders, the challenge is to make theoretically a distinction between the two orders,

---

99 ILA Report, *supra* note 66, at 28-29, The Principle of Good Governance, para. 6.1.

100 *Id.* at 29, para. 6.3.

101 *Supra* note 66; KONRAD GINTHER ET AL., SUSTAINABLE DEVELOPMENT AND GOOD GOVERNANCE, XX, 12-14 (1995) [hereinafter GINTHER].

while keeping in mind their practical linkage and the need to make them subject to evaluation by common standards.[102]

As of 1996 the World Bank applies six aggregate Worldwide Governance Indicators (WGIs) in assessing the quality of governance in both developed and developing countries: viz. Voice and Accountability; Political Stability; Government Effectiveness; Regulatory Quality; Rule of Law; and Control of Corruption.[103] The WGIs have been developed by the World Bank Institute (WBI) – a global connector of knowledge, learning and innovation for poverty reduction – and are updated every two year.[104] They are stored in the WGI data base which now provides information on the progress in respect the above six dimensions of governance over the period 1996-2012 in more than 200 countries.[105] The data concern governance as the set of traditions and institutions by which authority in a country is exercised:[106]

> This includes the process by which governments are selected, monitored and replaced; the capacity of the government to effectively formulate and implement sound policies; and the respect of citizens and the state for the institutions that govern economic and social interactions among them.

By themselves the WGIs do not qualify governance in a specific country as good or bad. Such a conclusion may be drawn, however, from linking data. For that reason they are under discussion.[107] Be this at it may, the use of the WGI data basis has shown that

- Governance can be measured;
- The qualification of governance as better or worse may apply to both developed and developing countries;

---

102 Konrad Ginther, *Sustainable Development and Good Governance: Development and Evolution of Constitutional Orders*, in GINTHER 163.

103 www.info.worldbank.org/governance/wgi/index.aspx#home, The Worldwide Governance Indicators (WGI) project.

104 *Id.*; Weiss & Sornarajah, *supra* note 88 at 517, para. 6.

105 www.info.worldbank.org/governance/wgi/index.aspx#countryReports rs.

106 www.info.worldbank.org/governance/wgi/index.aspx#home.

107 Weiss & Sornarajah *supra* note 88 at 517 paras. 7 and 8.

- It is possible to improve governance and curb corruption substantially.[108]

The WGIs thus substantiate good governance and sustainable development as principles of international law. For that reason it may somewhat surprise that the OHCR publication on Human Rights Indicators only mentions the WGI data base in a list of additional data-bases of the UN and other IGOs.[109] Anyhow, the OHCR publication Essays[110] does not even do that!

4 Global Governance in Silver Perspective

In silver perspective international law will have to cope with global governance and the evolving rights and responsibilities of states and peoples to that end. Although States bear the primary responsibility to protect their people(s), the rising society for all will result in an increasing secondary responsibility of the international community, particularly for preventing humanitarian catastrophes. This takes shape in the content of a global administrative law.

4.1 *Global Governance*

4.1.1 Rights and Responsibilities of States

States have not been able to agree on the right of States to choose their political system without foreign intervention. They could accept it as a principle of international law.[111] On the day it celebrated its silver anniversary – October 24, 1970 – the UNGA affirmed that each State has the right to choose and develop its political, economic, social and cultural systems, without interference in any form by another State but in the context of the principle of the sovereign equality of States.[112] In 1986 the

108 www.siteresources.worldbank.org/NEWS/Resources/wbi2007-report.pdf, *A Decade of Measuring the Quality of Governance: Worldwide Governance Indicators, 1996-2006* 3.

109 OHCR, HUMAN RIGHTS INDICATORS A Guide to Measurement and Implementation 169 (2012).

110 *Supra*, note 54.

111 Sergio M. Carbone and Lorenzo Schiano di Pepe, *States, Fundamental Rights and Duties, in* MPEPIL IX, 566, paras. 14 and 15.

112 G.A. Res. 2625 (XXV), principles VI para. 2 sub e. in conjunction with III para. 4.

ICJ confirmed that right. Moreover, it declared that it could not contemplate the creation of a new rule opening up a right of intervention by one State against another on the ground that the latter has opted for some particular ideology or political system.[113]

The judgement dates from a time when international law paid hardly any attention to democracy simply because the choice of a political system was the inalienable right of every State.[114] But this situation had radically changed after the fall of the Berlin Wall.[115] In 1993 the World Conference on Human rights solemnly adopted the Vienna Declaration and Programme of Action, according to which the international community should support "the strengthening and promoting of democracy, development and respect for human rights and fundamental freedoms in the entire world."[116] The then U.N. Human Rights Commission accepted the challenge. In 1999 it adopted a resolution on promotion of the right to democracy. The resolution affirmed that the rights to democratic governance include, inter alia, the freedoms of opinion and religion, political participation, the rule of law, universal and equal suffrage and the right of citizens to choose their governmental system through constitutional or other democratic means. It did so with only two abstentions,[117] albeit that the votes in favour were accompanied by doubts about the practicability.[118]

4.1.2 Rights and Responsibilities of People(s)

On 24 October 1970 the UNGA marked the end of the colonial system by declaring that all peoples have the right freely to determine, without external interference, their political status and to pursue their economic, social and cultural development and that every State had the duty to respect this right in accordance with the U.N. Charter.[119] Since then the

---

113 Military and Paramilitary Activities in und against Nicaragua (Nicaragua v. United States of America). Merits, Judgment. I.C.J. Reports 1986, 131, para. 258 and 133 para. 263.

114 See *infra* at note 150.

115 Gregory H. Fox & Brad R. Roth, *Democracy and International* Law 327 Vol. 27 REVIEW OF INTERNATIONAL STUDIES (2001), available at un.org/en/globalissues/democracy/human_rights.shtml.

116 A/CONF.157/23 of July 12, 1993, para. 8.

117 CHR Res. 199/57 of April 27, 1999, para. 2. The resolution was adopted by a roll call vote of 51 votes to none, with 2 abstentions (China and Cuba).

118 E/CN.4/1999/SR.57 of April 30, 1999.

119 G.A. Res. 2625 (XXV), principle V, para. 1.

discussion focussed on whether peoples have a right to democracy towards their States. The freedoms of opinion and religion do not imply or secure by themselves a democratic disposition of citizens in their choice of the governmental system indeed. Neither does the rule of law, as long as different cultures and political systems are only able to agree on a formal scope and content, word-wide.[120]

Even in the cradle of democracy – Europe – the notion of rule of law has not been developed in legal texts and practice as much as the other pillars of the Council of Europe, human rights and democracy.[121] As for democracy, the European Convention for the Protection of Human Rights and Fundamental Freedoms [hereinafter ECHR] does not lay down a right to democracy but refers to democracy in its Preamble and that to political democracy only.[122] The very first Protocol to the ECHR raised in 1952 a corner of the veil regarding scope and content of an effective political democracy in its article 3 on the right to free elections: "The High Contracting Parties undertake to hold free elections at reasonable intervals by secret ballot, under conditions which will ensure the free expression of the opinion of the people in the choice of the legislature."[123] The ECHR thus identifies democracy with a democratic state, leaving in the middle what is understood by democratic society in the context of, amongst others, limitations to the freedoms set forth in it. As for balancing the freedom of association against the freedom religion in a democratic society, the European Court of Human Rights has given the impression that the decisive factor is whether or not a political party excludes the use of force as a means to reach its religious ends.[124] At the same time it holds the view that the introduction of sharia as a

120 Simon Chesterman, *Rule of Law*, in MPEPIL VIII 1016 para. 14.

121 CDL-AD(2011)003rev EUROPEAN COMMISSION FOR DEMOCRACY THROUGH LAW (VENICE COMMISSION) REPORT ON THE RULE OF LAW of April 4, 2011 14 para. 67 and 15: Annex: Checklist for evaluating the state of the rule of law in single states.

122 ECHR of November 4, 1950 as amended by Protocols Nos. 11 and 14 supplemented by Protocols Nos. 1, 4, 6, 7, 12 and 13, Preamble, para. 5.

123 Protocol to the Convention for the Protection of Human Rights and Fundamental Freedoms of March 20, 1952, art. 3.

124 Paul de Waart, *Judicial Supervision of Countering Terrorism: The Case of Palestine*, in SHARIF BHUIYAN ET AL., INTERNATIONAL LAW AND DEVELOPING COUNTRIES, ESSAYS IN HONOUR OF KAMAL HOSSAIN 103-105 (2014).

political aim is hardly compatible with the democratic ideal underlying the ECHR as a whole.[125]

In sum, there is no consensus on the existence of a right to democratic governance, let alone the international protection of such right.[126] Nevertheless, it is said that there is an emerging right to democratic governance in the case of international administration of a territory, such as when the UN assumes political authority over territories like in Kosovo and East Timor.[127] Be this as it may, both public international law and international human rights law give no decisive answer as to whether such a right exist and if so, whether the focus is on procedure – elections and participation – or on substance: effective protection of a tolerant and pluralist society.[128] As for the latter, there is no consensus on the scope and content of the freedoms of opinion and expression as preconditions for the truly democratic character of a State.[129] All in all, "the wide spectrum of commitment to democratic governance provides an uncertain foundation for a global norm."[130] This may not surprise, since international human rights law is hardly concerned with corresponding human responsibilities. It is telling that no essay in the OHCR celebration book *Realizing the Right to Development* includes an entry on individual duties or responsibilities. [131] Neither does the MPEPIL![132]

---

125 Applications nos. 41340/98, 41342/98, 41343/98 and 41344/98, Judgment of February 12, 2003, Refah Partisi (The Welfare Party) and others v. Turkey [Grand Chamber - N° 50], paras. 123 and 132.

126 Gregory H. Fox, *Democracy, Right to, International Protection*, in MPEPIL III, 16 para. 4.

127 Markus Benzing, *International Administration of Territories*, in MPEPIL V 323-324 para. 38.

128 Fox, *supra* note 126, 25 para. 35.

129 Nicola Wenzel, *Opinion and Expression, Freedom of, International Protection*, in MPEPIL VII 993 para. 26; Peter Malanczuk, *Information and Communication, Freedom of, in* MPEPIL V 189 para. 28. See also CCPR/C/GC/34 of September 12, 2011, para. 11 and Communication No. 736?97 of May, October 18, 2000 *Malcolm Ross v. Canada*, para. 11.6 containing the observation of the Human Rights Committee that the exercise of the right to freedom of expression carries with it special duties and responsibilities/.

130 Fox, *supra* note 126, at 26 para. 36.

131 *Supra* note 54.

132 Paul de Waart, *Economic Sanctions Infringing Human Rights: Is There a Limit?*, in ALI.Z MAROSSI (ed.) UNILATERAL SANCTIONS IN INTERNATIONAL LAW ... (Forthcoming).

4.2 *Global Administrative Law*

4.2.1 Responsibility to Protect (R2P)

Tthe sovereignty of a State implies the right and especially the primary duty of a State to protect its people from atrocities, with a secondary responsibility of the international community. The massacres that ravaged hotbeds like Rwanda and former Yugoslavia in the 1990s had provoked the then U.N. Secretary General Kofi Annan to challenge the international community how to reconcile effectively, politically and legally, humanitarian intervention and State sovereignty.[133] His urgent appeal caused the Government of Canada to establish in 2000 the ad hoc International Commission on Intervention and State Sovereignty [hereinafter ICISS]. Its report *The Responsibility to Protect*, published in 2001 distinguishes between the responsibility to prevent – pillar I – to react – pillar II – and rebuild: pillar III. In doing so, the report let there be no mistake that the responsibility for protecting the lives and promoting the welfare of citizens lies first and foremost with the sovereign state, secondly with domestic authorities acting in partnership with external actors, and only thirdly with international organizations.[134]

The ICISS report also found less tension between intervention and sovereignty than expected.[135] This may explain the optimism of ICISS that enhancing the sovereign capacity of states and improving the ability of the international community to protect people in mortal danger – can be reconciled in practice.[136] There is a glimmer of hope indeed. It is now beyond doubt, that serious violations of human rights within States constitute a matter of concern of the international community as a whole. However, States are not in favour of the opinion that humanitarian emergency should give rise to a right to unilateral humanitarian intervention, let alone a duty to do so.[137]

All in all, in silver perspective the focus of the international community should be not so much on the responsibility to react – pillar II – as on the responsibility to prevent: pillar I. To that end, national capacities for effective, legitimate and inclusive governance should be built. For

---

133 Ingo Winkelmann, *Responsibility to Protect*, in MPEPIL VIII 965, para. 1; SIMMA, *supra* note 39, at 1201, para. 1.

134 ICISS, THE RESPONSIBILITY TO PROTECT 49 para. 6.11 (2001).

135 *Id.* 69 para. 8.2.

136 *Id.* 75 para. 8.32.

137 Vaughan Lowe and Antonios Tzanakopoulos, *Humanitarian Intervention*, in MPEPIL V, 57 para. 47.

that capacity-building are the following inhibitors from atrocity crimes essential, viz.:[138]

- Professional and accountable security sector;
- Impartial institutions for overseeing political transitions;
- Independent judicial and human rights institutions;
- Capacity to assess risk and mobilize early response;
- Local capacity to resolve conflicts;
- Media capacity to counteract prejudice and hate speech;
- Capacity for effective and legitimate justice

Otherwise the responsibility to react will be useless. The present dramatic situation in the Middle East is the writing on the wall. In this tormented region, "communities formerly belonging to the Turkish empire" – Iraq, Lebanon, Palestine and Syria – pay the price for the inability of the League of Nations to protect the well-being and development of the peoples living there as a sacred trust of civilization. [139] Palestine was still a mandate in 1946 when the League of Nations dissolved itself. It was not brought under the UN Trusteeship system by Great Britain as Mandatory Power. Not having been saddled with the Palestinian imbroglio, the U.N. trusteeship system is looked upon as a success, because "it has offered a distinctive model of internationalization, representing one of the most sophisticated occurrences of international territorial administration and good governance."[140] It has even given rise to international trusteeship law.[141]

4.2.2 Society for All

Enthusiasm for R2P as a binding legal principle may increase in silver perspective. But even if it remains a tool for slow normative change,[142] international administration of foreign territory will have the advantage of international trusteeship law. People in failing or failed States may count on that if they will be subjected to international administra-

138 A/68/947-S/2014/449 of July 11, 2014 *Fulfilling Our Collective Responsibility: International Assistance and the Responsibility to Protect*, Report of the Secretary-General 11-15 and 19, para. 77.

139 *Supra* note 90.

140 Andriy Melnyk, *United Nations Trusteeship System, in* MPEPIL X, 534 para. 39.

141 *Id.* para. 40.

142 SIMMA, *supra* note 3, at 1236 para. 82.

tion in the context of R2P.[143] The UN should take that into account when new States resulting from secession apply for membership.

Sovereign equality of States is still the cornerstone of global governance. Nevertheless, the right of State to freely choose its political, economic, social or cultural system has become subject to an increasing number of fundamental international standards in respect of important areas of global governance such as human rights, sustainable development, finance and trade.[144] The same standards apply, mutatis mutandis, increasingly to international organizations as well, and even to private actors[145] The growing interdependency of States and non-State actors in bearing responsibility for the common good has given rise to global administration by IGOs, transnational networks, hybrid public-private bodies and purely private bodies as well as domestic agencies.[146]

The emerging content of global administrative law concerns mainly procedural aspects like transparency, participation and review mechanisms. For there is still too much dissent between developed and developing countries whether the focus of substantial aspects should be on accountability within specific regions; protection of private rights; or entitlement to global democracy. Anyhow, in giving substance to procedural requirements greater sensitivity to their actual distributive consequences is required.[147] All in all, the "tasks of securing proper regard for the disregarded and the building of a more just and equitable system of global regulation are daunting."[148]

5 Global Sustainable Distribution of Wealth

So far sustainable development has been overtaken time and again by the rate of world population growth and the slowness of eradication of extreme poverty. As for the world population, the prognosis is that its size may reach a maximum of roughly 10 billion people in the second

143 *Id.* at 1865-1866: Revitalization of the Trusteeship System?

144 Kokott, *supra* note 83, at 584 para. 80.

145 Weiss & Sornarajah, *supra* note 88, at 526, paras.72 and 73.

146 Benedict Kingsbury and Megan Donaldson, *Global Administrative Law*, in MPEPIL IV, 471-473, paras. 15-20.

147 *Id.* at 479-480, paras. 57 and 58.

148 Richard B. Stewart, *Remedying Disregard in Global Regulatory Governance: Accountability, Participation, and Responsiveness*, AM.J.INT'L 211-271, at 270 (2014).

half of this century.[149] According to the World Bank, extreme poverty could be wiped out by 2030.[150] If both predictions have to become true indeed, fulfilment of the MDGs may come within reach more easily. They may pave the way for distributive justice through international taxation more effectively as a safety valve on the global free market.

Since the fall of the Berlin Wall, the fair distribution of wealth among nations has become the main responsibility of the capitalistic system, managed by an invisible because unpredictable hand.[151] In a much-discussed voluminous study of the role of capital, the French professor of economics Thomas Piketty concluded that the global inequality of wealth in the twenty-first century results from the central contradiction of capitalism, viz. that the rate of return on capital can be significantly higher than the income from labour.[152] Democracy should regain control over the globalized financial capitalism of this century by inventing new tools attuned to today's challenges. One of such tools is a global tax on capital.[153]

Almost simultaneously, the American professor of international law Joel P. Trachtman stated that the future of international law depends on the ability and flexibility of the international community to meet the changes resulting from globalization, development, demography, technology, and democratization. [154] According to him, these changes will ask for an increasing demand for international law. Conditions today exhibit this demand: "The most realistic, and practical response is to

149 www.unfpa.org/pds/trends.htm: Linking Population, Poverty and Development – Population Trends; Leonard Hammer, *World Population*, in MPEPIL X, 955 para. 2; ST/ESA/SER.A/236 WORLD POPULATION TO 2300 (2004). In the latest biennial update the prognosis for 2050 is a world population size of 9.6 billion. See ESA/P/WP.227, *World Population Prospects The 2012 Revision; Key Findings and Advance Tables* 1(2013).

150 World Bank, Ending Extreme Poverty Hinges on Progress in Fragile and Conflict-affected Situations, 30 April 2013, www.worldbank.org/en/news/feature/2013/04/30/ending-extreme-poverty-hinges-on-progress-in-fragile-and-conflict-affected-situations.

151 *Id.* at 9; PAUL DE WAART, *Legal Principle of Integration in the Doha Round: Embedding a Social Order in the Global Market*, in AGREEING AND IMPLEMENT THE DOHA ROUND OF THE WTO 247 (Harald Hohmann ed., 2008).

152 THOMAS PIKETTY, CAPITAL IN THE TWENTY-FIRST CENTURY 571 (2014).

153 *Id.* at 515-539.

154 JOEL P. TRACHTMAN, THE FUTURE OF INTERNATIONAL LAW: GLOBAL GOVERNMENT 70-82 (2013).

plan and establish structures than can increase global welfare in the light of these conditions."[155]

In this connection it is striking that the entry distributive justice in the MPEPIL refers to distributive effects of double taxation.[156] Other entries on taxation focus on taxation as a matter settled between States in bilateral treaties. However, the UN and the OECD have prepared models for such treaties that take into account the interests of developing countries.[157] To that end tax knowledge sharing fora have been created, among which the International Tax Compact, an informal and action oriented platform to strengthen international cooperation with developing countries to promote more efficient and equitable tax systems and fight tax evasion and avoidance.[158]

On the one hand, the achievement of the MDGs should take for granted good governance at both national and international levels. But on the other hand, good governance at the global level is an MDG itself. In silver perspective golden times may begin indeed, when the World Bank prognosis on the disappearance of extreme poverty and the stabilization of world population will be fulfilled within the foreseeable future. As for the Post-2015 debate on the eradication of extreme poverty, the focus may then shift to a more sustainable distribution of public spending in favour of the chronic, long-term poor.[159]

155 *Id.* at 289.

156 Yoram Margalioth, *Double Taxation*, in MPEPIL III, 228 paras. 36-39.

157 www.oecd.org/tax/treaties/oecdmtcavailableproducts.htm: OECD Model Tax Convention on Income and on Capital (2011); www.un.org/esa/ffd/tax/unmodel.htm: U.N. Model Double Taxation Convention between Developed and Developing Countries (2011).

158 Yoram Margalioth, *Taxation, International*, in MPEPIL IX, 781, para. 87; IMF, OECD, UN and WORLD BANK *Supporting the Development of More Effective Tax Systems*, A Report to the G-20 Development Working Group, 46-47 and 50 (2011), available at www.oecd.org/ctp/48993634.pdf. See also www.taxcompact.net/.

159 Andy Summer and Meera Tiwari, *What Issues Will (Re)define the Post 2015 Debate?*, in Malcolm et al. eds., *supra* note 25, at 380.

CHAPTER 2

Judicial Activism in Strasbourg

*Marc Bossuyt**

Based on its dictum that the European Convention on Human Rights is a "living instrument" that must be interpreted "in the light of the present day conditions", the Court of Strasbourg has attributed positive obligations to the rights and freedoms set forth in the Convention, transformed traditional freedoms into socio-economic rights, substituted its own appreciation to that of the competent national instances, recognized the indirect responsibility of states parties for the possible violation of some rights by other states, speculated about future events in other states and declared its interim measures binding. The question may be raised whether there are limits – other than self-imposed – to this continuous expansion of the jurisdiction of the Court beyond what has been assented to by the states parties.

The most relevant distinction between judges in a superior Court, be it international or national, is the one between judges taking an activist[1]

* Emeritus Professor of International Law, University of Antwerp, Emeritus President of the Constitutional Court of Belgium.

1 On the origin and the meanings of "judicial activism" in the USA, where this term originated, see Keenan Kmiec, *The Origin and Current Meanings of 'Judicial Activism'*, Calif. L. Rev., 2004, pp. 1441-1477. Concerning the Court of Strasbourg, other terms are sometimes used, such as "interventionist" or "violationist". The last term applies to judges who have, more than others, the tendency to find violations of the European Convention. As far as more in particular the Court of Strasbourg is concerned, see Paul Mahoney, *Judicial Activism and Judicial Restraint in the European Court of Human Rights: Two Sides of the Same Coin*, H. R. L. J., 1990, pp. 57-88; Erik Voeten, *The Politics of International Judicial Appointments: Evidence from the European Court of Human Rights*, Int. Org., 2007, pp. 669-701, & *Politics, Judicial Behaviour, and Institutional Design*, in Jonas Christoffersen & Mikael Rask Madsen, The European Court of Human Rights between Law and Politics, Oxford, 2013 (256 p.), pp. 61-76.

Karel Wellens (ed.), International Law in Silver Perspective: Challenges Ahead.
 ISBN 978-90-04-27167-8. pp. 31-56.

attitude and judges taking an attitude of restraint.[2] Activist judges have a tendency to adopt a large interpretation of the jurisdiction of their court and of the material provisions they have to apply. They believe that they are more qualified to interpret the applicable legal provisions than the original framers of these texts. Not seldom, they show a distrust of political organs such as the governments and parliaments that have approved these texts. Restrained judges, on the contrary, show more respect for the intentions of the authors of the treaties, constitution and laws they have to apply. They believe that political options should be made by politically responsible organs and that only when the manner by which those organs have translated those options into legal regulations manifestly contradicts superior legal principles, they are entitled to sanction such regulations.

In all courts, both types of judges are present. It is only the degree to which the one or the other category of judges dominates the court, which varies. The International Court of Justice is usually dominated by judges which – in conformity with the tradition of international law – exercise the jurisdiction of their Court with great restraint. The European Court of Human Rights,[3] mostly composed by judges not trained in international law, exercises its jurisdiction in an increasingly activist way.[4]

---

2 Cf. Voeten (*supra* note 2, Int. Org.): "activism-restraint is indeed the main dimension of contestation among judges" (p. 669) and "'activism – self-restraint' constitutes the most prominent divisions between ECHR-judges" (p. 695).

3 *See also* Marc Bossuyt, *Is the European Court of Human Rights on a slippery slope?*, in Spyridon Flogaitis et al., The European Court of Human Rights and its discontents: Turning criticism into strength, Cheltenham, 2013, 217 p., at pp. 27-36.

4 Voeten (*supra* note 2, Int. Org): "the ECHR's composition has grown more activist over time" (p. 697). This activism has been criticized by Lord Hoffmann (Leonard), *The Universality of Human Rights* (Judicial Studies Board Annual Lecture, Mar. 19, 2009), L. Q. Rev., 2009, pp. 416-432; Bernard Edelmann, *La Cour européenne des droits de l'homme: une juridiction tyrannique*, Rec. Dalloz, 2008, pp. 1946-1953; Jean-François Flauss, *Actualité de la Convention européenne des droits de l'homme, Act. jur. dr. adm.*, 2009, pp. 872-884. Léna Gannage, *A propos de l'"absolutisme' des droits fondamentaux*, in Vers des nouveaux équilibres entre ordres juridiques : Liber amicorum Hélène Gaudemet-Tallon, Paris, 2008, pp. 265-284; Yves Lequette, *Des juges littéralement irresponsables*, in Loïc Cadiet, Pierre Callé, Thierry le Bars & Pierre Mayer, (éds.), Mélanges dédiés à la mémoire du doyen Jacques Héron, Paris, 2008, pp. 309-330. For a more lenient approach, see Janneke Gerards, *The Prism of Fundamental Rights, EuConst.*, 2012, pp. 173–202; Jonas Christoffersen & Mikael Rask Madsen, *Post-scriptum: Understanding the*

First, some examples of activist behavior by the Court of Strasbourg are given. Then, some of the techniques used by the Court to engage in an activist behavior are indicated, as well as the main arguments invoked to justify it. Finally, attention is drawn to some of the dangers of this judicial activism.

1 Manifestations of Activist Behavior

1.1 *The Creation of Positive Obligations*

In their classical meaning, civil rights and fundamental freedoms entail only negative obligations for the state. The state is prohibited to torture someone, to hold someone in slavery or to discriminate in the enjoyment of the rights and freedoms set forth in the Convention, to arbitrarily deprive someone from his life and freedom, to interfere in someone's right to respect for privacy, to freedom of thought, of expression, of assembly and association, etc.[5] Only a few provisions explicitly impose positive obligations on the states parties.

Nevertheless, already in its judgment of July 23, 1968 on the merits of its third case (the *Belgian Linguistic* case), the Court stated – contrary to the Commission – that, despite the negative formulation of the right to education in Article 2 of the 1st Additional Protocol ("No person shall be denied the right to education"), "it cannot be concluded from this that the State has no positive obligation to ensure the respect for such a right".[6]

This was strongly criticized by the Norwegian Judge Terje Wold, who considered that inserting a positive obligation into that Article 2 was "not a valid interpretation". According to judge Wold, it would be embarking on "a very dangerous road"[7] to admit that the regulation of

Past, Present, and Future of the European Court of Human Rights in *id.*, *supra* note 2, pp. 230-249.

5 *See also* Marc Bossuyt, *Les droits sociaux: une catégorie spécifique de droits de l'homme?*, in Leif Berg et al, (Ed.), Cohérence et impact de la jurisprudence de la Cour européenne des droits de l'homme : Liber amicorum Vincent Berger, Oisterwijk, 2013, pp. 43-58.

6 *Case "relating to certain aspects of the laws on the use of languages in Belgium" v. Belgium (merits)*, The Law, I, B, para. 3.

7 In my Ph. D. thesis defended in 1975 (L'interdiction de la discrimination dans le droit international des droits de l'homme, Brussels, 1976, 262 p.), doubts were expressed that this "positive" interpretation corresponded to the will of the States

human rights "may vary in time and place according to the needs and resources of the community". In his view, "the human rights granted are absolute rights" which must be the same for everyone, since "everyone" is "every person on the earth". Once a freedom is protected by law against interference by the state, it is a "right". That does not imply, contrary to what was stated by the Court, that it implies positive obligations. As stated by judge Wold, "[i]mposing a negative obligation upon the State is important and has a full meaning".

Further criticism of the Court's approach was expressed by the British Judge Sir Gerald FITZMAURICE,[8] particularly in his elaborate separate opinion (34 p.) to the judgment *Golder* v. the United Kingdom of February 21, 1975, in which the Court decided that the right of access to a court is "inherent in the right stated by Article 6 of the Convention" (para. 36). In that opinion (para. 32), Sir Gerald FITZMAURICE did stress that:

> There is a considerable difference between the case of 'law giver's law edicted in the exercise of sovereign power, and law based on convention, itself the outcome of a process of agreement, and limited to what has been agreed, or can properly be assumed to have been agreed.

---

parties and it was stated that, in doing so, the Court took a path with "incalculable" dangers (*ibid.* p. 217).

8 John Graham Merrils, *Judge Sir Gerald Fitzmaurice and the Discipline of International Law*, The Hague, 1998, 340 p.; Sir Gerald Fitzmaurice, *Some Reflections on the European Convention on Human Rights – and on Human Rights*, in Rudolf Bernhardt et al., Völkerrecht als Rechtsordnung Internationale Gerichtsbarkeit Menschenrechte: Festschrift für Hermann Mosler, Berlin, 1983, pp. 203-219; Voeten (*supra* note 2, Int. Org.) notes that "The British Sir Gerald Fitzmaurice is estimated to be the most 'extreme' judge on the restraint side" (p. 687) in his "Figure 2: Estimates of levels of activism EHCR judges" (*ibid.*, p. 686), set up on the basis of the separate opinions expressed before June 2006, Sir Gerald Fitzmaurice occupies among 97 Judges the last place, immediately preceded by Judges Franz Matscher (Austria), Javier Borrego Borrego (Spain) and Thór Vilhjàlmsson (Iceland). The most "activist" Judges were : (1) Loukis Loukaidis (Cyprus), (2) Jan De Meyer (Belgium), (3) Françoise Tulkens (Belgium), (4) Giovanni Bonello (Malta), (5) Josep Casadevall (Andorra), (6) Dimitris Evrigenis (Greece) and (7) (the present President of the Court) Dean Spielmann (Luxembourg).

In another important judgment (*Marckx* v. Belgium, June 13, 1979), the Court attributed positive obligations to Article 8 of the Convention. In that judgment, the Court stated that the right to respect for family life "does not merely compel the State to abstain" from arbitrary interference by the public authorities:

> in addition to this primarily negative undertaking, there may be positive obligations inherent in an effective 'respect' for family life.

In a comment published in 1980 in the *Belgian Review of International Law*, it was stated that the Court had transformed a civil right into a social right requiring an active intervention by the legislator[9] and that, by neglecting the distinction between classical freedoms and social rights, the Court did risk exceeding its competence, which may not be done by way of interpretation. It was also observed that the method of interpretation of the Court would cause the legal counsels of the applicants quite some pleasant surprises.[10] Needless to say that for the counsels of the defendant governments those surprises are, on the contrary, particularly unpleasant.

Four months later, in another important judgment (*Airey* v. Ireland, October 9, 1979), the Court declared with respect to Article 6 of the Convention that

> the fulfillment of a duty under the Convention on occasion necessitates some positive action on the part of the State.

According to the Court, also in civil litigation, Article 6 of the Convention does

---

9 Marc Bossuyt, *L'arrêt* Marckx *de la Cour européenne des droits de l'homme, Belg. Int. L. Rev.*, 1980, pp. 53-81, at p. 68. The author assented (*ibid.*, p. 67) with the dissenting opinions of Sir Gerald in the cases *National Union of Belgian Police* (27 Oct. 1975) (see *id.*, *supra* note 8, pp. 233-240), and *Marckx* (June 13, 1979) v. Belgium (as did also François Rigaux, *La loi condamnée. À propos de l'arrêt du 13 juin 1979 de la Cour européenne des droits de l'homme*, J. T., 1979, pp. 513-524), but not with his dissenting opinions in the cases *Golder* (Feb. 21, 1975), *Tyrer* (Apr. 25, 1975) and *Ireland* (Jan. 18, 1978) v. the United Kingdom.

10 *Ibid.*, p. 79.

> compel the State to provide for the assistance of a lawyer when such assistance proves indispensable for an effective access to court.

Today, the Court has attributed positive obligations to virtually all Convention rights. At the time of the earlier judgments, the positive obligations were generally confined to the obligation to take legislative measures which did not entail considerable expenses. This did change,[11] when the Court decided in its judgment *Gaygusuz* v. Austria (September 16, 1996) that an emergency assistance in case of unemployment which was linked to the payment of contributions, was a pecuniary right for the purposes of Article 1 of Protocol nº 1 (the protection of property). The situation became worse when the Court, in its judgment *Koua Poirrez* v. France (September 30, 2003), decided that even a non-contributory social benefit for disabled adults must be considered to be a pecuniary right.

This interpretation of the right to property is designed to enlarge the jurisdiction of the Court to social rights, including social security regulations, in order to overcome the limitation to the rights and freedoms set forth in the Convention contained in the prohibition of discrimination provided for in Article 14 of the Convention. This interpretation was confirmed by the Grand Chamber of the Court in its decision on admissibility in *Stec and Others* v. the United Kingdom of July 6, 2005. In that decision, the Court declared itself competent to examine the applications of Ms Stec and others complaining that the Reduced Earnings Allowance scheme funded by general taxation and the Retired Allowance scheme treat men and women differently up to 2020.

It is true that the Court has recognized that in the field of social and economic rights the states parties enjoy a "wide" or a "broad" margin of appreciation.[12] As long as the Court sticks to this prudent approach, it may be questioned whether this praetorian extension of the Court's jurisdiction was worthwhile. But how long will it take before the so-called "dynamic" interpretation of the Court will lead to a stricter control of

11 Marc Bossuyt, *Should the Strasbourg Court exercise more self-restraint? On the extension of the jurisdiction of the European Court of Human Rights to social security regulations*, H. R. L. J., nº 28, 2007, pp. 321-332, at pp. 321-324.

12 *Stec and others* v. the United Kingdom (merits), GC, Apr. 12, 2006, para. 52, and *Andrejeva* v. Latvia, GC, Feb. 18, 2009, para. 89.

the infinite variety of distinctions that states parties have introduced in their economic and social legislation?[13]

1.2 *The Indirect Responsibility of States Parties for the Possible Violation of Some Rights by Other States*

This development started with the judgment *Soering* v. the United Kingdom of July 7, 1989. Based on the absolute character of the prohibition of torture, the Court decided that the extradition of Mr Soering for homicide to the United States, where he would run a real risk of spending years on death row, would violate that prohibition. On the basis of that judgment, the Court, starting with its judgment *Cruz Varas and Others* v. Sweden (March 20, 1991), engaged in the examination of applications by asylum seekers who complained that, if they would be expelled to their country of origin, they would run a real risk of being subjected to inhuman or degrading treatment.

Between 1989 and 2004, the Court rendered (in 16 years) 16 judgments concerning asylum seekers and found in 12 of those judgments concerning Article 3 of the Convention four (indirect) violations[14] of the absolute prohibition of torture and inhuman or degrading treatment or punishment.[15] However, after the Grand Chamber judgment in the case *Mamatkulov and Askarov* v. Turkey (February 4, 2005), there has been (in less than ten years) a sharp increase of the number (nearly 100)[16] of

---

13 Marc Bossuyt, *L'extension de la compétence de la Cour de Strasbourg aux prestations sociales : sur l'interprétation de l'article 14 de la Convention combiné avec l'article 1er du protocole nº 1 dans les affaires* Gaygusuz, Koua Poirrez, Stec et autres, Burden *et* Andrejeva, *Rev. Dr. Monég.*, 2009-2010, pp. 91-130, at p. 125.

14 *Soering* (July 7, 1989) and *Chahal* (Nov. 15, 1996) v. the United Kingdom, *Ahmed* (Dec. 17, 1996) v. Austria and *Jabari* (July 11, 2000) v. Turkey.

15 *See* Marc Bossuyt, Strasbourg et les demandeurs d'asile: des juges sur un terrain glissant, Brussels, 2010, 198 p.

16 *Ahmed* (Dec. 17, 1996) and *I.K.* (Mar. 28, 2013) v. Austria, *Garayev* (June 10, 2010) v. Azerbaijan, *Mubilanzila Mayeka and Kaniki Mitunga* (Oct. 12, 2006), *M.S.* (Jan. 31, 2012) and *Trabelsi* (Sept. 4, 2014) v. Belgium, *M.S.S.* (GC, Jan. 21, 2011) v. Belgium and Greece, *Al Hanchi* (Nov. 15, 2011) and *Al Hussin* (Feb. 7, 2012) v. Bosnia-Herzegovina, *Auad* (Oct. 11, 2011) and *M.G.* (Mar. 25, 2014) v. Bulgaria, *N.* (July 26, 2005) v. Finland, *Daoudi* (Dec. 3, 2009), *Y.P. and L.P.* (Sept. 2, 2010), *H.R.* (Sept. 22, 2011), *Mo.M* (Apr. 18), *Rafaa* (May 30), *M.E.* (June 6), *R.J.* (Sept. 19), *K.K.* (Oct. 10), *Z.M.* (Nov. 14) and *N.K.* (Dec. 19, 2013) and *M.V. and M.T.* (Sept. 4, 2014) v. France, *B.M.* (Dec. 19, 2013) v. Greece, *Shamaev and Others* (GC, Apr. 12, 2005) v. Georgia and Russia, *Saadi* (GC, Feb. 28, 2008), *Ben Khemais* (Feb. 24), *Abdelhedi, Ben Salah, Bouyahia, C.B.Z., Darraji, Hamraoui, O.* and *Soltana* (Mar. 24), *Sellem*

indirect violations of Article 3 of the Convention found by the Court in the event of an extradition or an expulsion of a person who had applied for asylum in a state party to the Convention.

In its Grand Chamber judgment *Mamatkulov and Askarov,*[17] the Court decided – contrary to its previous judgment of 1991 in *Cruz Varas and Others* and to its decision of March 13, 2001 in Čonka *and Others* v. Belgium – that its interim measures had become binding. By granting interim measures, the president of a section of the Court indicates that it is desirable not to extradite or to expel the applicants pending the procedure before the Court. In a sharp dissenting opinion, the Judges Lucius Caflisch (Liechtenstein), Riza Türmen (Turkey) and Anatoly Kovler (Russia) stated that the Court had not interpreted but amended the Convention. Indeed, contrary to the Statute of the International Court of Justice and to the Inter-American Convention on Human Rights, the

---

(May 5, 2009) and *Hirsi Jamaa* (GC, Feb. 23, 2012) v. Italy, *Said* (July 5, 2005), *Salak Seekh* (Jan. 11, 2007) and *A.* (July 20, 2010) v. the Netherlands, *Garabayev* (June 7, 2007), *Ryabikin* (June 19), *Ismoilov and Others* (Apr. 24) and *Muminov* (Dec. 11, 2008), *Khodzayev* (May 12), *Khaydarov* (May 20), *Kolesnik* (June 17), *Yuldashev* and *Abdulazhon Isakov* (July 8), *Karimov* (July 29) *Iskandarov* (Sept. 23), *Gaforov* (Oct. 21), and *Sultanov* (Nov. 4, 2010), *Yakubov* (Nov. 8) and *Ergashev* (Dec. 20, 2011), *Rustamov* (July 3), *Umirov* (Sept. 18), *Makhmudzhan Ergashev* (Oct. 16, 2012), *Zokhidov* (Feb. 5), *Azimov* (Apr. 18), *Savriddin Dzhurayev* (Apr. 25), *Nizomkhon Dzhurayev* (Oct. 13), *Ermakov* (Nov. 7) and *Kasymakhunov* (Nov. 14, 2013), *Pitsayeva and Others* (Jan. 9), *Ismailov* and *Gayratbek Saliyev* (Apr. 17), *Nizamov and Others* (May 7), *Egamberdiyev* (June 26), *Rakhimov* (July 10) and *Mamadaliyev* (July 24, 2014) v. Russia, *Labsi* (May 15, 2012) v. Slovakia, *Bador and Kandor* (Nov. 8, 2005), *R.C.* (Mar. 9) and *N.* (July 20, 2010), *S.F. and Others* (May 15) and *F.N. and Others* (Dec. 18, 2012), and *I.* (Sept. 5, 2013) v. Sweden, *A.A.* (Jan. 17, 2014) v. Switzerland, *Jabari* (July 11, 2000), *D. and Others* (June 22, 2006), *Abdolkhani and Karimnia* (Sept. 22), *Keshmiri* and *Tehrani and Others* (Apr. 13, 2009), *Z.N.S.* (Jan. 19), *Charahili* (Apr. 13), *Ahmadpour* and *M.B. and Others* (June 15), and *Dbouba* (July 13, 2010) and *Ghorbanov and Others* (Dec. 3, 2013) v. Turkey, *Soldatenko* (Oct. 23, 2008), *Kabulov* (Nov. 19, 2009) and *Bayakov and Others* (Feb. 18, 2010) v. Ukraine, *Chahal* (GC, Nov. 15, 1991), *NA.* (July 17, 2008), *S.H.* (June 15, 2010) and *Sufi and Elmi* (June 28, 2011) v. the United Kingdom.

17 Marc Bossuyt, *Judges on thin ice: the European Court on Human Rights and the treatment of asylum seekers, Int.Am. & Eur. Hum. Rts.*, 2010, pp. 3-48, at pp. 14-21, & *Le rôle de la Cour de Strasbourg à l'égard des demandeurs d'asile / Sur les arrêts* Čonka *et* Mubilanzila Mayeka et Kaniki Mutanga *c. Belgique*, Mamatkoulov et Askarov *c. Turquie*, N. *c. Finlande*, Saadi, N. *et* NA. *c. Royaume Uni et* Saadi *c. Italie*, R.u.d.h., 2007-2010, pp. 16-34, at 20-24.

European Convention does not contain any provision concerning interim measures. Moreover, proposals of the Parliamentary Assembly of the Council of Europe to include in an additional protocol a provision making interim measures binding, had been consistently rejected by the states parties.

What could be expected did happen. Year after year, the number of interim measures requested by applicants increased: 122 requests were made in 2006, 883 in 2007, 2,871 in 2008 and 4,786 in 2010.[18] The percentage of the requests granted by the presidents of the different sections of the Court increased even more. In a declaration of February 11, 2011, the President of the Court expressed his concern about the "alarming rise" in the number of requests for interim measures. At the Izmir Conference in April 2011, the member states of the Council of Europe recalled that "the Court is not an immigration Appeals Tribunal or a Court of fourth instance". With the exception of a decrease in the percentage of interim measures granted,[19] it does not appear that the Court takes this rebuke very seriously.

Particularly worrisome with respect to asylum is the Grand Chamber judgment *M.S.S.* v. Belgium and Greece of January 21, 2011.[20] Based on the EU Dublin Regulation, Belgium had transferred to Greece an Afghan interpreter, who had paid his smuggler 12.000 US$ for travelling to that country. By stating that asylum seekers that had entered the Schengen area in Greece may not be transferred to that country, the Court undermines the EU Dublin Regulation, a central piece of the Common European Asylum System.[21] In this case, the Court condemned Greece, directly responsible for the violation of Article 3, to pay 1,000 euros to the

18 According to the annex to the declaration of the President of the Court on Feb. 11, 2011.

19 From 1,443 (38 percent) in 2010 to 103 (5 percent) in 2012 and 108 (11 percent) in 2013.

20 Marc Bossuyt, *Belgium condemned for inhuman or degrading treatment due to violations by Greece of EU Asylum Law,* M.S.S. *v. Belgium and Greece, Grand Chamber, European Court of Human Rights, January 21, 2011*, E.H.R.L.R., 2011, pp. 581-596.

21 The situation has been worsened by the endorsement of this view by the Court of Justice of the European Union in its judgment of Dec. 21, 2011 in the cases C-411/10 and C-493/10 (*see* Geert De Baere, *The Court of Luxembourg acting as an Asylum Court*, in André Alen et al., Liberae Cogitationes: Liber amicorum Marc Bossuyt, Antwerp, 2013, pp. 107-124, at p. 117: "By adopting and endorsing the ECtHR's analysis, the ECJ profoundly unsettled the principle of mutual confidence that

applicant, while Belgium, which was only indirectly responsible, had to pay 24,900 euros.

Other developments in this judgment raising concern are:

(1) The continuously lowering of the threshold of Article 3: not every ill-treatment amounts to torture, or even to inhuman or degrading treatment; a particular level of severity (the threshold) has to be attained. In the first judgments, finding that the conditions of retention of an asylum seeker violated Article 3, the conditions considered "unacceptable" lasted for several months (from 17 months in *Dougoz* v. Greece, March 6, 2001, down to 2 or 3 months in several judgments, also mainly against Greece); however, in *M.S.S.* and in other recent judgments, such conditions lasted only four days or even less: two days in *Rahimi* v. Greece (April 5, 2011) and even maybe only two hours in *Tehrani and Others* v. Turkey (April 13, 2010). Is that compatible with the absolute character of the prohibition of torture which allows no exception, no restriction and no derogation "not even in time of war or other public emergency threatening the life of the nation"? It is, however, the absolute character of that prohibition that justifies the indirect responsibility for its violation by other states.

(2) The expansion of the list of "particularly vulnerable groups", such as "mentally disabled" in *Orsus and Others* v. Croatia (March 16, 2010) and "Roma" in *Alajos Kiss* v. Hungary (May 20, 2010), with a self-elected category: asylum seekers. Indeed, every foreigner who decides to apply for asylum is an asylum seeker, regardless his personal condition or his motives for applying. Other groups deserving special attention are women in Afghanistan (in *N.* v. Sweden, July 20, 2010) and children (in *Nunez* v. Norway, June 28, 2011, and *Kanagaratnam and Others* v. Belgium, December 13, 2011). In doing so, the Court is shifting from protecting civil rights of the universal human being towards protecting social rights of specific categories of persons having particular needs. According to the Court, persons belonging to one of those categories are entitled to an active intervention of the State beyond the level required for other persons with respect to civil rights and fundamental freedoms. The question arises how many more specific categories will the Court discover in the near future?

underlies the CEAS and, by extension, the entire edifice of European integration".

(3) The extension of the applicability of Article 3 to the living conditions of asylum seekers: the Court has transformed the civil right by excellence (the absolute prohibition of torture is an obligation not to do something, an obligation that has to be and *can* be respected regardless the available resources) into an obligation to provide social benefits to asylum seekers which requires considerable expenditures. Since the resources available for social benefits are not unlimited, this implies that, despite the deep financial crisis in Greece, that country should, according to the Court, give priority to the needs of asylum seekers.[22]

In its judgment *Sufi and Elmi* v. the United Kingdom (June 28, 2011),[23] the defendant government was considered indirectly responsible for a violation of Article 3 of the Convention if the applicants, two Somali sentenced several times in Britain on account of a variety of criminal offences, would end up in a settlement in Somalia or in a refugee camp in Kenya. The Court was of the opinion that the conditions in those camps were "sufficiently dire to amount to treatment reaching the threshold of Article 3 of the Convention". If a foreigner, even when he has committed criminal offences, may not be returned to his country when the conditions of living in that country are not sufficiently decent in the eyes of the Court, it will become very difficult to pursue an "effective – and not a merely cosmetic or illusory – migration control".[24]

Such a control is neither facilitated by the Grand Chamber judgment in *Hirsi Jamaa* v. Italy (February 23, 2012), which awarded 15,000 euros in respect of non-pecuniary damage to 11 Eritreans and 13 Somalis each, who had tried to reach Lampedusa by boat but were sent back to Libya by the Italian navy. It certainly will not discourage migrants to under-

---

22 Neither the Greek Government, nor the troika (composed of the European Commission, the European Central Bank and the International Monetary Fund) seem to respect this priority obligation imposed by the Court which remains (three years after the judgment) without implementation. After the judgment *Suso Musa* v. Malta (July 23, 2013), Joseph Licari, former Ambassador of Malta to the Council of Europe, raised the following question: "Does it mean that the Finance Minister should put the welfare of refugees and illegal immigrants as his budget's top priority?" (The Sunday Times of Malta, Sept. 15, 2013, p. 22).

23 Marc Bossuyt, *Strasbourg et les demandeurs d'asile* (M.S.S. *c. Belgique et Grèce, et* Sufi et Elmi *c. le Royaume-Uni*)", VI Ann. int. dr. h. 2011, Athens, 2012, pp. 663-676, at pp. 668-676.

24 *Cf.* the dissenting opinion of Judges Ljiljana Mijović (Bosnia-Hercegovina) and Vincent A. De Gaetano (Malta) in *Nunez* v. Norway (Feb. 14, 2012).

take such a perilous journey at the risk of their lives and it raises a number of intriguing questions relevant to the mission of Frontex (the EU agency managing European border control).

In other recent judgments, the Court has extended the indirect responsibility for acts of foreign states to possible violations of Article 6 of the Convention (the right to a fair trial). In its judgment *Othman (Abu Qatada)* v. the United Kingdom (January 17, 2012), the Court decided that the extradition of the applicant to Jordan would not violate Article 3 but Article 6 "on the account of the real risk of the admission at the applicant's retrial of evidence obtained by torture of a third person". It is this judgment that prompted the British Prime Minister on 25 January 2012 before the Parliamentary Assembly of the Council of Europe to state, referring to persons who intend to harm one's country, that "there are circumstances in which you cannot try them, you cannot detain them and you cannot deport them". It is quite obvious that this development will, in the future, prohibit extraditions to a great number of countries and hamper international judicial cooperation.

In a later judgment (*El Haski* v. Belgium, September 25, 2012), the Court attributed even further reaching extra-territorial effects to Article 6 by judging that that Article was violated since the applicant was condemned in Belgium on the basis of material provided by Morocco while it was not excluded that it could have been obtained in violation of Article 3 of the Convention. In the first case, Jordan could not obtain the extradition of Abu Qatada due to Jordan's own actions; in the second case, Belgium could not condemn El Haski due to actions of another country (Morocco).

1.3 *Some Other Large Interpretations of the Rights Set Forth in the Convention*

In its judgment of *Hatton and Others* v. the United Kingdom (October 2, 2001) concerning complaints of an increase in the level of noise caused at the applicants' homes by aircraft using Heathrow airport, the Court stated that

> the applicants' complaints fall to be analysed in terms of a positive duty on the State to take reasonable and appropriate measures to secure the applicants' rights under Article 8 § 1 of the Convention

and that, in the particular case at hand, the defendant Government had

> failed to strike a fair balance between the United Kingdom's economic well-being and the applicants' effective enjoyment of their right to respect for their homes and their private and family lives.

That judgment was overturned on July 8, 2003 by the Grand Chamber of the Court, which decided that the authorities "had not overstepped their margin of appreciation". Indeed, it would be far reaching,[25] if Article 8 would empower judges – having as only terms of reference a provision stating that "*Everyone* has the right to respect for his private and family life" – to decide where airports should be located and which runways airplanes should use for take-off and landing. Severely criticized in Great Britain is also the judgment *Hirst* v. the United Kingdom (October 6, 2005),[26] in which the Court decided that the law banning convicted prisoners from voting was in breach of Britain's obligation to hold free elections at reasonable intervals by secret ballot.

As far as Article 8 of the Convention is concerned, the Court went particularly far by imposing positive obligations to states parties in finding violations of that provision in its judgment *Georgel and Georgeta Stoicescu* v. Romania (July 26, 2011),[27] because the government had not taken concrete measures to tackle the serious problem of public health and threat to the physical integrity of the population by a great number of stray dogs in Bucharest (para. 61), and in its judgment *Di Sarno and Others v.* Italy (January 10, 2012), because the government felt short of taking adequate measures to ensure the regular functioning of the ser-

---

25 Hoffmann, *supra* note 5, para. 32: "[it] sounds about as far from human rights as you could get".

26 *See* David Davis, *Britain must defy the European Court of Human Rights on prisoner voting as Strasbourg is exceeding its authority* in Flogaitis et al., *supra* note 2, pp. 65-70; *see also* Koen Muylle, *Prisoners' right to vote: the* Hirst *case law of the European Court of Human Rights and its application by the Belgian Constitutional Court, Liberae Cogitationes, supra* note 22, pp. 403-418.

27 In his dissenting opinion, Judge Luis López Guerra (Spain) did not find it justified to require that the authorities should "adopt all necessary measures to protect all people from all forms of danger in general. The public powers are required to meet practically unlimited needs with inevitably limited means. They must provide vital services such as clean water, sewer systems, waste disposal, health care, traffic safety and public safety, among many others. And the numbers of victims of the faulty delivery of those services may be considerable. But it is the competent authorities of each country and not this Court who must establish priorities and determine preferences when allocating efforts and resources".

vice of collection, treatment and elimination of waste in the commune Somma Vesuviana (para. 109).[28]

As far as Article 10 of the Convention is concerned, mention can also be made of the judgment of the Court in the case of *Lautsi* v. Italy,[29] in which a Chamber of the Court unanimously decided that the presence of crucifixes in schools in Italy violated the freedom of religion of two school boys. This judgment of November 3, 2009 caused uproar from several states parties which decided to intervene in that case: Armenia, Bulgaria, Cyprus, Romania, the Russian Federation, Greece, Lithuania, Malta, Monaco and San Marino. In its judgment of March 18, 2011, the Grand Chamber of the Court reversed its position by deciding that this matter fell within the margin of appreciation of the state party concerned. In his concurring opinion attached to that judgment, Judge Giovanni Bonello (Malta) referred to "a court in a glass box a thousand kilometres away" which had been "engaged to veto overnight what [had] survived countless generations".

As far as criminal law in Belgium is concerned, particularly important are the judgments *Salduz* v. Turkey (April 26, 2007; GC, November 27, 2008),[30] and also – be it to a lesser extent – *Taxquet* v. Belgium (January 13, 2009; GC, November 16, 2010) which provoked in continental law countries considerable legal uncertainty and a high increase in the cost of criminal justice.

As far as terrorism related cases are concerned, the Court found, in its judgment *M.S.* v. Belgium (January 31, 2012), a violation of Article 3, despite the absence of indications that the applicant, an Iraqi national

---

28 In his dissenting opinion, Judge András Sajó (Hungary) stated that he was not convinced that persons not having their residence in that commune could pretend that they were victims in the enjoyment of their private life and their home.

29 *See* Jean-Marc Piret, *Limitations of Supranational Jurisdiction, Judicial Restraint and the Nature of Treaty Law*, in Jeroen Temperman (ed.), *The Lautsi Papers: Multidisciplinary Reflections on Religious Symbols in Public School Classroom*, Leiden, 2012, pp. 59-89.

30 *See also* Egbert Myjer, *One* Salduz *a year is enough. Associative Thoughts on Judge Rozakis' Judicial Activism and the* Salduz *Judgment*, in The European Convention on Human Rights, a living instrument: Essays in honour of Christos L. Rozakis, Louvain-La-Neuve, 2011, pp. 419-430, and Janneke Gerards, *The scope of ECHR rights and institutional concerns – the relationship between proliferation of rights and the caseload of the ECHR*, Ghent University, Mar. 12-13, 2012 (nog yet published) : "the judgment has caused great confusion and controversy in many legal systems" (p. 9).

condemned for terrorism, was ill-treated after his forced return to Iraq, after having received 10,000 euros from the Belgian authorities.[31] In its judgment *Trabelsi* v. Belgium (September 4, 2014), the Court found a violation of Article 3 in the extradition of the applicant to the USA, on charges for offences relating to Al Qaeda-inspired acts of terrorism, in the absence of a review mechanism that would require the US authorities to ascertain, whether, if a life sentence would be imposed upon him, he, while serving his sentence, would have changed and progressed to such an extent that continued detention could no longer be justified on legitimate penological grounds. Belgium was to pay 60,000 euros in respect of non-pecuniary damage.

Finally, mention can be made of the judgment in *B.* v. Belgium (July 10, 2012) which resulted in rewarding a mother for the legal kidnapping in the United States of her five year old child, in disregard of the Hague Convention of 1980 on the civil aspects of child abduction and of the well-reasoned judgment from the Court of Appeal of Ghent, as recognized in the joint dissenting opinion of Judges Ms Isabelle Berro-Lefèvre (Monaco) and Ms Isil Karacas (Turkey). As the Court is rendering about 1,500 judgments a year, there may be quite a number of such judgments largely unknown even to most students of the European Convention.

2 The Techniques Used by the Court to Engage in an Activist Behavior and the Main Arguments Invoked to Justify Such a Behavior

In important speeches delivered in Strasbourg at the European Court[32] and in London at the Barnard's Inn Reading,[33] both in 2011, Baroness Hale of Richmond, Justice at the Supreme Court of the United Kingdom,

---

31 Marc Bossuyt, You cannot try them, you cannot detain them and you cannot deport them (*Observations sous C.E.D.H.,* M.S. *c. Belgique, 31 janvier 2012*), J. T., 2012, pp. 351-355.

32 Baroness Hale of Richmond, in European Court of Human Rights, Council of Europe, Dialogue between judges 2011, Strasbourg, pp. 11-19.

33 www.gresham.ac.uk/lectures-and-events/beanstalk-or-living-instrument-how-tall-can-the-european-convention-on-human-rights-grow, published also under the title *Common Law and Convention Law: The Limits to Interpretation*, in E.H.R.L.R., 2011, pp. 534-543.

identified four different ways in which the Convention jurisprudence has developed beyond the expectations of the original parties:

(a) The autonomous concept (a concept used to avoid that European norms would vary according to the different meaning they may have in different states parties):

According to Baroness HALE, there is no problem when the language of the Convention is applied

> to situations which may not have been contemplated by the original framers, but which are entirely capable of being covered by the language used and are consistent with its underlying principles and purpose.

However, the concept "civil right", e.g., has been developed in a way that has, in her view, now reached its natural limits. In her opinion,

> claims for services, which require a high degree of discretionary judgment on the part of officials, are not readily susceptible to court-like adjudication on the merits.

(b) The concept of implied rights:

According to Baroness HALE, some decisions of the Court are

> examples of an evolution in the Court's jurisprudence which, however admirable it may be from some points of view, does risk going further than anything the member States committed themselves to at the time.

And, while accepting that the Convention may develop beyond its original intentions, she is of the opinion that

> those developments should be foreseeable, for otherwise States might be landed with obligations which they would not have signed up had they known.

(c) The development of positive obligations:

In the opinion of Baroness Hale, this is "the more controversial area" because they oblige the States parties "to provide some benefit which [they] could not otherwise be obliged or wish to provide". She wonders whether we are beginning to see "the emergence of socio-economic rights" and whether that is "a good thing or a bad thing".

(d) The narrowing of the margin of interpretation:

On this issue, Baroness HALE referred to Lord BINGHAM (Britain's former senior Law Lord), who believes that respect should be shown to "the considered judgment of a democratic assembly" and that

> the democratic process is liable to be subverted if opponents of an Act achieve through the courts what they could not achieve in Parliament.

(e) Conclusion:

Baroness Hale concluded: "there must be some limits".

The problem is, however, that the only limitations to its jurisdiction that the Court seems to accept, are self-imposed limitations.[34] It would help if the Court would clearly indicate that it is not competent to extend its jurisdiction to

> the creation of rights not enumerated in the Convention, however, expedient or even desirable such new rights might be.[35]

At the end of the 70's, the Court relied on the so-called "present-day" interpretation of civil rights in order to condemn judicial corporal punishment of children (in *Tyrer* v. the United Kingdom, April 25, 1978), the distinction between legitimate and illegitimate children (in *Marckx* v. Belgium, June 13, 1979) and the absence of indispensable legal assistance in a civil procedure (in *Airey* v. Ireland, October 9, 1979). All this, however, is very modest compared with the more recent extension of the jurisdiction of the Court to the field of social security by relying on a property protection provision, as in *Gaygusuz* (1996), *Koua Poirrez* (2003) and *Stec and Others* (2005).

The Court justifies the extension of its jurisdiction mainly by quoting its *Tyrer* judgment (para. 31) in which it stated that the Convention is "a

34 Bossuyt, *supra* note 12, p. 328.

35 Dissenting opinion of Judge Egbert Myjer (Netherlands) in *Munoz Diaz* v. Spain (Dec. 8, 2009), quoted in Egbert Myjer, *Why much of the criticism of the European Court of Human Rights is unfounded*, in Flogaitis *et al.*, *supra* note 4 (pp. 37-53), p. 50.

living instrument" which must be interpreted "in the light of the present day conditions", and its *Airey* judgment (para. 24) in which it stated that

> [t]he Convention is intended to guarantee not rights that are theoretical or illusory but rights that are practical and effective.

According to Lord HOFFMANN,[36] the concept of a "living instrument" is

> the banner under which the Strasbourg court has assumed power to legislate what they consider to be required by 'European public order'

and according to Rosalind ENGLISH, on the *UK Human Rights Blog* of July 6, 2010, it is

> a Trojan horse for judicial activism, giving Strasbourg judges the liberty to find what they want to find in the interstices of Convention rights.

Nevertheless, the living instrument doctrine is not without validity for the material provisions of the Convention. Notions as "discrimination", "torture", "family life" etc., to mention only a few, should not be interpreted nowadays as they were understood in 1950. There is no major problem when the Court interprets the civil rights and fundamental freedoms guaranteed by the Convention "in the light of present day conditions", as long as the Court remains within the borders of its jurisdiction. However, the Court is exceeding its jurisdiction when it transforms – by way of interpretation – a civil right into a social right.

A civil right loses its very nature when positive obligations are attributed to it which entail expenditures that many states cannot afford and that require choices and priorities at the expense of other rights or other categories of persons. It is disputable to admit that the member states of the Council of Europe have accepted that positive obligations can be imposed upon them – without the intervention of the legislature – when it is not possible – in good faith – to take it for granted that they are inherent or implied in the civil rights and fundamental freedoms guaranteed by the Convention.

---

36 Hoffmann, *supra* note 5, para. 39.

The jurisdiction of an international court[37] is determined by the states parties in its constitutive treaty. The legal basis for the binding character of the states parties' obligations lies in the acceptance of that treaty. To disregard, willingly and knowingly, the intentions of the authors of a treaty is incompatible with the principle of good faith, the cardinal principle of any legal interpretation. Moreover, it amounts to a limitation of state sovereignty without democratic legitimation.[38]

Sometimes reference is made to the existence of a "consensus"[39] in order to impose a particular interpretation of the rights guaranteed by the Convention.[40] A comparative law research indicating that certain regulations have been adopted in several other member states cannot suffice to conclude that derogatory regulations in a particular member state violate the Convention. Each national regulation should be evaluated on its own merits in the light of the Convention. It is up to the Court to enforce respect for minimum norms and not to harmonise the domestic legislation of the states parties.[41] Nor should the finding of a violation depend on the resistance expected or not from governments of states parties.[42] Those are political considerations and the political authorities have entrusted judges with the protection of human rights precisely in order to have such decisions based on legal (rather than political) considerations.

---

37 On the jurisdiction of the Court of Strasbourg, *see* Marc Bossuyt, *Des limites* à la juridiction de la Cour de Strasbourg?, *L'homme et le droit: En hommage au Professeur Jean-François Flauss*, Paris, 2014, pp. 117-127.

38 Bossuyt, *supra* note 12, p. 330.

39 On consensus, *see* Kanstantsin Dzehtsiarou, *Does Consensus matter? – Legitimacy of European Consensus in the Case Law of the European Court of Human Rights*, Publ. L., 2011, pp. 534-553; Dean Spielmann, *Consensus et marge d'appréciation nationale*, J. T., 2012, pp. 592-593.

40 Having noted (with reference to Dzehtsiarou) that the Strasbourg judges leave the consensus method aside, when its application would lead "to results that go against their own strong personal convictions" (p. 950), Tom Zwart (*Why the Strasbourg judges, like Odysseus, should tie themselves [to the mast to be able to resist the Sirens of subjective interpretation]*, Liberae Cogitationes, *supra* note 22, pp. 943-959, at p. 946) concludes: "a court that is prepared to set aside its canons of interpretation cannot be distinguished from political bodies" (p. 952).

41 Hoffmann, *supra* note 5, para. 27: "[The Court] has been unable to resist the temptation to aggrandise its jurisdiction and to impose uniform rules on Member States".

42 *Cf. supra*, *sub* 1, c, the Grand Chamber judgment in the case *Lautsi*.

3 The Dangers of His Judicial Activism

3.1 *As Far as the Creation of Positive Obligations*[43] *is Concerned*

(1) A first casualty of the positive obligations doctrine is democracy itself. It is up to the national constitutions to determine which organs are granted which powers. In conformity with the Separation of Powers principle, it is up to political organs to create the rules and to the judiciary to apply them. The Court is entitled to interpret the rules, not to extend its own competences by creating new rules. According to the text of the Convention, the power of the national legislators is limited by negative obligations. There is no clear basis in the Convention empowering the Court to impose positive obligations upon the states parties without the intervention of their parliaments.

Moreover, the concept of positive obligations is open-ended. The Court does not indicate what are the limits of those positive obligations. With respect to the negative obligations, several paragraphs of the Convention provide, in the second paragraph of the articles concerned, for the possibility of restricting those negative obligations of the state on the condition that they are "prescribed by law", "necessary in a democratic society", taken in the interest of a number of goals specifically mentioned in the relevant paragraph and, all this, in a non-discriminatory way. It is not feasible to apply the same conditions to positive obligations: e.g. a state cannot be required to demonstrate the necessity in a democratic society to restrict a particular rather than another social right to all or to certain categories of persons. In case of scarcity of resources, it is up to the political authorities of the state to set up priorities as far as the rights, their beneficiaries and the timetable of their realization is concerned, without having to justify that a particular restriction rather than another is "necessary in a democratic society".[44]

---

43 On positive obligations, *see* Hugues Dumont & Isabelle Hachez, *Les obligations positives déduites du droit international des droits de l'homme: dans quelles limites?* in Yves Cartuyvels et al., Les droits de l'homme, bouclier ou épée du droit pénal?, Brussels, 2007, pp. 45-73; Khanlar Hajiyev, *The evolution of positive obligations under the European Convention on Human Rights by the European Court of Human Rights*, in Essays Rozakis, *op. cit.*, pp. 207-218; Dimitris Xenos, The Positive Obligations of the State Under the European Convention of Human Rights, Oxon, 2012, 272 p.

44 Bossuyt, *supra* note 12, p. 325, note 50.

The Court has appropriated itself the power to judge to what extent it may impose positive obligations on the states parties. It is also since the attribution of positive obligations that cases of conflicts between human rights have multiplied, giving the opportunity to the Court to expand its powers by balancing the one right against the other.

(2) It is not only problematic that those positive obligations are created by a court, but even more so that they are created by an international court. A national constitutional court functions within the framework of the national constitution and is composed of nationals of the state, which are familiar with the economic, social, cultural and political environment of the national community upon which the constitutional court exercises its jurisdiction. An international court is composed in its overwhelming majority by non-nationals which are much less familiar with the national environment in which the decisions it controls are taken.

Moreover, at any time, the competent political authorities can amend the laws and even the constitution when the interpretation of domestic courts goes beyond what is considered appropriate. As an amendment of the European Convention requires 47 ratifications, it is practically impossible for the states parties to counter the Court's judicial activism. The knowledge that the jurisdiction of the Court is based on an agreement given by the states parties in the form of an international treaty, should induce the Court to exercise its jurisdiction with great restraint rather than continuously trying to extend it beyond the limits expressed by the negative formulation of the rights set forth in the Convention.

As long as the Court applies the rights and freedoms of the Convention in conformity with their negative formulation, the lack of familiarity of foreign judges with the national environment of the state parties concerned is generally not problematic. However, when attributing positive obligations to those rights, the Court needs an overall view of the factual and legal situation in the country concerned, taking into account the whole of the national context, including the other interests of the state and of other citizens and groups and not in the least the budgetary implications of its judgments.

(3) The extension of the Court's jurisdiction to economic and social rights leads to the development of a purely regional human rights standard, unattainable by many countries, and depriving human rights of their universality, which is one of the strengths of the traditional con-

cept of human rights. Indeed, as the realization of those social rights depends on the availability of resources in the state concerned, there is no universal standard, not even a common regional standard among states parties to the Convention ranging from Albania to Switzerland or from Monaco to Moldova.[45]

(4) The extension of the Court's jurisdiction to economic and social rights also enlarges the applicability of the prohibition of discrimination guaranteed in Article 14 of the Convention. The general prohibition of discrimination provided for in the 12th Additional Protocol has only been the subject of ratification by a minority of the members of the Council of Europe.[46] This number will not increase rapidly if states become aware of the fact that the application of the prohibition of discrimination to economic and social rights amounts to relinquishing a considerable degree of sovereignty from the national legislator to the international judge, much more than is the case with respect to civil rights and fundamental freedoms.

This is particularly the case since the Court, when examining differences of treatment, attaches great weight to the element of proportionality. In a *Festschrift* published in 2010 – in honour of the former German Judge at the Strasbourg Court, Renate JAEGER –, Paul MAHONEY, former Registrar but at present the British Judge at the Strasbourg Court, expressed his worries over the

> interventionist tendency whereby the principle of proportionality becomes merely the means by which a small group of international judges substitute their own personal view as to the desirability of the regulatory policy chosen for that of the democratic institutions of the country, judicial as well as executive and legislative.[47]

45 *Ibid.*, p. 329.

46 This Protocol has only been ratified by 18 of the 47 member states of the Council of Europe: 11 East-European (Albania, Armenia, Bosnia and Herzegovina, Georgia, Croatia, Montenegro, Romania, Serbia, Slovenia, de Former Yugoslav Republic of Macedonia, Ukraine) and seven Western-European (Andorra, Cyprus, Finland, Luxembourg, Netherlands, San Marino and Spain) member states.

47 Paul Mahoney, *Reconciling Universality of Human Rights and Local democracy – the European Experience* in Grundrechte und Solidarität. Durchsetzung und Verfahren, Festschrift für Renate Jaeger, Kehl-am-Rhein, 2010, pp. 147-161, at p. 158.

(5) The reliance of the Court on EU regulations and directives, as in its *M.S.S.* judgment, to define the extent of the positive obligations the states are supposed to have assumed by becoming parties to the Convention, is highly questionable. The obligations accepted by the states parties to the Convention are minimum obligations. According to the preamble of the Convention, the governments signatory thereto were resolved to take the "first steps" for the collective enforcement of "certain" of the rights stated in the Universal Declaration.

In any case, the Court cannot rely on those regulations and directives to interpret the Convention with respect to the 19 states parties which are not members of the European Union. And the Court may neither interpret the extent of the obligations applicable to the 28 member states of the European Union differently from those applicable to the 19 other states parties to the Convention. Finally, it is not up to the Court in Strasbourg – but to the Court of Justice in Luxembourg – to interpret the extent of the EU regulations and directives and to sanction their non-respect.

3.2 *As Far as the Asylum Cases are Concerned*[48]

Based on the absolute character of the prohibition of torture, the Court moved into the direction of finding indirect and potential violations of the Convention: indirect violations, because the states parties are held responsible for treatment inflicted by other states, generally non states parties, and potential violations, because very often the prohibited treatment has not taken place yet but could take place if a person has to leave the territory of a state party.

As a consequence,

(1) the Court does not assess facts that did happen but speculates about events that could happen;
(2) the Court must be familiar not only with situations and regulations of states parties to the Convention but also of non-states parties;
(3) the Court does not only rely on primary sources but also relies heavily on secondary sources.

Quite often the Court substitutes its own appreciation of the credibility of an asylum seeker and of the risk he could face in case of return to his

48 Marc Bossuyt, *The Court of Strasbourg Acting as an Asylum Court*, *EuConst.*, n° 8, 2012, pp. 203-245, at 241-242.

country of origin, to that of the competent national authority. *Quid* if the Court would also in criminal cases substitute its own appreciation to that of the competent national criminal jurisdictions?

It is particularly in the field of asylum and immigration that the Court quite often indicates interim measures. The Court intervenes in the daily exercise of the migration policy of the states parties,[49] based on a unilateral request, at very short notice and without giving the defendant government the opportunity to state its case. Not only is, as already stated, the legal basis for such an intervention shaky, it is also very likely that, if the state party abides to those interim measures, an irreversible situation is created: chances are indeed very low that in a later stage the applicant will still leave the territory of the state party. By deciding that the interim measures had become binding, the Court has attracted a sharp increase of the applications by asylum seekers contributing to the overall increase of applications submitted and to a backlog which makes it extremely difficult for the Court to discharge its duties "within a reasonable time".

The backlog of applications pending before the Court did increase from 97,300 on January 1, 2009 up to 160,200 on September 1, 2011. It is true that now, three years later, thanks to the new single-judge procedure instituted by the 14th Additional Protocol, that backlog went down (on June 30, 2014) to 84,850 pending applications. When the remaining cases which are not clearly inadmissible or which cannot be struck out without further examination, will be dealt with in a near future, it may be estimated that about 50,000 cases which are not clearly inadmissible nor belonging to one of the categories of prioritisation, will be left over. As observed by Judge Mahoney, last year at a conference in The Hague on the Court and its discontents:

> It is inconceivable that the Court [...] should have the material capacity to look fully into the merits of all unresolved human rights

49 As noted by Pieter van Dijk, Ben Vermeulen and Aleidus Woltjes (*It's a livin' thing'. The European Convention applied in Strasbourg and at the domestic level: cooperation and dialogue*, Liberae Cogitationes, *supra* note 22, pp. 817-830, at p. 827: "this self-claimed exclusive competence with binding force entails heavy responsibilities, since it may constitute a serious intervention in the execution of a domestic court decision or a decision of the executive". However, fortunately, "the increased number of requests for interim measures has urged the Court to mitigate an overenthusiastic use of this instrument".

> violations within a Convention community of 47 states and 800 million people.[50]

What could be done and what should be done to meet this challenge is not the subject of the present contribution.

4 Conclusions

The present analysis may raise concern, particularly with those unfamiliar with the activity of the Court. Some may wonder what might be the appropriate reaction. More important is to state what would not be an appropriate reaction. Inappropriate is any suggestion of withdrawing from the Council of Europe or denouncing the European Convention. Even suggesting that some of the judgments of the Court should not be implemented is ill advised. Europeans are proud to belong to a region that shares common values. Upholding the Rule of law and respect for human rights are some of the most cherished common values and the Convention and the Court are expressions of those values.

But, this should not preclude criticizing judgments which deserve it, particularly when they are typical for a tendency which gives rise to concern. The long standing reluctance to criticize the Court is one of the main reasons why the Court is continuously advancing on what appears to be "a slippery slope". The only hope to stop this unfortunate development is by subjecting the judgments of the Court to strict scrutiny and to assist the judges of the Court to become aware that more restraint is necessary to enhance its credibility.

Criticizing judgments of the Court of Strasbourg should not be a taboo.[51] It is not blasphemy and it should be possible without running the risk of being labeled a "populist". In an "open European society" it should be possible to engage in a free and frank dialogue, not the kind of "self-inflicted monologue"[52] in which the Strasbourg Court tells the national courts what they should do, but a genuine dialogue in which the national courts and the governments of the states parties, the Court

---

50 Paul Mahoney, *The European Court of Human Rights and its ever-growing caseload: Preserving the mission of the Court while ensuring the viability of the individual petition system*, in *Flogaitis et al., supra* note 2, pp. 18-26, at p. 22.

51 *See also* Bossuyt, *supra* note 16, pp. 103-104.

52 Muylle, *supra* note 27, p. 416.

of Luxembourg and the Court of Strasbourg alike should participate in mutual respect. It should be done in the spirit of the former President of the Court, Luzius WILDHABER (Switzerland), who stated at the same The Hague conference last year:

> institutions and states will perish, if those who love them do not criticize them and if those who criticize them do not love them.[53]

53 Luzius Wildhaber, *Criticism and case-overload: Comments on the future of the European Court of Human Rights*, in Flogaitis et al., *supra* note 2, pp. 9-17, at p. 10.

CHAPTER 3

Reflections on the Future of International Criminal Law

*Harry H.G. Post**

Predicting developments and even reflecting on the future of a field of law is not something lawyers are usually very keen to do. The simple reason for this reluctance is perhaps a combination of the lack of legal security and the interference of too many extra-legal factors. Or, to say it in other words: too many technological, economic, political and other factors from outside the 'normative science' have a decisive impact on the development of a legal field. Also in the case of international criminal law, it is not so easy to choose an elegant way around this kind of problem. For instance, the continuous developments in arms technology (robots, cyber war aspects, missile technology, etc.) and their potential impact on the conduct of armed conflict will, firstly influence the state of international humanitarian law and then, inescapably also have its impact on the development of international criminal law. Moreover, the presence in armed conflict of extremist groups like Al Qaida or the Islamic State will have an important impact on the application and non-application of international criminal law with respect to those conflicts. I have tried to diminish as much as I can the 'external' problems just mentioned by taking the recent history of international criminal law as my starting point and focus on the 'logistical' development of the field rather than on the material development. That focus will make it somewhat less hazardous to look into the future although still risky enough in particular because some daring comments on external inferences,

* Ph.D. (Queen's Univ., Kingston, Canada); Visiting Professor of International Law, *Faculté Libre de Droit, Université Catholique de Lille* (France) and at the *Facoltà di Scienze di Giurisprudenza, Università degli Studi di Sassari*; Italia; Professor of International Law, ret., School of Law, University of Exeter (UK). I wish to thank Dr Erik Koppe for his most valuable and inspiring comments and suggestions.

Karel Wellens (ed.), International Law in Silver Perspective: Challenges Ahead.
 ISBN 978-90-04-27167-8. pp. 57-95.

notably in respect to the state of international humanitarian law cannot be completely avoided.

There can be no doubt that the surprisingly dynamic development of international criminal law of the last decades could only have taken place because a quite well-developed, international humanitarian law was available to be applied in international and national criminal procedures. It needed an institutional mechanism to be applied including a proper procedural law, in particular to make it effectively applicable as international criminal law. That was provided, firstly by the foundation and more importantly the functioning of the UN Tribunals, and, secondly, by a more stabilized embedding of the field in a permanent International Criminal Court and its Statute. The 'complementary' nature of the ICC meant that not only this permanent criminal court was created but also that a great impetus was given to the role of domestic courts in the administration of international justice. The increased jurisprudence of domestic courts on the administration of international justice provides, besides the foundation of the *ad hoc* tribunals and the resulting case-law, and the creation and foundation of the ICC itself, a third important factor in the development of international criminal law. I will argue here that this domestic jurisprudence on the longer run is likely to be the most promising force strengthening international criminal law, which anyway seemed to have acquired its remarkable surge in success in particular due to the case-law that was produced during the last two decades. This jurisprudence interpreted and explained the available international humanitarian law and identified the rules, including on the level of international customary law, the violation of which incurred individual criminal responsibility.

The ICC was from the start a rather surprising success: its Statute entered into force after 4 years and it has in the meantime reached a membership of over 120. The ICC Statute seemed soon enough to function as a 'basic law' for international criminal law, and the ICC Prosecutor became a remarkable and weighty figure in the international theatre. However, less fortunate aspects also began to emerge rather soon. Important states like China, Russia and the United States for various reasons explicitly refused to become a member of the Court. Moreover, the number of cases effectively decided upon remained rather low, were all African and their progress was often marred with difficulties. A major reason for these problems seems to be that Prosecution and Court are so dependent on the faithful co-operation of states and that co-operation is not always easy to get. The Prosecutor is not only a prominent but has also become a controversial actor on the international scene.

Now that the most important international tribunals, the ICTY, ICTR as well as the Special Court for Sierra Leone are closing (or closed) and the ICC itself, although not at all 'beaten', is going through difficult times, in my view the most promising development in international criminal law on the longer run is to be expected from the area of domestic trials on international crimes, including the trials before internationalized court.[1] In the following pages I will focus on this third factor in the development of international criminal law. Administration of international justice by domestic courts is a slow process, primarily as a consequence of considerable procedural and legislative obstacles that virtually everywhere had and have still to be overcome. This is not to say that I do not fully appreciate the important contributions already made in some countries, notably The Netherlands and Canada. The quality of the domestic jurisprudence so far produced may be called promising which is not much more than an impressionistic remark. After all, the important and considerable task of monitoring the rapidly increasing domestic jurisprudence on war crimes in view of the general international criminal law standard has, as yet, hardly been taken up.

In section 1 the remarkable rise to general political and legal prominence of international criminal law is briefly reviewed. Section 2 identifies some of the reasons why the developments in domestic adjudication of international crimes have not really materialized much although states did assume international obligations to that extent. The Dutch experience will be used as the major example to illustrate the slowness if not reluctance to engage domestically with international crimes. In section 3 recent 'stagnation' at the international level is discussed in respect to the future of *ad hoc* tribunals and of the ICC itself. The section is concluded with some remarks on the development of the 'twin' of in-

1 Also referred to as 'hybrid' courts: like the Special Panels in East Timor, the War Crimes Chamber in the Court of Bosnia &Herzegovina and the newly agreed Extraordinary Chambers within the Courts of Senegal (although the Chambers will have a rather limited international input). The Extraordinary Chambers in the Court of Cambodia, the Special Tribunal for Lebanon and even the Special Court for Sierra Leone have also been classified as such internationalized courts (see, e.g., Gerhard Werle, *Principles of International Criminal Law*, 2dn ed., The Hague TMC Asser Press, 2009, p. 26). In the following pages I have at times made liberal use of my "International Criminal Law: Reflections on Monism and Dualism", 43 Israel Yearbook of Human Rights, 2013, Leiden-Boston, pp. 321-353.

ternational criminal law, international humanitarian law. Section 4 assesses the 'new' and promising domestic contribution to the administration of international justice. Finally, a reflective section 5 will conclude the preceding thoughts and considerations.

1 The Dynamic Development of International Criminal Law

Armed conflict usually leads to many victims and devastating destruction. It also tends to produce a multitude of crimes, many of them with quite a scope and often involving great cruelty to innocent civilians. Since the Second World War and the wave of criminal trials that took place in its wake, both at the domestic and the international level, no grand scale attempts at trying war criminals have been undertaken until the International Criminal Tribunal for the Former Yugoslavia (ICTY) was created by the UN Security Council. The ICTY was soon followed by the International Criminal Tribunal for Rwanda (ICTR), the Special Court for Sierra Leone (SCSL) and in particular by the foundation of a permanent International Criminal Court.

The ICTY has indicted 161 individuals for serious violations of international humanitarian law, all those persons were arrested and proceedings against 141 of them (December 2014) have so far been concluded. However, estimates of the number of war crimes committed during the Balkan War of 1991-1993 reach into the hundreds of thousands. At the ICTY, only some of the most important perpetrators of these crimes have been brought to trial. The remaining thousands should be brought to justice, primarily, in the States where they allegedly committed their crimes, or by the States whose nationality they hold. Other domestic courts can in principle also have a role in this prolonged process of administering justice.

However, in practice not much activity could be noticed at the domestic level until the emergence of the *ad hoc* tribunals and in particular since the permanent ICC began to function.

The Preamble of the ICC Statute states:

> Affirming that the most serious crimes of concern to the international community as a whole must not go unpunished and that their effective prosecution must be ensured by taking measures at the national level and by enhancing international cooperation,
>
> …

> *Recalling* that it is the duty of every State to exercise its criminal jurisdiction over those responsible for international crimes,
>
> ...
>
> *Emphasizing* that the International Criminal Court established under this Statute shall be complementary to national criminal jurisdictions, ...[2]

These passages thus announce that the impunity for committing such 'serious crimes of concern to the international community as a whole' is to be achieved first at the national level and by national courts. These passages and in particular the reiteration in Article I of the ICC Statute[3] and the explicit reference in Article 17(1) on "issues of admissibility" tend to lead, primarily, to an examination of the consequences of complementarity for the admissibility of a case in the Court in view of the most appropriate national justice system being "unwilling or unable genuinely to carry out the investigation or prosecution" (Article 17(1)(a)).[4] But complementarity at the same time has another, more legal policy side to it. It implies that the States Parties to the Statute also undertake to make such national investigations, prosecutions and court cases possible, and, in addition, that they actually take place. In the words of Ilias Bantekas: "...it (...) entails the strengthening of all domestic criminal laws and enforcement mechanisms, thus rendering the ICC a court of last resort".[5]

Strengthening and enforcing the domestic legal instruments in this sense has often been a very considerable task, if not a mission. As will be briefly argued in the next section, at the beginning of this century

---

2 Rome Statute of the International Criminal Court, 1998, 2187 *U.N.T.S.* 3 [hereinafter: Rome Statute, Rome Treaty].

3 Art. 1 of the ICC Statute (*id.* note 2) expresses the 'principle of complementarity': "An International Criminal Court ("the Court") is hereby established. It shall be a permanent institution and shall have the power to exercise its jurisdiction over persons for the most serious crimes of international concern, as referred to in this Statute, and shall be complementary to national criminal jurisdictions..."

4 The term has been introduced in the International Law Commission's 1994 Draft, (UN Doc. A/49/10), and has from the outset primarily been discussed in terms of admissibility. *See, e.g.,* W. Schabas, *An Introduction to the International Criminal Court* 174-86 (3rd ed., 2007). *See also* M.M. El Zeidy, *The Principle of Complementarity in International Criminal Law: Origin, Development and Practice* (2008); J.K. Kleffner, *Complementarity in the Rome Statute and National Criminal Jurisdictions* (2008).

5 I. Bantekas, *International Criminal Law* 429 (4th ed., 2010).

these conditions existed only to a (very) limited extent in national legal orders. But quite a number of the State Parties to the 1998 Rome Treaty of the ICC[6] have expressed willingness to change their criminal laws where needed, and nationally, indeed, make this all happen (see below).

During the last twenty odd years we have thus witnessed an unprecedented number of trials before *ad hoc* international criminal tribunals, the beginning of trials before the ICC and, perhaps in particular, a spectacular increase in domestic trials for international crimes or thereto related crimes.[7]

These domestic trials were rather diverse in nature. It can be argued that they mark a *transition* from an attempt, often successful, to make better use of existing laws to the use of legal instruments more specifically enacted for the 'complementarity' objective of the ICC Statute. Here we will illustrate this transitional phase, mainly by way of the development in Dutch case law which to quite some extent played almost a 'model' role in this transitional phase.

The largest number of international criminal law cases, were (and are) of the "classic" kind: the international crimes were committed in the country where the trial takes place, or involve a perpetrator with its nationality; the jurisdiction of the domestic courts in such a case is usually not a problem, but the special character of international crimes may be. The trials in several Balkan States, or in Rwanda, belong to this category.

Another number of trials took (and are taking) place outside the State where the international crimes were committed, but the suspects had the nationality of the State where the trial takes place. Examples are the *Van Anraat* case and the *Kouwenhoven* case in The Netherlands: both defendants had Dutch nationality. The jurisdiction of the local court is not the problem, but, again "international crimes" may be.[8]

---

6 *Supra* note 2.

7 For an overview of relevant domestic cases, *see* the International Crimes Data base (www.internationalcrimesdatabase.org). This databank contains over 650 International cases, decided before international, 'hybrid' (or internationalized) and domestic courts and tribunals.

8 For *Pros. v. van Anraat, see*: International Crimes Database (ICD): http://www.internationalcrimesdatabase.org/Case/178/Van-Anraat (translated in English). For *Pros. v. Kouwenhoven, see*: ICD: http://www.internationalcrimesdatabase.org/Case/887/Kouwenhoven (all judgments with the exception of the 2010 judgment of the Supreme Court in the *Kouwenhoven* case –which is only summarised in English – are translated in English). Boot-Matthijssen & Van Elst rightly empha-

Finally, there were (and are) domestic trials involving defendants who do not have the domestic nationality and who are accused of international crimes that took place abroad. Here there is obviously a jurisdiction issue. In most domestic legal systems such trials require a form of universal jurisdiction regarding the crimes at issue, presuming (again) that they are punishable under the domestic criminal law.[9] Examples of such cases, if we limit ourselves again to the Dutch situation, were the *Hesam* case and the *Jalalzoy* case, decided by the Hague District Court in 2005. Both suspects were Afghan generals (with Afghan nationality) residing in The Netherlands, while the crimes they were accused of allegedly took place in Afghanistan.[10]

Along these international and also some domestic lines international criminal law has developed not only unusually rapidly but at the same time profoundly. In some 20 years, a situation with almost "European" legal characteristics, and this time not only applicable in Europe, but universally, has developed in a completely transformed international criminal law. The penetration of this part of international law, now also through the constitutional sovereignty crust of quite a number of States into their municipal law has often been creative and remarkable in particular in view of the past. In quite a number of cases, the result is thus that municipal courts can be seen applying and interpreting interna-

---

size that one of the merits of the 2003 Dutch International Crimes Law (the *WIM*, *see* below) made possible that Dutch suspects of international crimes could now effectively be tried. In the past such cases could easily lead to acquittal. They illustrate: "It turned out to be impossible to try a self-confessed Dutch mercenary who claimed to have killed dozens of civilians when he was a member of an Albanian militia serving in Serbia" (M. Boot-Matthijssen & R. van Elst, "Key Provisions of the International Crimes Act 2003", [2004] *Netherlands Y.B. Int'l L.* 257.

9 Just like the universal jurisdiction principle, the passive personality principle is probably acceptable in international law, at least where international crimes are at stake. But the latter principle is not accepted everywhere in municipal law, for example not in The Netherlands. *See International Criminal Law in The Netherlands* (B. Swart & A. Klip eds., 1997) 58.

10 For *Prosecutor v. Hesam*, *see*: ICD: http://www.internationalcrimesdatabase.org/Case/1020/Hesam/ (all judgments translated in English). For *Prosecutor v Jalalzoy*, *see*: http://www.internationalcrimesdatabase.org/Case/1025/Jalalzoy/ (all judgments translated in English). A variety of this category (and of all the other categories) is provided by trying a suspect *in absentia*. The *Bouterse* case, again in The Netherlands, provides an example. *See* English text in: [2001] *Netherlands Y.B. Int'l L.* 282-96, and a commentary by L. Zegveld, "The Bouterse Case", *id.*, 97.

tional law, i.e., international criminal law but also of course the international humanitarian law that international criminal law expresses. In fact, these courts for all practical purposes are indeed functioning as international criminal courts (of sorts). In doing so they tend to be guided directly by the jurisprudence of the international criminal tribunals (and the ICC) in the way they interpret the international criminal and humanitarian law in the cases before them. The ICC Statute and the extensive interpretation instrument contained in Article 9 of the Statute, the "Elements of Crimes", play a prominent and 'guiding' role.

2 The Domestic Level 'As It Was'

2.1 *The Implementation of International Obligations*

If we move back to the situation as it was in this part of international law before the 1990s, it is fair to argue that it was unlikely that any "revolutionary" change would take place regarding international crimes in domestic law. As said above, States parties to some conventions certainly had explicitly assumed the obligation to enact domestic legislation in order to fulfil their international obligations under these treaties. Under Article V of the 1948 Genocide Convention the Contracting Parties undertook

> ... to enact, in accordance with their respective Constitutions, the necessary legislation to give effect to the provisions of the present Convention and, in particular, to provide effective penalties for persons guilty of genocide or of any of the other acts enumerated in article III.[11]

Many among the numerous parties to the Genocide Convention have, indeed, done so, and in a wide variety of ways as the Convention left them discretion. Some States, like Norway, believed that no change in their laws was really necessary.[12] Flaws or potential weaknesses of these national arrangements became only apparent when legislation in respect to genocide actually had to be applied. And it took almost fifty

11 Convention on the Prevention and Punishment of the Crime of Genocide, 1948, 58 *U.N.T.S.* 277.

12 Schabas gives an excellent overview of the various ways Parties to the Convention believed they fulfilled their obligation under Art. V; W. Schabas, *Genocide in International Law* 405-409 (2nd ed., 2009).

years, until the international developments incurred that; only then some parties to the Genocide Convention, like Norway, found out that their choice of giving effect to the municipal duties with respect to the crime of genocide, in practice were not so satisfactory at all. At least, in the case of Norway an international criminal tribunal decided for that reason not to defer a suspect to Norway. Apparently there was an urgent need to update domestic law in view of the new requirements under modern international criminal law.[13]

In the relevant Articles of the four 1949 Geneva Conventions on "grave breaches",[14] the High Contracting Parties are held to a similar duty as under the Genocide Convention. Article 49 of Geneva Convention I, states in its first paragraph:

> The High Contracting Parties undertake to enact any legislation necessary to provide effective penal sanctions for persons committing, or ordering to be committed, any of the grave breaches of the present Convention defined in the following Article.[15]

Thirty years later, in Article 85(5) of the 1977 Additional Protocol I to the Geneva Conventions,[16] the High Contracting Parties agreed that such grave breaches "shall be regarded as war crimes".

With respect to the duty to enact legislation, the activities of the Parties since the Geneva Conventions entered into force have often been qualified as inadequate and ineffective. Until recently, national prosecutions for grave breaches have been scarce and impunity still appears to be the norm. Indeed, even if states occasionally prosecute acts that

---

13 *Id.*, 408-409, referring to the rather embarrassing *Bagaragaza* case (*see, infra*, note 56).

14 *See*, Art. 49(1) of Geneva Convention [I] for the Amelioration of the Condition of the Wounded and Sick in Armed Forces in the Field, 1949, 75 *U.N.T.S.* 31; Art. 50(1) of Geneva Convention [II] for the Amelioration of the Condition of the Wounded, Sick and Shipwrecked Members of Armed Forces at Sea, 1949, 75 *U.N.T.S.* 85; Art. 129(1) of Geneva Convention [III] Relative to the Treatment of Prisoners of War, 1949, 75 *U.N.T.S.* 135; Art. 146(1) of Geneva Convention [IV] Relative to the Protection of Civilian Personsin Time of War, 1949, 75 *U.N.T.S.* 287.

15 *Id.*

16 Protocol Additional to the Geneva Conventions of 12 August 1949 and Relating to the Protection of Victims of International Armed Conflicts (Protocol I), 1977, 1125 *U.N.T.S.*, 3.

might constitute grave breaches within the grave breaches regime, they may do so under a different criminal legal heading.[17]

Few States among the many parties to the four 1949 Geneva Conventions actually enacted specific legislation in order to punish the perpetrators of the grave breaches of the Geneva Conventions; several others considered their criminal law as adequate to cope with them, or otherwise did nothing.[18] Just like for the crime of Genocide, with some rare exceptions, the adequacy of domestic legislation regarding war crimes was again not really tested until well after 1990.[19]

How easily a municipal criminal law system could stay closed in particular to "foreign" cases can be illustrated by the example of the Netherlands.[20] If anything, the Dutch legal system had a reputation of

---

17 W. Ferdinandusse, "The Prosecution of Grave Breaches in National Law", [2009] *J. Int'l Crim. Just.* 724 (Special Issue on the Grave Breaches Regime in the Geneva Conventions: A Reassessment – Sixty Years On). Ferdinandusse gives three examples of such prosecutions in Denmark, Switzerland and the United Kingdom (crimes committed in 1992, 1994 and 2003, respectively). If states prosecute grave breaches under other criminal legal headings, he comments: "This is not necessarily problematic, as long as the limits posed by international law are respected" (*id.*, sec. 5).

18 *See*, F. Kalshoven & L. Zegveld, *Constraints on the Waging of War* 81 (ICRC, 4th ed., 2011).

19 In respect to the much later 1984 UN Torture Convention (UN Convention Against Torture and Other Cruel, Inhuman or Degrading Treatment or Punishment, 1984, 1465 *U.N.T.S.* 85) the picture is brighter. Many parties took steps to modify their domestic legislation. In The Netherlands the Torture Convention Implementation Act entered into force in 1989. In 2004 the first conviction in The Netherlands based on universal jurisdiction took place. The Rotterdam District Court found Nzapali guilty on one count of torture under the Torture Convention Implementation Act, committed in the Dem. Rep. of Congo in 1996. It sentenced him to 2½ years imprisonment. *See* M. Kamminga, "First Conviction under the Universal Jurisdiction Provisions of the UN Convention Against Torture", [2004] *Netherlands Int'l L. Rev.* 439 (the issue contains a translation in English of the verdict). *See* for the Supreme Court judgment and the procedural history (in English), of this rather complicated case which does not seem to have ended, as yet (*see* ICDB: http://www.internationalcrimesdatabase.org/Case/1128/Nzapali/).

20 The somewhat peculiar way general international law is treated in Dutch law has been the subject of considerable commentaries and detailed discussions. In view of the scope of this article they will be left aside. For an excellent explanation and review in English, *see* E.A. Alkema, "Netherlands", in *International Law and Domestic Legal Systems* 407-28 (D. Shelton ed., 2011). With respect to crimi-

openness to international law, of being more 'monistic' than 'dualistic'. At least with respect to criminal law, that may be somewhat of an exaggeration.

2.2 *The Example of The Netherlands*

The Dutch legal order incorporates both rules of treaty law and international customary law. Both are valid but they have a remarkably different status.[21] The relevant Articles of the Dutch Constitution are:

> Article 93
> Provisions of Treaties and of Resolutions by International Institutions which may be binding on all persons by virtue of their contents, shall become binding after they have been published.
>
> Article 94
> Statutory regulations in force within the Kingdom shall not be applicable if such application is in conflict with provisions of Treaties that are binding on all persons or of Resolutions by International Institutions.

Article 94, in particular, stating the explicit superiority of (self-executing) provisions of treaties and of (equally self-executing) resolutions of international institutions, can be said to be a "monist" trait of the relationship between international and Dutch law according to the Constitution.

But the position of customary rules does not fit such a qualification. There is no reference whatsoever to international customary law in these core provisions, nor explicitly elsewhere in the Dutch constitution. In its famous (for part of the doctrine un-famous) 1959 judgment in the *Nyugat* case, the "Hoge Raad" (the Dutch Supreme Court) argued

---

nal law, *see* W. Ferdinandusse, *Direct Application of International Criminal law in National Courts* 66-70 (2006).

21 *See, e.g.*, (in Dutch): J. Fleuren, "Directe en Indirecte Toepassing van Internationaal Recht Door de Nederlandse Rechter" [Direct and Indirect Application of International Law by the Dutch Judge], in Preadviezen, 131 *Mededelingen van de NVIR* 69, 76 (2005). *See also* L. Besselink, "Internationaal Recht en National Recht", *Handboek Internationaal Recht* 47-78 (2007). The translation of articles 93 and 94 can be found on the site of the Netherlands judiciary (http://www.rechtspraak.nl/English/Legislation/Pages/default.aspx).

that Dutch courts are not allowed to review Dutch law in the light of international customary law or treaty rules that are not self-executing. Before this judgment, Dutch courts were supposed to have discretion to do so. This new, more restrictive point of view was confirmed by the Dutch Government and Parliament on the occasion of the 1983 constitutional review.[22] Hence, also today international customary rules are excluded from superior rank in the Dutch legal order. This explicit exclusion of rules of international customary law can perhaps be called an even more remarkable "dualist" side of the Dutch legal order than the "monist" aspect of the superior status of self-executing treaty rules.

With respect to the application of international norms in Dutch criminal law, the so-called "legality" principle provides an additional barrier – and perhaps an even more formidable one for that matter – to the application of international customary law. Article 16 of the Constitution (and, identically, Article 1(1) of the Dutch Penal Code) formulates it as follows: No offence shall be punishable unless it was an offence under the law at the time it was committed. The *nullum crimen sine lege* principle can of course in some form or another be found, explicitly or implicitly, in virtually all national criminal laws as well as in several international instruments, like the Statute of the ICC. The principle is part of customary international law, but the question remains in what definition precisely.[23] In Article 22(1) of the ICC Statute this principle is formulated as follows:

22 The *Nyugat* Judgment (English translation in [1957] *I.L.R.* 24) is in reference to the 1956 Constitution. Articles 66 and 67 of the 1956 Constitution have been renumbered as 93 and 94 in the 1983 Constitution. Dutch courts are allowed to review by-laws and other lower regulations in light of customary law or non-self-executing provisions of treaties (*see, e.g.*, Fleuren, *supra* note 21, at 83-84). See, also, in detail, the Supreme Court judgment of 18 September 2001 in the *Bouterse* case (ICD: http://www.internationalcrimesdatabase.org/Case/1082/Bouterse/).

23 This is a point of controversy, *see, e.g.*, M.C. Bassiouni, *Introduction to International Criminal Law* 198 (2003); or Bantekas, *supra* note 5, at 21-28. The principle has been included in human rights and humanitarian law treaties, like the 1966 International Covenant on Civil and Political Rights, Art. 15 (999 *U.N.T.S.* 171); the 1950 European Convention on Human Rights, Art. 7 (213 *U.N.T.S.* 211); and the 1949 Geneva Conventions, *supra* note 14 [(III) in Art. 99(1), and (IV) in Art. 67]; as well as in the 1977 Additional Protocol I to the Geneva Conventions, Art.75 (4)(c), *supra* note 16.

> (1) A person shall not be criminally responsible under this Statute unless the conduct in question constitutes, at the time it takes place, a crime within the jurisdiction of the Court.[24]

Article 22(2) of the Statute provides an additional guarantee of certainty:

> (2) The definition of a crime shall be strictly construed and shall not be extended by analogy. In case of ambiguity, the definition shall be interpreted in favour of the person being investigated, prosecuted or convicted.[25]

Article 16 of the Constitution in The Netherlands is seen as to bar international custom as a basis for criminal prosecution.[26] In 1997, the Supreme Court interpreted the principle of legality rather strictly, holding that it involves a "criminalization to be formulated and published in Dutch". This pronouncement in fact re-states one of the more general requirements of Article 93 of the Constitution, i.e., "after they have been published". In modern times, 'formulated and published in Dutch' can be called rather remarkable. Anyway, most international criminal law would fulfil such a publication condition (that is, if the 'in Dutch' is ignored). Since the detailed Statute of the International Criminal Court and the even more detailed jurisprudence of the tribunals – widely published for that matter – the crimes there subsumed are at least "sufficiently familiar" for any potential defendant's lawyers. Still, even if international customary criminal law could be argued now to meet the criteria of Article 93, it would still not attain the "supremacy" position

---

24 *Supra* note 2.

25 *Id.* In the Statutes of the International Criminal Tribunal for the Former Yugoslavia, 1993 (ICTY) [32 *I.L.M.* 1203 (1993)] and the International Criminal Tribunal for Rwanda, 1994 (ICTR) [33 *I.L.M.* 1598 (1994)] this principle has not found an explicit place. Cassese points out – in my view correctly – that Arts. 1-8 of the ICTY Statute, as well as par. 29 of the UN Secretary-General's Report to the UN Security Council on the establishment of the Tribunal (S/25704) can be seen as honouring the principle adequately (A. Cassese, *International Criminal Law* 41, n. 18 (2nd ed., 2008)). The same could be argued for the ICTR Statute, Arts. 1-7.

26 *See, inter alia,* (in Dutch) W. Ferdinandusse *et al.,* "Origineel of Reproductie? Internationale Strafbaarstellingen in de Nederlandse Rechtsorde", [Original or Reproduction? International Criminalization in the Dutch Legal Order], [2002] *Nederlands Juristen Blad* 343-44.

of (self-executing) criminal law treaty provisions under Article 94.[27] But Ferdinandusse, following a careful study of the matter, concludes that "[today] there are few examples of treaty provisions with a penal content being directly applied" and, furthermore, "[i]t should be noted that the Dutch government has on several occasions denied the possibility of direct application of treaty-based offences".[28] In Dutch jurisprudence as well there are hardly any examples to be found where direct application of such treaty provisions has played a relevant role in proceedings.[29] In view of this state of affairs, Dutch prosecutors and courts could easily convey the impression of being more interested in how not to pass judgment on suspects of international crimes than to try and contribute to the administration of international criminal justice. But this has all changed as we will see.

But such passivity might also have adverse results in the wider area of foreign policy. After all, over the years one of the objectives of Dutch foreign policy was to persuade international organisations to have their seat in The Netherlands, and that objective included international courts and tribunals. This policy was crowned with considerable success, in particular from the 1990s on. With the presence of the International Court of Justice, the ICTY, which Appeals Chamber is also the Appeals Chamber of the ICTR, the ICC, the Special Tribunal for Lebanon, and the most important trial before the Special Court for Sierra Leone, *The Prosecutor v. Taylor*, taking place there, The Hague effectively has become the world's international legal centre. For a (much) more successful contribution to the administration of international justice by the Dutch courts than so far outlined, "political action" was required: it was decided that the relevant domestic law needed to be changed. That has

27 As has been confirmed in both the *Bouterse* case (the Supreme Court judgment of 18 September 2001, *see* ICD: http://www.internationalcrimesdatabase.org/Case/1082/Bouterse/); and the 2002 Amsterdam Court of Appeals judgment in In re Zorrequita *et al.* (not yet published; *see* Ferdinandusse, *supra* note 20, at 69, n. 439.

28 *Id.*, 68. With respect to these Dutch government statements he also comments that they "clearly contravene established practice" (*id.*), but does not make clear what this "established practice" involves (*see* his n. 429, at 68 for some examples).

29 Although in the 2001 Supreme Court judgment in the *Bouterse* case the Court endorsed the direct application of criminal law treaty provisions over the national principle of legality, for other reasons such direct treaty application did not take place in that case (*supra* note 27).

happened with the enactment and entry into force of the 2003 International Crimes Act, or "*WIM*" (*Wet internationale misdrijven*).

However as much as such a policy motive probably played a role in order to change Dutch criminal law, this was a change that took place within the context of the entry into force in 2002 of the Rome Statute of the International Criminal Court. Quite a number of 'willing' states parties to the Rome Treaty had decided that it was time to adapt their criminal law so that it conformed to the Statute, making it possible nationally to adjudicate the international crimes as they were defined in Articles 6-8 of the ICC Statute. The Dutch situation as described in this section 2 cannot be called a standard way of executing international obligations, and national legal systems differ considerably anyway in this respect. Still, in virtually all other parties to the Genocide Convention or the Geneva Conventions the net result has been quite similar to The Netherlands: only very sparsely did domestic prosecution for war crimes, genocide or crimes against humanity take place. If it occurred at all then World War II crimes were usually the subject matter allowing special post War legislation still to be applied.

Following a short overview in section 4 of the situation in a few other countries, I will return in that section to the development of the application of international criminal law by Dutch courts in the decade after the *WIM* entered into force. It is perhaps a little exaggerated to say that the changes in Dutch law have served as an example or even a model for other 'willing' states but the Dutch activities have led to, or at least accompanied, a remarkable surge in activity in the domestic administration of international justice since the beginning of this century.[30]

3 Stagnation at the International Level?

Before we return to the domestic level and its impact on the administration of international justice, we will firstly, discuss the developments and likely developments at the international level itself. Here, it may be fair to say, some stagnation can be observed. There are a number of

---

30 'The Long Arm of Justice; Lessons from Specialized War Crimes Units in France, Germany, and the Netherlands', Human Rights Watch 2014 singles out the approach chosen in The Netherlands as highly successful and effective including the accompanying efforts by Dutch police and prosecution services (*see*, in particular, pp. 6 and 7).

reasons that may account for a lull in the development of international criminal law at this level, including in the near future. In this section three important ones will be addressed.

In the first place, the activity of special *ad hoc* criminal tribunals is 'winding down' and the establishment of new tribunals (by the UN) is not very likely (section 3.1). Secondly, the ICC has difficulty to produce important judgments (section 3.2). Finally, there seems stagnation in the development of international humanitarian law, perhaps the twin (although not *monovular*) of international criminal law and certainly 'feeding' it. At least at the treaty level there seems to be a lack of inspiring development in international humanitarian law (section 3.3).

As a result of these developments there seems to be a shift of contributions to international criminal law from the international to the domestic level. No doubt this shift takes only place in a gradual way and for the time being in particular in a 'quantitative' sense: while international judgments will diminish in number, there is already a wave of relevant domestic case law and its volume is likely to increase. This trend is strengthened if we include at the domestic level the continuing production of cases and decisions by 'hybrid' courts, i.e., domestic courts with (substantial) international participation in one form or another

3.1 *The Winding Down of the* Ad Hoc *Criminal Tribunals*

It is not so difficult to find general arguments why it is that the 'heydays' of *ad hoc* criminal tribunals are likely to be over. The ICTY and the ICTR are winding down. What will remain of these tribunals is the 'Mechanism for International Criminal Tribunals' (MICT). This new body, established by the UN Security Council in 2010, since 1 July 2012 and 1 July 2013 with a branch for each tribunal, will finish the remaining tasks of the tribunals when they have completed their mandate.[31] The

31 The MICT is established by way of UN SC Resolution 1966 of 22 December 2010; see also: International Residual Mechanisms, Second Annual Report to the UN General Assembly and Security Council, 1 Aug. 2014 (A/69/226–S/2014/555). Neither of the two tribunals was able to complete its work by 31 December 2014, the date they were foreseen to have done so. The ICTR did complete all its trial cases, its Appeals Chamber completed all but one (*Pros. v. Nyiramasuhuko, et al.*). The ICTR is scheduled to be closed in 2015 (see 19th Annual Report of the ICTR to the Security Council of 13 October 2014). In his address to the UNSC of 12 Dec. 2014 the President of the ICTY anticipates 2017 as the year when the ICTY will be closed; see also S/2014/827, p. 3. During the initial period of the Mechanism's work, there will be a temporal overlap with the ICTR and the ICTY as these in-

Mechanism is expected to prosecute the most senior persons arrested after those dates, or those who interfere with the administration of justice. However, although the Mechanism will be able to conduct review proceedings, supervise the enforcement of sentences and decide on pardon or commutation of sentences, it cannot issue new indictments and at most may be called a comprehensive court. Since 2013 the Residual Special Court for Sierra Leone performs similar functions for the Special Court for Sierra Leone which in that year completed its mandate.[32] As said above, the ICTY, ICTY and SCSL have produced a very impressive case-load which has transformed international criminal law in a most profound way. When also the ICTY and ICTR will have closed down, The Extraordinary Chambers in the Courts of Cambodia (ECCC) and the Special Tribunal for Lebanon (STL) are the remaining *ad hoc* tribunals.[33] They will continue to function for an as yet not determined number of years. Although interesting and important decisions may certainly be expected from these two courts, their contribution will be of a different magnitude than what ICTY, ICTR and SCSL have produced. This assessment holds true, I believe, also if we include the cases to be decided by the two branches of the MICT, and even those continuing before the ICTY, notably of *Radovan Karadžić* and *Ratko Mladić,* however fascinating and important. It remains also the case if any of the three very prominent fugitives of the Rwanda massacres, *Félicien Kabuga, Protais Mpiranya* and *Augustin Bizimana* will be apprehended and brought to trial before the MICT.[34]

---

stitutions complete outstanding work on any trial or appeal proceedings which were already pending as of 1 July 2012 and 1 July 2013, respectively. The ICTY, *e.g.*, will continue the trials of *Radovan Karadžić, Ratko Mladić* and *Goran Hadžić*, whereas their eventual appeals proceedings will take place in the ICTY branch of the MICT.

32 Residual Special Court For Sierra Leone; *see*: 2012 Residual Special Court For Sierra Leone Agreement, at: http://rscsl.org/Documents/RSCSL-Act.pdf.

33 The Special Tribunal for Lebanon, created in 2010 is an independent judicial body composed of Lebanese and international judges, which is not a United Nations tribunal and does not form part of the Lebanese judicial system. The ECCC founded in 2006 is an *ad hoc* Cambodian court with international participation. In terms of doctrine the ECCC and the Lebanon Tribunal may also be seen as the 'top' of the hybrid or internationalised courts (*see, infra,* note 1).

34 If apprehended the other six remaining fugitives indicted by the ICTR are to be brought to trial in Rwanda.

It is not too likely that notably the UN Security Council will see reasons to establish new *ad hoc* criminal tribunals although one of course never knows where politics may lead. In addition to prohibitive costs and other external reasons, the SC power to refer an issue to the ICC and the increasing activity of domestic courts are probably additional reasons why new *ad hoc* tribunals are unlikely to be established in the near future. In summary, I believe that it is no exaggeration to say that the contribution to the development of international criminal law from *ad hoc* criminal tribunals will diminish rather considerably in the coming decade.

Will the administration of international justice therefore shift to the ICC?

3.2 *The Case-Law of the ICC*

The further development and re-enforcement of the ICC seems stagnating. Several factors can be identified here. The first one is the increasing political pressure from African countries complaining that the ICC is unduly focusing on their continent. The African Union (AU) has made itself the voice of this criticism. For example, in October 2013, at an extraordinary summit on the ICC the AU unanimously adopted a resolution that no sitting African president should be tried in international courts while in office and that the trials against the sitting presidents Al Bashir and Kenyatta should be postponed.[35] In several sensitive and important matters among which notably the Darfur conflict stands out but also problems in respect to Libya and Kenya should be mentioned, the ICC complaints about less than ideal support from the Security Council. In the opinion of Mrs Fatou Bensouda, the ICC Prosecutor, notably the level of 'practical' support by the Council is in comparison much more limited than the support the ICTY and ICTR got. In her recent statement before the UN Security Council she declared:

> I respectfully call on this Council to consider using stronger language in its referrals, similar to the language used in past Council resolutions requiring cooperation from all States with the United Nations International Criminal Tribunal for the former Yugoslavia and the International Criminal Tribunal for Rwanda. The language

35 http://summits.au.int/en/icc. Moreover there is some pressure towards the establishment of a regional African Criminal Court.

> of the Darfur and Libya resolutions leaves a fair amount of ambiguity as to whether all States are obliged to cooperate.[36]

Besides the lack of full backing by the Security Council, the ICC anyway suffers from less than faithful co-operation from some states, notably in the Libya and Sudan/Darfur cases. But the state of the Kenya/*Kenyatta* case is even more worrisome. On the 3rd of December 2014, the Trial Chamber even declined to further adjourn the trial of Uhuru Muigai Kenyatta, President of Kenya. The Judges of Trial Chamber V (B) of the International Criminal Court (ICC) noted that the Government of Kenya had failed to adequately cooperate with the Prosecutor's investigations in this case. In its ruling the Chamber stated: "[it] finds that, cumulatively, the approach of the Kenyan Government [...] falls short of the standard of good faith cooperation" and "that this failure has reached the threshold of non-compliance" required under the Rome Statute. The Chamber further found,

> [...] that the Kenyan Government's non-compliance has not only compromised the Prosecution's ability to thoroughly investigate the charges, but has ultimately impinged upon the Chamber's ability to fulfil its mandate under Article 64, and in particular, its truth-seeking function in accordance with Article 69 (3) of the Statute.[37]

On the same 3 December the ICC Prosecutor drew the consequences and filed a notice of withdrawal of the charges against Kenyatta, albeit declaring that in doing so she did not prejudice the possibility of bringing a new case should additional evidence become available.[38]

On a brighter note, the Court could announce that the 2012 verdict and sentence in the case of Thomas Lubanga Dyilo on 1 December 2014

36 Prosecutor of the ICC, Statement to the United Nations Security Council of 23 October 2014 on the Subject of "Working Methods of the Security Council." par. 9.

37 ICC Trial Chamber V(B) Decision of 3 Dec. 2014, in the case of *The Prosecutor v. Uhuru Muigai Kenyatta*, ICC -01/09-02/11. On 10 December 2014, Pre-trial Chamber I decided that Libya had not complied with requests for co-operation in the case of *The Prosecutor v. Saif Al-Islam Gaddafi* and referred the matter to the Security Council, ICC-01/11-01/11.

38 ICC Statement of the Prosecutor of 5 Dec. 2014 in the case of *The Prosecutor v. Uhuru Muigai Kenyatta*, ICC -01/09-02/11.

were confirmed by the Appeals Chamber.[39] Reactions to the judgment, mainly for the time being from NGO's in the human rights field, were certainly positive. Generally speaking the same can be said, including academic comments, about the trial judgment.[40] It seems therefore that the ICC faces primarily a problem of 'quantity' as the *Lubanga* case is the very first completely finished case before the ICC. After twelve years that is perhaps not precisely what was hoped for.

3.3 *International Humanitarian Law*

International criminal law and international humanitarian law are related, even in such a significant way that one may be tempted to call them 'twins'. Robert Cryer even talks about 'a risk of identifying one with the other, even though the norms of one are not coterminous with the norms of the other'. He does so after observing as we have done here as well, that there has been 'a huge swing toward the use of international criminal law to deal with violations of international humanitarian law'.[41] I think that identifying the two so much, albeit understandable, is also an unhelpful exaggeration. Certainly, a crucial part of modern international criminal law is erected on the international crimes of genocide, crimes against humanity and war crimes which primarily, although not totally occur during armed conflict and have found their origin in the criminalization of rules of humanitarian law. But other important international crimes bear a more remote relationship to armed conflict, although certainly occurring frequently in such circumstances, notably torture crimes. Moreover, more traditionally, international criminal law (or perhaps we should say transnational criminal law) relates to co-operation between states in criminal matters by way of such instruments as extradition, rules on transfers, including of documents, and the like. In view of increased co-operation between states in criminal matters,

39 ICC Appeals Chamber, Judgment of 1 December 2014 in the case of *The Prosecutor v. Thomas Lubanga Dyilo,* ICC-01/04-01/06 (http://www.icc-cpi.int/iccdocs/doc/doc1877186.pdf) with a Dissenting Opinion of Judge Anita Ušacka and a partly dissenting opinion of Judge Sang Hyun-Song.

40 *See, e.g.*, Kai Ambos extensive note 'The First Judgment of the International Criminal Court (*Prosecutor v. Lubanga*): a comprehensive analysis of the legal issues', in 12 International Criminal Law Review 2012, 115-153, which is critical but not negative.

41 Robert Cryer, 'The role of international criminal prosecution in increasing compliance with international humanitarian law'; in 44 Israel Yearbook on Human Rights 2014, p. 247.

also regarding crimes with none or a rather remote relationship with armed conflict, these latter parts of international criminal law will undoubtedly grow and extend further, assuming also institutional forms as developments in the European Union witness.[42]

But having said that, international humanitarian law will undoubtedly continue to 'feed' and 'inspire' the development of international criminal law. It can safely be argued, I believe, that it is the most important feed to international criminal law at the international level, both in a formal and a more informal way.[43] The potential development in international humanitarian law therefore deserves some (brief) comments here. As said above: that is a daring undertaking and will be done without pretention and very modestly.

In broad terms: international humanitarian law will on the one hand, continue to 'float' on the developments in warfare techniques both in terms of methods and in terms of means of warfare, and on the other hand, will be subject to the ever-lasting pressure to codify the law and to 'humanize' armed conflict. 'Cyber' warfare and ever more sophisticated 'robot' arms technology are just two modern examples of new technological developments in warfare techniques that demand or may demand changes in the law of armed conflict. Academic discussion of such changes is regularly taking place.[44]

---

42 By way of the Treaty of Lisbon a (European) Public Prosecutor was inserted in Article 86 of the Treaty on the Functioning of the European Union. There probably is still a way to go before such an institution will be operational, but progress is made as the European parliament voted on 14 March 2014 in favour of a Commission proposal to set up the office. The Public Prosecutor would have the exclusive task of investigating, prosecuting and bringing to judgement crimes against the EU budget. *See, e.g.*, Claus Kreß on the variety of meanings of international criminal law including transnational criminal law and even supranational criminal law (in: Max Planck Encyclopedia of Public International Law, www.mpepil.com).

43 International human rights law may be classified as 'a good second'. Human rights, of course, also have their own 'humanizing effect' on the development of humanitarian law (*see, e.g.*, Theodor Meron, The Humanization of International Law, Leiden-Boston, 2006, Ch. 1).

44 In publications, as well as during conferences, like the annual Round Table of the International Institute of Humanitarian Law in San Remo, Italy. See, e.g., on the developing law on 'cyber war', the contributions in 43 Israel Yearbook on Human Rights, 2013, pp. 1-169, reporting on the International Law Conference: 'Cyber War and International Law' (held at the US Naval War College in June 2012).

In the area of attempts to 'humanize' armed conflict, the great interest in the law of non-international armed conflict can be noticed. The increase in scope of the law of non-international armed conflict involves a further identification of rules of the law of armed conflict also applicable to non-international armed conflict as was initiated by the well-known *Tadić* Appeals decision.[45] It also includes attempts to agree on a comprehensive set of rules specific for that part of the law of armed conflict as presented in the 2006 Manual on the Law of Non-International Armed Conflict.[46] Such attempts toward 'private' codification have continuously taken place inspired and instigated, in particular by the International Committee of the Red Cross (ICRC) and the International Institute of Humanitarian Law.[47]

Although experts in the field of humanitarian law thus undertake great efforts to agree on manuals and other codifications of rules on new warfare technologies or on old forms of warfare that are much in need of new regulation *inter alia* because of such technological (but also other) developments, states may be said to have been less active. Since the two 1977 Protocols additional to the 1949 Geneva Conventions a few more specific instruments have been added to the general body of international humanitarian law. The 1993 Convention on the Prohibition of the Development, Production, Stockpiling and Use of Chemical Weapons and on their Destruction,[48] is probably the most important of these treaties, closely followed by the 1980 Convention on Certain Conventional

---

45 ICTY Appeals Chamber, Decision of 2 October 1995 in *Prosecutor v. Tadić*, par. 128 ff.

46 As prepared for the San Remo International Institute of Humanitarian Law (IIHL), Leiden-Boston, 2006. The subject is academically (and otherwise) still very much centre-stage. The annual Round Table of the San Remo Institute in 2015 is, *e.g.*, entitled 'The Relationship between International Armed Conflict and Non-International Armed Conflict'.

47 The 2005 ICRC study by Jean-Marie Henckaerts and Louise Doswald-Beck, Customary International Humanitarian Law (Cambridge, 2005), whereas the 1995 San Remo Manual on International Law Applicable to Armed Conflict at Sea is an earlier example to which the Manual on the Law of Non-international Armed Conflict (*see, supra,* note 46) is a sequel. The Program on Humanitarian Policy and Conflict Research at Harvard University (HPCR) is another of such 'private' projects. It produced the Manual on International Law Applicable to Air and Missile Warfare (Cambridge, Mass., 2009).

48 1992 Convention on the Prohibition of the Development, Production, Stockpiling and Use of Chemical Weapons and on their Destruction 1974 *UNTS*, 45.

Weapons (CCW), in particular its Protocols.[49] But both Conventions and Protocols are rather specific in their subject matter. The same can be said of the 1997 Ottawa Convention on Anti-personnel mines[50] and of the 2007 Dublin Convention on Cluster Weapons.[51] If we take inclusion of rules in the Statute of the ICC as a criterion for their status in international criminal law, the consequences of these new treaties so far have been limited. The rules contained in Articles 6-8 of the Statute have only once been amended and not in view of rules in these treaties. The General Assembly of States Parties to the ICC in 2010 in Kampala, Uganda, adopted a resolution to extend three existing provisions under war crimes in international armed conflict of Art. 8, paragraph 2 (b) also to non-international armed conflict. All three crimes thus added to Article 8, paragraph 2 (e) of the Statute are referred to in the Resolution as 'serious violations of the laws and customs applicable in armed conflict not of an international character, as reflected in customary international law'.[52] The 2010 ICC General Assembly did amend the Statute in a fundamental way, *i.e.*, by inserting the Crime of Aggression in a new Article 8 *bis,* but this amendment has no relationship to new treaty instruments in international humanitarian law and its consequences are still very much to be seen.[53]

---

49 1980 UN Convention on Prohibitions or Restrictions on the use of Certain Conventional Weapons which may be deemed to be excessively injurious or to have indiscriminate effects, and Protocols I-III, 1980, 1342 *UNTS*, 137; Protocol IV, 1995 and Amended Protocol II, 1996, 35 *International Legal Material* (1996), 1206; Protocol V, 2003, 2399 *UNTS,* 100.

50 http://www.unog.ch/80256EDD006B8954/(httpAssets)/8DF9CC31A4CA8B32C12571C7002E3F3E/$file/APLC+English.pdf.

51 http://www.unog.ch/80256EDD006B8954/(httpAssets)/CE9E6C29A6941AF1C12574F7004D3A5C/$file/ccm77_english.pdf.

52 Resolution RC/Res.5 (with 2 Annexes) adopted by consensus by the Assembly of States Parties; *see* Depositary Notification C.N.651.2010 Treaties-6, dated 29 November 2010 (at http://treaties.un.org). It concerns new rules in Art. 8, par. 2 (e) (xii) on Employing poison or poisoned weapons; (xiv) on Employing asphyxiating, poisonous or other gases, and all analogous liquids, materials or devices; and (xv) on Employing bullets which expand or flatten easily in the human body, such as bullets with a hard envelope which does not entirely cover the core or is pierced with incisions." As said in the Resolution, all three rules reflect customary law, in respect to both international and non-international armed conflict.

53 Resolution RC/Res.6 (with 3 Annexes) adopted by consensus by the Assembly of States Parties; *see* Depositary Notification C.N.651.2010 Treaties-8, dated 29

4 Domestic Contributions to the Administration of International Justice

As argued already above: There seems one consolation for those hoping for improvement in the administration of international justice in the world, although the process will be slow and by way of case-law, hence, not comparable to the acceptance of new treaties like the Statute of the ICC was. The state of international criminal law is likely to be enhanced, including perhaps in terms of quality by the (strongly) increased contribution of domestic courts to the administration of international justice, including from cases before internationalised courts and cases resulting from the transfer to national courts by international criminal tribunals or by residual mechanisms. An important question is: what will be the quality of this rapidly increasing case-load? Part of this increase in domestic jurisprudence will not in all respects be up to standard, as it might be motivated mainly by political or power considerations or by sheer vengeance, although the proceedings are clad in ICL terminology. Examples like the 2005 Supreme Iraqi Criminal Tribunal (established in 2003 as the Iraqi Special Tribunal), the 2008 International Crimes Division in the Courts of Uganda[54] or the 2009 Bangla Dash International Crimes Tribunal come to mind. Carefully monitoring the activities of proceedings in such 'complementary' tribunals (*e.g.* under Art. 17.2 of the Statute) would be a considerable challenge for the ICC Prosecutor. Doing the same for other 'complementary' proceedings in perhaps less 'suspect' courts may be an increasingly demanding task now that the domestic contribution to the administration of international justice is clearly increasing.

4.1 *Complementarity at the National Level*

War crimes, crimes against humanity and genocide are not ordinary crimes. They have a broad scope and magnitude and tend to require an expansion of domestic jurisdiction to prosecute them in any effective way. The complications and special nature of such crimes had become

---

November 2010 (at http://treaties.un.org). The amendment will enter into force for those states parties who have accepted it at the earliest in 2017.

54 The International Law Division has been established in July 2008 in accordance with the 2010 ICC Act of Uganda. It is, in principle, a court of 'complementarity' with respect to the ICC. (*see* http://www.judicature.go.ug/data/smenu/18/International_Crimes_Division.html).

clear as a result of their application in ICTR and ICTY to the slaughter in Rwanda and the atrocities in the Balkan War. Judges and prosecutors came across criminal offences that they were unlikely to encounter in national proceedings. Still, there was not too much reason to predict any remarkable development on the domestic front as a result of the ICC Statute. Differently than, *e.g.*, the Genocide Convention or the 1949 Geneva Conventions, the ICC Statute does not establish any explicit obligations with respect to the way the relevant substantive international criminal law is to be incorporated into national (criminal) law.

> Neither Statute provisions nor the underlying principle of complementarity oblige state parties to enact criminal legislation or even to 'copy' the ICC Statute...[55]

This may be called somewhat curious as the Statute explicitly embraces the notion of a de-centralised administration of international justice in national courts by stating in Article 1 that the ICC "shall be complementary to national criminal jurisdictions". The Statute approach therefore did not look too promising. However many States Parties to the Rome Treaty, "like-minded" like the Netherlands assumed that by becoming a State Party criminalizing international crimes in national law, where that was not yet adequately done, was now required. And that is what a number of States in different ways set out to do. One option, not excluded in the Rome Treaty, is not to do anything and just apply "ordinary" criminal law when a case is at stake. It has been argued that leaving States this "soft" option, has even contributed substantially to the number of ratifications to the Treaty. From a policy point of view that may be wise, but in view of ending impunity for international crimes, "no action" did not appear to fit these special crimes very well or to contribute to the quality of the administration of international justice, as the rather embarrassing example of the *Bagaragaza* case has shown.[56] Ad-

55 *See* Werle, *supra,* note 1, p. 118.

56 The *Bagaragaza* case involving Norway (and the Netherlands) is by now the "classic" case. The Appeals Chamber of the ICTR decided that it "cannot sanction the referral of a case to a jurisdiction for trial where the conduct cannot be charged as a serious violation of international humanitarian law" (*Prosecutor v. Bagaragaza,* Case No. ICTR-05-86- AR11bis, Decision on Rule 11bis Appeal, 30 Aug. 2006, par. 18). Also in Norway specific legislation is now in the process of being enacted. *See* M. Harlem, "Importing War Crimes in Norwegian Legisla-

judicating international crimes is so much more complicated than the well-established practices of trying "normal" national crimes that the criminal law procedures and substance that are already in place usually are inadequate even in States where incorporation of an international treaty like the Rome Treaty would perhaps be the "natural" approach. Also when the choice was made to enact a national statute transforming the ICC Statute or its main duties directly into national law, practical cases can still pose numerous legal problems and pitfalls.

Quite a number of States have already enacted legislation or are intending to enact legislation to make the international crimes of Articles 6-8 punishable under their national law. Apart from the approach indicated of just relying on the already available domestic criminal law, these crimes are then specifically incriminated in domestic law. States have done this by way of an open-ended reference to the relevant international treaties to which they are a party and to international customary law (like Canada), or by criminalizing each specific international crime separately within their criminal law system (Germany, the Netherlands, and France), or aiming for a combination of the two (as in the case of Finland). All kinds of variations are further possible, and, as said are in principle allowed under the ICC Statute, from more "static" to more dynamic approaches. In the former potential problems with the principle of legality (see above) can easier be avoided than in the latter. If other details like the specific range of penalties or the provisions on jurisdiction are taken into account, further differences are possible. Nevertheless, in view of the existing situation characterised by a high level of impunity for international crimes, considerable modification of criminal legal systems to allow municipal adjudication for such crimes seems already achieved and is likely further to be extended.

Here it will suffice to illustrate the emerging situation by way of some examples. The Dutch cases are discussed in somewhat more detail below. In Germany, like the special *WIM* statute in the Netherlands, a German Code of Crimes against International Law (*Völkerstrafgesetzbuch*) has been enacted. It entered into force in 2002. The entry into force of the Statute did not lead to an increase in the number of domestic German cases where international crimes in the sense of the ICC Statute were adjudicated. In fact, in the period before 2002, the German courts

tion"; Ch. 6: "Importing Core International Crimes Into National Law", *Forum for International Criminal and Humanitarian Law* [FICHL] 33-34 (Pub. Ser. No. 1, 2nd ed., 2010).

seemed to have been more effectively occupied with such cases than in the subsequent period. Under the old German law, the universality principle was already applicable to genocide and war crimes. This facilitated considerable efforts before 2002. Werle reports that: '[s]ince 1996, the German judiciary has complied with more than 600 requests for judicial assistance from the Yugoslavia Tribunal; in the same period over 100 investigations were initiated in Germany in connection with the events in the former Yugoslavia. Several convictions were obtained, including some for genocide'.[57] For the period from 2003-2009, no cases of this kind reached beyond a (preliminary) investigation. This can be surprising as the German Statute has a very considerable scope.[58] An explanation for the (initial) lull in these kind of court proceedings may be that the German Federal Prosecutor's Office interprets its jurisdiction to be rather strictly as "subsidiary" in the sense that it should only be exercised if States nearer to the place where the crime took place, or nearer to the suspects, are not prepared or unable to adjudicate.[59] But in 2009 *Ignace Murwanashyaka*, residing in Germany where he was granted asylum, was arrested and in 2010 became the first person indicted under the Code of Crimes against International Law. Since 4 May 2011 *Murwanashyaka,* alleged President of the Forces Démocratiques de Libération du Rwanda (FDLR), and his alleged deputy, *Straton Musoni,* are tried before the Higher Regional Court ('Oberlandesgericht') in Stuttgart . Both are accused of crimes against humanity and a variety of war crimes committed in the Democratic Republic of Congo.[60]

---

57 Werle, *supra,* note 1, at 126, nn. 700-701. This is information from the German Federal Ministry of Justice as of 12 Apr. 2005 and 7 June 2007.

58 *See* Werle, *id.*, in particular, at 127-35. Germany, *e.g.*, decided in its adaptation of the law to include the permission to extradite German nationals with respect to the international crimes to which the Code of Crimes against International Law applied.

59 *Id.,*135. Another explanation is that the complaints leading to investigations by the Prosecutor were all against foreign high officials of State, like the Chinese President Jiang Zemin, and the former US Secretary of Defence D. Rumsfeld. The decisions not to prosecute were based on lack of evidence or the suspect's legal immunity. For entirely different reasons the Federal Prosecutor decided not to prosecute in a military case concerning an attack in Afghanistan. *See*: the *Klein* case, ICD: http://www.internationalcrimesdatabase.org/Case/1035/Klein/.

60 This is a rather complicated if not controversial case which in 2014 still 'drags on'; see also, in English, the Status Report February 2012 of the European Center for Constitutional and Human Rights, and, recently, http://www.taz.de/!146415/d

Australia has enacted two Acts upon becoming a party to the Rome Treaty. The 2002 Australian International Criminal Court Act – with the ICC Statute as its first schedule – covers the co-operation between Australia and the ICC. The 2002 International Criminal Court (Consequential Amendments) Act adapts the Australian Criminal Code.[61] Division 268 of the latter law is entitled: Genocide, crimes against humanity, war crimes and crimes against the administration of justice of the International Criminal Court. The crimes in this Division follow the ICC Statute as is already indicated in 268.2 of the Division: "... offences in this Division (...) are also crimes within the jurisdiction of that Court" [*i.e.*, the International Criminal Court]. So far no cases under the Act have been reported.

Canada has not adapted its national criminal law by defining crimes in an international context but has decided to base its 2000 Crimes against Humanity and War Crimes Act directly on international law. Historically Canadian courts have had difficulty with applying "core" crimes in cases before them: in the 1980s and 1990s every case involving such crimes was lost, for reasons not only of unsatisfactory evidence but also due to a certain lack of experience of the courts with the special requirements of such cases.[62] As a result of these unfortunate experiences the Canadian government decided to enact the 2000 Crimes against Humanity and War Crimes Act. This Act draws heavily on the ICC Statute. It contains in an Appendix the text of Articles 6, 7 and 8(2) of the Statute.[63] In addition, the Act tries to prevent some of the evidentiary problems earlier Canadian cases of this nature had caused. In the *Mugesera* case, the new Act played a secondary role although the basic crime at stake was incitement to commit genocide or crimes against

---

(in German). Murwanashyaka had been under investigation in Germany before. His case got an impetus when Rwanda in 2008 issued an arrest warrant.

61 It is sub-titled: An Act to Amend the Criminal Code Act 1995 and Certain Other Acts in Consequence of the Enactment of the International Criminal Court Act 2002, and for Other Purposes.

62 Four Second World War cases failed, all for reasons of insufficient evidence. Notably the *Finta* case provided a negative precedent. The Supreme Court of Canada put the evidentiary requirements to prove international offences so high as in effect barring further attempts to prosecute such offences. *See* Forum for International Criminal and Humanitarian Law [FICHL], *Importing Core International Crimes Into National Law* (Ch. III – The Canadian Model) 13-14 (Pub. Ser. No. 1, 2nd ed., 2010) [hereinafter: *Importing Core International Crimes*].

63 *Supra* note 3.

humanity. *Mugesera* tried unsuccessfully to prevent his deportation to Rwanda where he is currently being tried for allegedly having committed such a crime.[64]

It has been argued that the advantage of the Canadian approach is "... that Canada will never be out of step with new developments in the international sphere. These new developments automatically become part of Canadian law without the need of legislative amendments".[65]

The first application of the 2000 Act in the 2009 *Munyaneza* case demonstrates this by extensive references to applicable international law. The Montreal Superior Court observed:

> [65] *Contrairement à l'ensemble des lois canadiennes qui punissent des infractions commises sur le territoire canadien, la Loi prévoit qu'une personne ayant commis à l'étranger un crime de génocide, crime contre l'humanité ou un crime de guerre peut être poursuivie au Canada si elle y réside.*
>
> [66] *Un des buts avoués de la loi est de lutter contre l'impunité de criminels de guerre comme celle qui a existé après la seconde guerre mondiale.*[66]

After a detailed analysis of the state of international jurisprudence the Court found *Munyaneza* guilty of genocide, crimes against humanity and war crimes. He was sentenced to life in prison with no chance of parole for 25 years, the severest penalty available under Canadian law. The sentence was confirmed on Appeal on 7 May 2014.[67]

---

64 Supreme Court of Canada, Decision of 28 June 2005, in 2 *Sup. Ct. Rep.* 100, and, *see* ICD: http://www.internationalcrimesdatabase.org/Case/1070/Mugesera-v-Canada/. The case against *Mugesera* serves since 2012 before the High Court in Kigali.

65 J. Rikhof (Senior Counsel and Manager of the Law in the Crimes against Humanity and War Crimes Section of the Canadian Department of Justice), as quoted in *Importing Core International Crimes, supra* note 61, at 17.

66 *See* Montreal Superior Court (Crim. Div.), *R. v. Munyaneza*, 22 May 2009, [2009] *Q.C.C.S.* 2201available at: http://www.jugements.qc.ca/ and at ICDB: http://www.internationalcrimesdatabase.org/Case/1176/Munyaneza/ (*see*, in part. para. 81 ff). Judge A. Denis observed: "*Les procès relatifs aux crimes contre l'humanité et aux crimes de guerre sont extrêmement rares hors l'enceinte des tribunaux pénaux internationaux. C'est à ma connaissance une première dans les deux Amériques*".

67 The Quebec's Court of Appeal rejected the grounds of appeal and confirmed the first instance judgment on 7 May 2014. Currie and Stancu, commenting on the

That all actors in criminal prosecutions continually have to be up to date with changes in the international jurisprudence has been noted as a disadvantage of the Canadian approach.[68] The judgment of the Montreal Superior Court shows that for a Canadian court this is not necessarily a big problem. The judgment contains extensive knowledge of the relevant international law and an awareness of the foreign context where the international crimes were supposed to have been committed.[69]

France has a large number of cases pending concerning serious international crimes, mainly related to the Rwandan massacre. In view of this case-load, necessary changes in French criminal law have only relatively recently been enacted.[70] Since 2012 a specialized war crimes unit consisting of prosecutors and investigative judges has been operational.[71] In 2014 a specialized police unit the 'Office central de lutte contre les crimes contre l'humanité', has been formed. On 14 March 2014 at the 'Tribunal de Grande Instance' in Paris *Pascal Simbikangwa* was sentenced to 25 years.[72] During the 1994 massacres *Simbikangwa* was the

---

Superior Court judgment, conclude: 'The Munyaneza judgment strengthened the effectiveness of Canada'sapproach, and the overall good work it will do as a partner in the worldwide battle against impunity"; R. Currie & I. Stancu, "*R. v. Muyaneza*: Pondering Canada's First Core Crimes Conviction"; [2010] *Int'l Crim. L. Rev.* 854, *also at*: http://papers.ssrn.com/sol3/papers.cfm?abstract_id=2121670).

68 Rikhof, *supra,* note 64, at 17.

69 In the *Mugesera* decision (*supra* note 63) the Supreme Court of Canada showed also considerable awareness of relevant international law (and jurisprudence).

70 Loi nº 2010-930 du 9 août 2010 ("ICC Implementing Legislation"). The law entered into force on August 11, 2010. See: http://www.legifrance.gouv.fr/affichTexte.do;jsessionid=DA7956739FD101F26E23CD144B032676.tpdjo02v_1?cidTexte=JORFTEXT000022681235. See for an excellent overview in English: The Legal Framework for Universal Jurisdiction in France, Human Rights Watch 2014 (12 p.).

71 Local courts in other parts of the country retain jurisdiction over international crimes cases but can refer them to the specialized unit in Paris. In practice, nearly all cases since 2012 have been handled by the specialized unit. Relevant extradition cases are still dealt with by courts in the districts where the suspects are located. The Office of the Paris Prosecutor, on an on-going basis, deals with requests for mutual assistance in matters of international crimes from other countries and international tribunals (including the ICC). *See also* 'The Long arm of Justice..., *supra,* n. 30, pp. 69-85 on the way France has organised its approach and, on pp. 104-109, for an overview of French cases.

72 *See* the ICD, at http://www.internationalcrimesdatabase.org/Case/2241/Simbikangwa/.

head of the 'Service Central de Renseignement', the Rwandan central intelligence agency. He was indicted in Rwanda in 2008 for genocide and complicity in genocide, conspiracy and organized crime. *Simbikangwa* had fled Rwanda and was eventually arrested on the French island of Mayotte. This was the first case brought to trial by the newly established war crimes unit. Important other cases before the Paris 'Tribunal' are expected to begin in 2015.[73]

4.2 *The Dutch* WIM*; The Role of Prosecutors and Judges*[74]

Has the *WIM*, the 2003 Dutch International Crimes Act, indeed, changed the legal system of The Netherlands to the extent that it is now something like a 'model' for the administration of international justice along the lines of what the ICC Statute foresees, perhaps even to be followed by others? According to a recent Human Rights Watch assessment (*see* below), we may, indeed, believe this to be the case.

The *WIM* (the International Crimes Act) involves in essence a way of applying complementarity as included in Article 1 of the ICC Statute, to Dutch criminal law. The logical consequence of complementarity in the sense of Article 1 of the Statute can be formulated as follows: In order for national authorities to invoke their primacy entitlement it is imperative that they adopt legislation that transposes all the offences in the ICC Statute – although they are under no obligation to do so – otherwise their courts will be unable to assert jurisdiction over the relevant offences.[75]

The Dutch Government in its Explanatory Report to the *WIM* agrees: Although this is not expressly stated in the Statute, a majority of States, including the Kingdom, always assumed that it followed from the principle of complementarity that States that are parties to the Statute are obliged to criminalize the offences that are subject to the jurisdiction

73 It concerns the cases against two Rwandan genocide suspects, *Octavien Ngenzi* and *Tita Barahirwa*, former mayors in Eastern Rwanda. For both cases the judicial investigation reportedly has been completed.

74 Within the scope of the subject matter of this article reviewing the "legal history" of the WIM with proper attention for the often highly interesting legal "finesse" can unfortunately not be undertaken. The WIM has been amended in 2012 adding, a.o., an Article 21 (4) retro-actively extending the jurisdiction of the courts over genocide to 1970. *See* for the English text of the 'WIM': https://www.icrc.org/applic/ihl/ihl-nat.nsf/a24d1cf3344e99934125673e00508142/2a6d559625223f62c12577d0003be499/$FILE/60466371.pdf/Neth.

75 Bantekas, *supra*, note 5, at 429.

of the International Criminal Court in their own criminal law and to establish extra-territorial, universal jurisdiction, empowering their national criminal courts to try these offences, even when such offences have been committed abroad by non- nationals.[76] By way of the *WIM*, the Netherlands is supposed to be able to make a contribution to the administration of international justice, in particular in view of the international crimes mentioned in Articles 6 to 8 of the Statute of the ICC to which the Netherlands had become a Party in 2001. The Act subsumes the already existing penalization of wartime offences (in the 1952 Wartime Offences Act, or *WOS*), of Genocide (the 1970 Genocide Convention Implementation Act) and Torture (in the 1989 Torture Convention Implementation Act), adds Crimes against Humanity and provides universal jurisdiction for all these crimes. Ever since its entry into force, several Dutch and foreign nationals have faced trial before The Hague District Court. The Hague District Court has been singled out for this purpose.[77] In doing so it was hoped that concentration would help to develop the necessary specialised expertise. The *WIM* recognizes universal jurisdiction over these four crimes but does require a suspect to be present on Dutch territory, or a Dutch victim.[78] From 2003 to 2014, The Hague District Court has delivered judgments in quite a number of rather diverse cases. In terms of nationality, four of these cases involved defendants with a foreign nationality: three with Afghan nationality, one with Rwandan nationality. The so-called *LTTE* (*Liberation Tigers of Tamil Elam*) cases concerned five persons from Sri Lanka, of Tamil origin, with Dutch nationality. The *Besabya* case, concerned a defendant from Rwanda who had obtained Dutch nationality.

---

76 Bijl. Hand. II 2001/2002, 28337, No. 3, at 2; English text in [2003] *Netherlands Y.B. Int'l L.* 233 (cited in Boot-Matthijsen & Van Elst, *supra* note 8, at 255). Hence, national courts (although the same can be argued for other "officials" like prosecutors in particular) function, not only as national, but also as international agents. On such "role splitting" *see* Post, "International Criminal Law: Reflections on Monism and Dualism", 43 Israel Yearbook of Human Rights, 2013, Leiden-Boston, 364 ff.

77 The District Court Arnhem (or mobile military courts) has specific jurisdiction under the Administration of Military Criminal Justice Act over criminal offences committed by Dutch soldiers.

78 *WIM*, Art. 2. *See* for an assessment of the characteristics of the WIM, Boot-Matthijsen & Van Elst, *supra* note 8; W. Ferdinandusse, 'The Dutch Experience', in M.C. Bassiouni, III *International Criminal Law* (*International Enforcement*) 385 (2008).

The defendants in the *Van Anraat* and *Kouwenhoven* cases[79] have Dutch nationality. On 23 December 2005, The Hague District Court found *Frans van Anraat*, a Dutch businessman, guilty of complicity in violating the laws and customs of war. He was acquitted of complicity in genocide for which he was also indicted, as there was insufficient evidence that he knew about the genocidal intent of Saddam Hussein's regime. He was sentenced to 15 years imprisonment (later after appeal and cassation to 16 ½). *Van Anraat* was the main supplier of chemicals necessary to fabricate the gas used in attacks in Iraq and Iran, among them on the Kurdish town of Halabja (Iraq) on 16 March 1988 in which an estimated 3000-5000 people died and many more were injured. His conviction was confirmed on appeal (including by a judgment of the European Court of Human Rights).

Kouwenhoven, another Dutch businessman, was accused of war crimes by Liberian troops and militia during armed conflicts in Liberia and Guinea. The Hague District Court acquitted him of those accusations on the basis of insufficient evidence, but convicted him of another accusation: complicity in violating the arms embargo against Liberia prohibited on the basis of Dutch law implementing UN Security Council Resolutions (Resolutions 1343 and 1408) and measures taken by the Council of the European Union. He was sentenced to the maximum penalty of eight years imprisonment. On appeal, however, The Hague Court of Appeals acquitted *Kouwenhoven* also of this latter violation. But on 20 April 2010 the Supreme Court quashed that judgment and ordered a re-trial at the Court of Appeals in Hertogenbosch (where it is pending).

Of the two Afghan generals *Hesam* and *Jalalzoy*,[80] the first was convicted by The Hague District Court on 14 October 2005 of co-perpetration to torture and of complicity in the violation of the laws and customs of war. He was sentenced to twelve years in prison. General *Jalalzoy* was convicted on the same day by the same Court for co-perpetration in vio-

79 *See* for both cases: *supra* note 8. *See* on some of the legal questions the *Van Anraat* case has raised: H.G. van der Wilt, "Genocide, Complicity in Genocide and International v. Domestic Jurisdiction", [2006] *J. Int'l Crim. Just.* (JICJ) 239, and of the same author, "Genocide v. War Crimes in the Van Anraat Appeal", [2008] *ibid.*, 557. *See also* Ferdinandusse, *supra* note 17, Sec. 5, who discusses, critically, the interesting divergence of opinion between prosecutor and the Hague District Court on the application of a national or an international standard of liability in the case of a suspect with Dutch nationality (i.e., *Van Anraat*).

80 *See*, for both cases, *supra*, note 10.

lating the laws and customs of war. He got nine years imprisonment. All these crimes had been committed in Afghanistan in the 1980s. The judgments and sentences were confirmed in appeal, and appeal in cassation at the Dutch Supreme Court was dismissed.

Another Afghan general, *Faqirzada*, like the other two residing in the Netherlands, was acquitted (confirmed on appeal) by The Hague District Court on 25 June 2007. He had been charged with war crimes and crimes against humanity involving torture. Although the Court found that acts of violence, cruel and inhumane treatment and torture had clearly taken place, it had insufficient evidence for his individual involvement or command responsibility.

On 23 March 2009 *Mpambara*, a Rwandan, was convicted of complicity in different acts of torture.[81] He had also, alternatively, been accused of war crimes, but The Hague District Court did not find that a relationship with the on-going armed conflict in 1994 in Rwanda was adequately proven. The Court imposed a 20-year prison sentence. On 7 July 2011, The Hague Court of Appeals found *Mpambara* also guilty of co-participation in breaching the laws and customs of war, committed several times, as part of systematic terror against the Tutsi-population of Rwanda. The Court of Appeals saw *Mpambara*'s crimes, as the gravest crimes tried in Dutch courts since World War II. It sentenced him to life imprisonment. This means that unless being pardoned, *Mpambara* is supposed to spend the rest of his life in prison as there is no possibility of parole or early release for such a sentence in Dutch criminal law. The case is on appeal in cassation before the Dutch Supreme Court.

The counts *Mpambara* was charged with, were initially also charged as constituting genocide. But, by an interlocutory decision of 24 July 2007, The Hague District Court had barred prosecution with respect to genocide, since the laws applicable in 1994 in its view provided neither direct nor indirect jurisdiction to do so. This decision (albeit on different grounds) was confirmed on appeal.

This decision in the *Mpambara* case had a somewhat remarkable consequence. In the meantime another Rwandan suspect, *Bagaragaza*, had been transferred by the ICTR to the Netherlands, after a transfer to Norway had already been rejected by the ICTR (see above). He was to be prosecuted for war crimes or genocide. However, after the *Mpambara*

81 For the *Publ. Prosecutor v. Mpambara* case, ICD: http://www.internationalcrimesdatabase.org/Case/748/Mpambara/ (some of the judgments have only been summarised in English).

case, it had become clear that in the Netherlands he in fact could be adjudicated for war crimes but not for genocide. The ICTR decided to have *Bagaragaza* returned and that is what happened.[82]

On 21 October 2011, The Hague District Court delivered judgments against five Dutch nationals from Sri Lankan descent and Tamil origin resident in the Netherlands. They were accused of extortion through blackmail and threats in order to benefit the *LTTE* (*Liberation Tigers of Tamil Elam*), a group listed by the EU as a terrorist organization.[83] The defence held that they were freedom fighters in the non-international armed conflict that had been raging in Sri Lanka. The Court found that there was not enough evidence that the *LTTE* had as its objection to commit terrorist crimes. Also, in a detailed analysis, it concluded that the crimes were, indeed, related to the armed conflict in Sri Lanka and, on the basis of Article 6(2) of the 1977 Additional Protocol II to the 1949 Geneva Conventions, could therefore not be prosecuted in the Netherlands.[84] Because it was placed on the EU list of terrorist organizations, certain business transactions on behalf of the *LTTE* the five had been involved in were per se forbidden under Dutch law. Their actions were not considered extortion under Dutch criminal law but the suspects did force people to contribute money. They were convicted to sentences varying from two to six years' imprisonment. The cases are pending before the Court of Appeals.

On 1 March 2013, the Hague District Court convicted *Yvonne Basebya* to 6 years and 8 months imprisonment for incitement to genocide (on multiple occasions), the maximum sentence possible in the Netherlands for this crime. In 2007 Basebya had been sentenced *in absentia* to life imprisonment by a so-called 'gacaca' court for her role in the Rwanda killings.[85]

In *The Netherlands (Ministry of Defence and Ministry of Foreign Affairs) v. Hasan Nuhanović*, a civil case, the Dutch Supreme Court decid-

82 On 17 Aug. 2007 the referral order was revoked by the ICTR Prosecutor. On 17 Nov. 2009, the ICTR convicted *Bagaragaza* to eight years imprisonment for complicity in genocide. He was released early on 24 Oct. 2011 (*see also supra*, note 56).

83 ICD: http://www.internationalcrimesdatabase.org/Case/202.

84 Protocol Additional to the Geneva Conventions of 12 August 1949 and Relating to the Protection of Victims of Non-International Armed Conflicts (Protocol II), 1977, 1125 *U.N.T.S.* 609.

85 For the *Besabya* case, *see* ICD: http://www.internationalcrimesdatabase.org/Case/971.

ed on 13 September 2013 that in principle The Netherlands and the UN could both have had effective control over the same wrongful conduct of a Dutch UN contingent ('Dutchbat') which held the town of Srebrenica under assault of Bosnian Serb forces. It made this finding on the basis of a detailed analysis of relevant international law.[86] Attributing such control to The Netherlands did in no way, according to the Court prejudice the possibility of the UN also having control. As a result The Netherlands could be held responsible for conduct of 'Dutchbat' and is therefore responsible for the death of three men who were later executed in the Srebrenica massacre. In this case the Hague District Court also had a role albeit more minor. On 10 September 2008 the Court had attributed exclusive control of 'Dutchbat' to the UN and on that basis had rejected the claim against The Netherlands. However, on 5 July 2011 the Court of Appeals had quashed the earlier judgment and presented basically the arguments later upheld by the Supreme Court.

In many respects these Dutch cases provide a good example of how complementarity in the sense of the ICC Statute can be given effect. Tentatively, it can be argued that The Hague District Court and the prosecution service have done a serious and often impressive job trying defendants accused of international crimes.[87] Also, tentatively, it seems that the performance of, in particular, Dutch and Canadian courts (and prosecutors) indicate that according to an acceptable standard the administration of international justice can be undertaken in national courts as long as the municipal law provides adequate instruments.[88] The jurisprudence shows that the Dutch courts, like their Canadian counterparts have no particular problem applying international law (international criminal and humanitarian law), keeping up with the (inter-

86 *See* ICD: http://www.internationalcrimesdatabase.org/Case/1005/The-Netherlands-v-Nuhanovi%C4%87/ in par. 3.7 to 3.10 of the judgment, on the basis of an analysis of the 'rules developed in unwritten international law' (par. 3.7), *i.e.*, the 2001 ILC Draft Articles on State Responsibility and the 2011 Draft Articles on the Responsibility of International Organisations. The Supreme Court clearly assumes that these Draft articles correctly reflect rules of customary international law. This is generally accepted to be the case for the rules from the 2001 Draft that the Court refers to. However, in respect to the rules from the 2011 Draft this status is quite debatable.

87 It is probably accurate to say that these laudable activities have been 'inspired' by the *WIM* as all the cases referred to have in fact been decided on the basis of other legislation; the facts took place before the new Act entered into force.

88 *See* on the Dutch efforts also: 'The Long Arm of Justice...' *infra*, note. 30, pp. 32-51.

national) jurisprudence and as far as possible with relevant events and developments in the world. Perhaps, concentrating and pooling the considerable knowledge needed, as has been done in The Netherlands and in France is likely to enhance the quality of the administration of this kind of justice. However, in the end it should not be left out of sight that for the quantity and quality of national adjudication of international crimes, apart from the organization, the willingness, role and approach of the prosecutors and the judges is of the greatest importance.[89]

5 Concluding Remarks

In the preceding pages the remarkable expansion of international criminal law in the last 2 decennia has been reviewed. The main impulse for this expansion has been the foundation of special *ad hoc* criminal tribunals in the early 1990s. The successful apprehension and adjudication of a large number of suspects of gruesome crimes (in the case of the ICTY – miraculously: all suspects) has left a lasting impression. The resulting very considerable and detailed jurisprudence has led to a profound explanation and, in several cases, elaboration of the already available international humanitarian law instruments and customary international humanitarian law including their translation and individual application in international criminal law. Moreover, the operation of the tribunals have produced a substantial body of procedural law which is now available to serve as an example for future international or domestic criminal adjudication. The case law of the tribunals, and increasingly, of 'hybrid' and even of domestic courts, after two decades has led to a *corpus* of international criminal law which might be characterized as that of a young adult.

However, the core question that had to be addressed here is what the perspective is for the further development of this young adult? In the

89 Boot-Matthijsen & Van Elst (*supra* note 8, at 257) quote the Dutch Government in a statement included in their Report regarding the role of the Dutch UN contingent at Srebrenica that "the public prosecutor had been 'too passive', lacked the initiative necessary to guarantee that information about possible criminal conduct by the Dutch military would be received timely and handled adequately, and even choose a 'restrained attitude'". *See* for an account of the many problems and demands these cases generate: R. van Rossum, "Adjudication of International Crime in the Netherlands", [2011] *Int'l J. of Legal Information* 194, at 198-207.

previous pages I have argued that the prospects are perhaps not as glorious as could be hoped for on the basis of its initial years, at least no longer at the international level where international criminal law has grown so successfully. Without being too presumptuous, one can argue that the hey-days of *ad hoc* criminal tribunals are likely to be over. The SCSL has closed down, the ICTR will soon follow suit and the ICTY is now scheduled to be closed in 2017. On the one hand the existence of the ICC as an alternative of sorts does not encourage the establishment of new tribunals, which anyway are now known to be a costly undertaking. On the other hand, on the shorter term one should be careful not to exaggerate the point: the Residual Mechanisms of the tribunals are likely still to produce some noteworthy judgments, e.g., in the Appeals stage of the *Karadžić* and *Mladić* cases of which the ICTY is to finish the trial stage. In that sense the contribution to the development of international criminal law by *ad hoc* tribunals is certainly not yet over. In addition the EEEC and the Special Tribunal for Lebanon continue to function and might produce noteworthy judgments.

Still, I have tried to show above that on the somewhat longer term, it is likely that the main point of gravity in the development of international criminal law will gradually shift to relevant domestic jurisprudence. The efforts by some 'willing' states to adapt and use their national legal systems for war crime procedures are noteworthy and have begun to bear fruit. In particular, but not solely, the jurisprudence produced by Canadian and Dutch courts is most promising. Much more, and in many more countries, is to come as the strong increase in cases undertaken all over the world suggests. In that sense a major increase in the domestic administration of international justice, as foreseen in the ICC Statute seems to be on its way. Whether this is good for the state of international criminal law will depend, of course on the quality of the jurisprudence generated. If that quality is good, domestic case-law may continue to lead to the identification of customary humanitarian law and the explanation of treaty obligations and their application in criminal law procedures.

What will the role of the ICC be in this process? In the first place, the Court is the main inspiration for the increase in domestic cases by way of the 'complementarity' principle enshrined in the Statute. The principle has been 'embraced' now by a number of willing states. In addition, the ICC Statute serves like a kind of informal base law for international criminal law. It seems that this 'indirect' aspect of the ICC undertaking is more successful than the Court's direct contribution on the international level by way of its own cases. In that respect the ICC increasingly has faced obstacles on its path. The level of support from the UN Security Council has been a source of even official complaints. Moreover, the ICC Trial Chambers have joined the Prosecutor in her complaint about the (much) less than faithful compliance and co-operation by individual states, notably Kenya and Libya. Partly as a result of the political configuration in which in particular the Prosecutor has to work, the Court has now completed only one full case, i.e., including the Appeals phase. Without more stringent support from the Security Council the 'vulnerability' of the ICC can hardly be solved notwithstanding the recommendable efforts of its organs.

This situation suggests a limit to the contribution the ICC can make to the further development of international criminal law. We have instead argued that such a contribution is more likely to be expected from the expansion that seems on its way of domestic cases on international crimes. The development in the relevant jurisprudence in some willing countries, like The Netherlands and Canada, and now also France seems promising enough including from the essential point of the quality of the cases and the eventual judgments. It is to be hoped that the ICC will see it also as one of its real, as opposed to 'formal', responsibilities to monitor this rapidly expanding domestic administration of international justice against a strict quality standard. After all, the quality of the domestic jurisprudence will in the end determine whether or not the state of international criminal law really benefits from this development.

CHAPTER 4

Sixty Years in the Life of an International Lawyer Both as a Teacher and a Practitioner

*Eric Suy**

1 Introductory Remarks

Any legal order, lest it may sooner or later become ineffective and obsolete, should reflect, as much and as precise as possible, the living realities within the society of which it tends to organize its structures and regulate the relations between its members. This is also true of the international legal order that purports to regulate the social fabric of the relations between its members (the States) through an immense network of general and special norms covering a steadily growing amount of issues. As the Permanent Court of International Justice stated in one of its earlier Advisory Opinions: "The question whether a certain matter is or not solely within the domestic jurisdiction of a State is an essentially relative question: it depends upon the development of international relations". Ever since this dictum of 1923, the necessities of interstate relations became so intense and so overwhelming that the States felt that a closer organization of the international community had become necessary. In 1945, 'only' fifty-one States were present at the birth of the United Nations Organization. Today, way into the second decade of the twenty-first century, the international community has close to two hundred member States organized in a nearly cluttered amount of universal and regional organizations dealing with nearly all aspects of life. There are virtually no more matters that fall within the exclusive jurisdiction of a State.

When I started the study of international law in the early fifties of the twentieth century, international law was mainly limited to what was then called *The Law of Nations* to use the title of J. L. Brierly's fascinating "introduction to the international law of peace". Similarly, the an-

* Emeritus Professor of International Law , Catholic University of Leuven (KUL), former Under-Secretary-General of the United Nations, the Legal Counsel, Member of the Institute of International Law.

Karel Wellens (ed.), International Law in Silver Perspective: Challenges Ahead.
 ISBN *978-90-04-27167-8. pp. 97-108.*

nual general courses of international law at The Hague Academy dealt with the *Principes généraux du droit international de la paix*. Gradually, Public International Law, Droit International Public, became a more fascionable title, while German scholars seem to continue to use the expression *Völkerrecht*, although the Max Planck Institute decided to publish the *Encyclopedia of Public International Law* as the successor of the two previous editions of the *Wörterbuch des Völkerrechts*.

The need to manage the increasing complexity of a global international society led to the introduction of new words and expressions into the vocabulary relating to the sociology of international relations. Thus, at the outset of the twenty-first century, '*global governance*' has become a learned concept of political sociology, covering a wide range of disciplines, but lacking the necessary precision so as to be labelled as scientific. Anyway, it is a far cry from the law governing international relations or international law, and has become a vague, but sometimes convenient, notion used in debates by politicians and 'experts' to hide their ignorance of the real issues.

As of late, my granddaughter, born at the turn of this century, confessed to me that she wants to become an international lawyer. I explained to her that, contrary to the time when I became fascinated by international law, nowadays international law has proliferated in as many distinct branches as there are aspects of international relations. Is she thinking of classical public international law or the law of nations? Or does she have in mind international commercial or trade law, - criminal law, - economic law, - environmental law, - fiscal law, - monetary law, - humanitarian law, - labor law, - air and space law, - intellectual property law, - human rights law, - private law or conflicts of law, etc....? She was amazed when I showed her the immense collection of the *Treaties Series* of both the League of Nations and the United Nations. I also told her that scientific institutions had immensely contributed – and still continue to do so - to the development of both public and private international law. I mentioned in particular the Reports and Resolutions of the *Institut de Droit International*, founded in Ghent (Belgium) in 1873, and of which I am a member since 1975. I added that the *Institut* was awarded the Nobel Peace Price in 1910. This impressive amount of information led us to discussing the codification of international law.

1.1 *Codifying International Law: Highlights and Pitfalls*

Treaties are the primary sources of international law. Therefore, it was felt necessary to elaborate the problems and rules governing the procedures leading to the making of treaties, from their negotiation till their entry into force. The result was the *Vienna Convention on the Law of Treaties, 1969*, largely codifying state practice and custom.

Another major source of international law – at least according to traditional doctrine and reflected in the Statute of the International Court of Justice – is *custom*, based upon state practice and the so-called *opinio iuris*. I never was a follower of this subjective element in the formation of customary law. I rather feel that a given state practice is based on the conviction of state actors that this conduct is *necessary* for a smooth development of international relations. Therefore, *opinio necessitatis* seems to be the more clarifying element. Customary international law, sometimes also called 'general international law', reflects, by definition, a great degree of generality, vagueness and uncertainty that is obnoxious for peace and security among nations. Codification of general international law should avoid doubt, exclude uncertainties and contradictions, thus creating a clear and more reliable set of rules for states.

After World War I, the League of Nations made a first attempt at codifying some aspects of general international law without any serious success. The Charter of the United Nations took over this idea of codifying international law, and it entrusted the General Assembly of the new Organisation with the task of, *inter alia*, "progressive development and codification" of international law. To this end, the General Assembly created the subsidiary organ called: *International Law Commission*, which became the focal point of the codification effort. Ever since 1947, the year in which the ILC was founded, the path of codification through the ILC has been a most impressive one with such benchmarks as the first conventions on the various aspects of the law of the sea, adopted in 1958 in Geneva. At that time, the Convention on the continental shelf was the most significant example of what was, still in 1958, a largely controversial notion of 'progressive development'. Codification indeed does not mean the simple writing down of existing rules and regulations. That may have been a Napoleonic concept of the late eighteenth century. The success of every codification, of either internal or international law, depends on the ability and wisdom of the drafters to grasp the realities of social events that are constantly moving. It would therefore seem that the results of any attempt to codify international law, in the form of either an international convention or of a solemn declaration, should be subject to a possible revision or adaptation to new developments in the fabric of interstate relations: a *rebus sic stantibus* clause that should therefore be inserted in all general international agreements with a view to proceed to a possible reconsideration of the rules previously adopted and recognized as valid at earlier times and under previously prevailing conditions.

Overlooking the results of the codification of international law – and of its progressive development – the following remarks come to mind.

First, there can be no doubt that, the works and achievements of the International Law Commission during the last seventy years are to be admired and praised. This admiration and praise have to be shared with the Special Rapporteurs in charge of preparing the sometimes lengthy and voluminous reports and drafts. Similarly, members of the Codification Division of the United Nations Office of Legal Affairs play an important role in the preparation and organization of the ILC's works.

Second, some important benchmarks of the codification could not have been brought to a successful result without the invitation of some member states of the United Nations to host codification conferences. The Vienna Conventions on diplomatic (1961) and consular relations (1963), the Vienna Convention on the Law of Treaties (1969) stand as milestones on the path of codification. Similarly, codification conferences held in Vienna resulted in the adoption of conventions on the Succession of States in respect of Treaties (1973) and on some other aspects such as State Property, Archives and Debts (1983). Yet, the preparatory works for the codification of aspects of state succession were ill conceived: the approach focused too heavily on state succession following decolonization, and did not sufficiently take into account the 'traditional' devolution problems which re-emerged only in the 1990's after the breakdown of the Federal Republic of Yugoslavia. The limited number of ratification of these two conventions seems to confirm the view that this phase of codification cannot be viewed as successful, although some of the recorded principles may be useful as guidelines during devolution negotiations. Another Vienna Convention was adopted in 1975, and dealt with the Representation of States in their Relations with International Organizations of a Universal Character.

Third, as a consequence of the near universality of the United Nations, member states are clearly no longer willing or able to issue invitations for the organization of the mammoth conferences of longer duration. The series of Vienna Conventions ended in 1986 with the adoption of the Convention on the Law of Treaties between States and International

Organizations or between International Organizations. Thus, it appears that the era of codification conferences has come to an end, and that the United Nations General Assembly has become the only appropriate forum where codification can be successful.

Fourth, codification conventions or treaties, though, need a sufficient number of ratifications in order to enter into force. Therefore, they may very well never enter into force. What then is their value as codified customary or general rules? The longer the entry into force is delayed, the weaker will become the argument of the universal validity of the codified existing norms. In the long run, the distinction between rules of progressive development and those of a customary nature may become fluid. Un-codified customary rules of international law remain more flexible and malleable by the moving sands in international relations. Once codified, however, these general rules become more fixed, clearer and therefore more reliable in their application and interpretation by States. But does this not imply immobility and stagnation, unless recourse can be had to some correcting mechanism? Renegotiating manifestly antiquated treaties is perhaps the ultimate method, and was used in 1949 when the so-called Red Cross conventions of 1929 were replaced by the four new Geneva conventions on international humanitarian law. These, in turn, were adapted to the new warfare techniques by the 1977 two Additional Protocols. The 1952 European Convention on Human Rights and Fundamental Freedoms is regularly and successfully adapted through the adoption of Protocols. Several treaties in the field of disarmament contain provisions calling for regular revision conferences where the parties proceed to an evaluation of the results, although the main purpose of this evaluation process may very well be to exercise pressure on the major powers to speed up efforts towards disarmament.

These various methods or techniques, the effect of which is the 'modernisation' of the treaty commitments and their adaptation to the changing conditions of international relations, are absent in codification treaties. As indicated earlier, it may perhaps be useful to think of some means of adjusting these treaties, without running the risk of reopening them constantly to new challenges. A clause opening the possibility for a revision after, say, at least thirty years, may offer a reasonable solution to keep the codification up to date.

Fifth, on 21 November 1947, the General Assembly of the United Nations adopted Resolution 174 (II) on the *Statute of the International Law Com-*

mission. This Statute was amended in 1950, in 1955 (twice) and in 1981 for the sole purpose of increasing the number of members in the Commission. This number now stands at thirty-four. The distinction between 'progressive development' and 'codification', as confirmed in the Articles 16 and 18 to 24 of the Statute, has become mostly blurred. Thus, time has perhaps come for a substantial overhaul of this Statute. In its present version the Statute spells out the various possibilities for the General Assembly to finalize the codification procedure of any given topic. Article 33 of the Statute mentions the following actions the International Law Commission may recommend to the General Assembly: to take no action after the publication of the ILC's report, to take note of, or to adopt the report, to recommend the ILC's draft to member states with a view to concluding of a convention, and, finally, to convoke a conference to conclude a convention. All these options have been adopted by the General Assembly during these last five decades. A complete survey can be found in the website of the ILC, under *Texts, instruments and final reports*.

1.2 *International Trade Law*

In 1966, the U.N. General Assembly created a Commission on International Trade Law (UNCITRAL) for the purpose of harmonizing and unifying rules of international trade law. During half a century since its establishment, this body, supported by the works of its secretarial body, the Trade Law Branch in the Office of Legal Affairs, has produced an impressive volume of conventions, rules and reports that can also be found in the Commission's Annual reports to the General Assembly. I am fully aware that, at first glance, the achievements of this Commission are somewhat dwarfed by those of the World Trade Organization (WTO), and by the prospects of the negotiations on international commerce and investments between the European Union and other global players (Canada and the United States), and by the negotiations on the Trans-Pacific Partnership. This leads me to a further suggestion: would it not be more reasonable to bring *Uncitral* and its secretarial services under the helm of the WTO ? I am fully aware how difficult it is to change the structure of an intergovernmental organ once it is created. But it is my earnest feeling, and even conviction, that the Commission could function in a more appropriate environment close to the World Trade Organisation and, in particular, to its Panel on the Settlement of Trade Disputes, which is, in fact, the World Trade Court.

This brings me to some aspects of another source of international law, i.e. decisions of international organizations, especially of the Security Council.

1.3 *Some Thoughts on the Reform of the Security Council*

In 2015, the United Nations 'celebrates' its seventieth year in existence. This is a new occasion for a thorough evaluation of its achievements, defaults and lacunae. Whenever and wherever I deliver lectures or conduct seminars and workshops on the Organization, attendants' reactions unavoidably focus on the role and the functioning of the Security Council. Students in high schools, colleges and universities, members of U.N. Associations and of other clubs seem to be only interested in two narrow aspects of this topic *viz.* the membership in the Council, and the voting system, in particular, the 'objectionable' veto right granted to the still five Permanent Members (PM) of the Council. Even former high officials of the United Nations and of its Specialized Agencies participate in this exercise of questioning the usefulness of the Security Council in its present structure.

Reforming the Security Council is not a new theme; it has been an obsession for over the last three decades. No new proposals or suggestions are on the table. Some of them are a far cry away from being realistic. In evaluating a proposal, one has to consider, first of all, if it implies an amendment of the UN Charter. This is certainly the case for adding new permanent members, or for abolishing the veto. Article 108 of the Charter determines that an amendment enters into force if it is accepted and ratified by two thirds of the Members of the United Nations "including all the permanent members of the Security Council". Obviously, these PM will never agree to abandon the privileges granted to them in 1945. Similarly, France and the United Kingdom of Great Britain and Northern Ireland will never accept to be replaced in the Security Council by the European Union (a proposal one frequently hears in debates, without realizing that the EU is not even a member of the Organization!). The permanent members will ultimately be the ones that decide which other States may be admitted to the status of PM. One may feel sorry for these realities that prevent the world body from adjusting to the necessities of the twenty-first century. Article 109 of the Charter mentions the possibility of a General Conference "for the purpose of reviewing the present Charter". But here again, the PM have the power to prevent any review that will affect their privileged positions. The hypothesis of a new world cataclysm, that would ultimately give birth to a new world order with a new constitution, seems to be, at least provisionally, premature. So, we have to continue to live with the old fashioned Charter.

The way out from this highly unsatisfactory situation of living with a constitution that has, to a large extent, become obsolete, is to search for *de facto* adaptations of the Charter that do not necessitate an amendment. This occurred in the past when Article 27, dealing with voting in the Security Council, was adapted to the effect that the abstention by a permanent member does not prevent a resolution of the Council to be validly adopted. An "affirmative" and "concurring" vote does not necessarily mean a 'positive' vote.

This subtle nicety of interpretation could also be used in other instances necessitating the advancement of political goals. Thus, concerning the election of non-permanent members in the Security Council, practice reveals that certain member states of the Organization have been elected more often than others to serve on the Council. Article 23, § 1, of the Charter refers to this possibility by mentioning that the General Assembly, in electing the non-permanent members of the Security Council, "due regard being specially paid, in the first instance, to the contribution of Members of the United Nations to the maintenance of international peace and security and to the other purposes of the Organization, and also to the equitable geographical distribution". The interpretation of this passage may open the way to admitting certain members of the Organization on a non-permanent basis more often than others... provided there is a consensus within regional groups to suggest candidates for the function.

In a remarkable Statement of 7 February 2015, *The Elders*, a group of senior statesmen and -women, suggested four proposals for the purpose of *Strengthening the United Nations*. A first suggestion deals with creating *A new Category of Members* of the Security Council. This proposal to create *de facto* a category of quasi-permanent members is a valid and workable one, but its realization lies, of course, in the camp of the regional groups. It is to be assumed that this solution would not do away with the exclusive veto right of the permanent members and their other privileges.

On this hot issue, *The Elders* come up with an entirely new proposal: *A Pledge by the Existing Permanent Members* "not to use, or threaten to use, their veto..." Instead, they should make "greater and more persistent efforts to find common ground, especially in crises where populations are being subjected to, or threatened with, genocide or other atrocity crimes". In explaining its negative vote, the permanent member "must refer to international peace and security, and not to the national interest of the state casting the veto, since any state casting a veto simply to protect its national interest is abusing the privilege of permanent membership".

This is a highly noble effort to tackle an issue that is probably foremost in the mind of all those who are trying to improve the authority of the Security Council and, hence, of the Organization itself. One may, however, ask what is the value of the proposed pledge. If it is not framed in a formal undertaking with a legally binding force, a pledge is nothing more than a moral commitment. *The Elders'* proposal emphasizes the importance of the explanation vote by a permanent member in casting the veto. The permanent member(s) involved will always find the right wording to explain why the negative vote on a given draft resolution, even if it affects its national interest, or the national interest of it(s) friend(s), is inspired by considerations of international peace and security.

This leads me to a peculiar aspect of the explanations of vote *viz.* their importance in determining the *legal* position of the participating state, especially if it happens to be a permanent member casting his veto.

1.4 *The Legal Importance of Explaining a* Veto *in the Security Council*

It is a generally accepted practice in parliamentary proceedings that participants in a voting procedure be allowed to explain their vote, before or after casting the vote. I do not wish to dwell on the various motives a voter may have had to cast his or her vote one way or the other. In international organizations, however, the participant in a vote is a state, and not an individual. Hence the importance of knowing the motive(s) that may induce a state cast its vote. Sometimes, the explanation of a vote may clarify important aspects in the conduct of the foreign relations of the state concerned. The United Nations Security Council has the main responsibility for the maintenance of international peace and security. Chapter VII of the Charter deals with *action* the Council can take in this respect. Members of the Council, and, in particular, permanent members, have a prevailing role in this endeavour. Therefore, the votes (including the *vetos*) of these permanent members are important to be observed and analysed. One example may serve as an illustration of this importance.

On 18 February 2011, the Security Council voted on draft resolution S/2011/24 dealing with Israeli settlement activities in the Occupied Palestinian Territory. The draft starts with reaffirming the applicability of the 1949 Geneva Convention relative to the Protection of Civilian Persons in Time of War to the Palestinian Territory, including East Jerusalem, and further reaffirms that all Israeli settlement activities in the Occupied Palestinian Territory, including Jerusalem, are illegal and constitute a major obstacle to the achievement of peace on the basis of the two-State solution. The draft further reiterates the Council's earlier demands that Israel, the occupying Power, immediately and completely ceases all settlement activities.

The voting result was: 14 in favour, to 1 against (United States of America). It is worth looking at the statement made by the US Representative, Ms. *Rice*:

> Our opposition to the resolution before this Council today should ... not be misunderstood to mean that we support settlement activity. On the contrary, we reject in the strongest terms the legitimacy of Continued Israeli settlement activity. For more than four decades Israeli settlement activity in territories occupied in 1967 has undermined Israel's security and corroded hopes for peace and stability in the region. Continued settlement activity violates Israel's international commitments, devastates trust between the parties and threatens the prospects for peace ... While we agree with our fellow Council members – and indeed with the wider world – about the folly and illegitimacy of continued Israeli settlement activity, we think it unwise for this Council to attempt to resolve the core issues that divide Israelis and Palestinians. Therefore, regrettably, have opposed this draft resolution (S/PV.6484).

This statement by the representative of the United States of America, in explanation of the negative vote on the draft resolution, calls for some brief remarks. *First*, it is crystal clear that the substance of the draft, *viz*. the applicability of the 1949 Geneva Convention in the occupied territories and the illegality of the Israeli settlement activity in all occupied territories were *unanimously* recognized by the Council and by the international community at large. *Second*, this statement is the expression of the legal position of the US, a major world player and otherwise strong supporter and ally of Israel. It therefore contributes to strengthening the rule of international law in this conflict. *Third*, this episode indicates that a vetoed draft resolution should not be dumped in the wastebasket of the Security Council. International lawyers, political scientists and students should have an easier access to the materials surrounding aborted resolutions for they mostly contain highly valuable information on the position of a state in any given conflict. A veto may perhaps kill a resolution, but it cannot destroy its spirit and underlying motivation.

21 March 2014

CHAPTER 5

New Developments in the Cyprus Question – The Beginning of the End, or the End of the Beginning?

*Neri Sybesma-Knol**

The UN News Centre, on 17 September 2014:

> The newly appointed Special Adviser to the Secretary-General on Cyprus, Espen Barth Eide of Norway, meets with leaders of the Greek Cypriot and Turkish Cypriot communities. They had reaffirmed their commitment to lead negotiations in an interdependent, results-oriented manner, – through a win-win approach – with the aim to reach a settlement as soon as possible and hold separate simultaneous referenda thereafter, in order to put an end to the unacceptable status quo.
>
> The United Nations works through the Good Offices of the Secretary-General to assist in the search for a comprehensive and mutually acceptable settlement to the Cyprus problem.
>
> The UN maintains a peacekeeping force in Cyprus, known as UNFICYP, which was deployed in 1964, when inter-communal fighting erupted on the Island.[1]

1 Fifty Years of United Nations Involvement

1.1 *An Ongoing Effort to Bring Peace*

In July 2014 the United Nations Peacekeeping Mission in Cyprus, UNFICYP, "celebrated" 50 years of presence on Cyprus.

* Emeritus Professor of the Law of International Organisations, Free University of Brussels (VUB).

1 The official United Nations website for UNIFICYP, <www.un.org/en/peacekeeping/missions/unficyp> contains background information, facts and figures and the Mission mandate.

Karel Wellens (ed.), International Law in Silver Perspective: Challenges Ahead.
 ISBN 978-90-04-27167-8. pp. 109-136.

That anniversary gives rise to questions as to the meaning and the functioning of this kind of missions. Are they to stay on as a semi-permanent feature in some situations? Without a final solution even remotely in sight?

As we will see, for a peacekeeping mission to play a useful role and to lead to success in solving a conflict, there are several prerequisites to be fulfilled. But in the first place there has to be an accompanying and parallel effort to find a political solution to the conflict.

As to the situation in Cyprus, we will discuss how for many years the Blue Helmets in Cyprus have been mainly in charge of supervising a *de facto* ceasefire, maintaining a buffer zone between the lines of the Cyprus National Guard and of the Turkish and Turkish Cypriots forces. in short: in containment.

On the other hand, from the beginning the Secretary-General in his Good Offices mission has appointed Special Representatives and Advisers to help him find a political solution, and has used his personal influence to persuade the parties to come to an comprehensive settlement.

Over the years, these efforts have been sometimes more and sometimes less intense. However, in the final analysis it is now clearly up to the parties involved to find their own way to end their difficulties and come to a "Cypriot-owned and Cypriot-led" comprehensive settlement.

2 What Happened Before

2.1 *A Troubled History*

From immemorial times, Cyprus has found itself at he crossroads of civilizations.

From years before Christ, when it it had been hellenized by Myceneans, to 58 BC when it became a Roman province, to the twelfth century when it became an independent empire, but was conquered by Richard I of England on his way to capture Acre. Later, the Island was sold to the Templar Order and at one time belonged to the Republic of Venice, until it became part of the Ottoman Empire in 1571.

However, following the opening of the Suez Canal (1869), in 1878 the British, in agreement with Turkey, took over the administration of the

Island, with a view to be able to protect their new sea route to India. Cyprus became a British Crown Colony in 1925.[2]

Already from 1931, riots broke out, the Greek Cypriots demanding Enosis: union with Greece. Martial law was declared, the Legislative Council abolished. At that time, the British Administration coined the terms Greek Cypriots versus Turkish Cypriots, to stem the demand for Enosis.

At the end of World War II, where Cypriots fought on de side of the Allied Powers, the Turkish Cypriots wanted British rule to continue, but the demand of the Greek Cypriots for Enosis grew stronger, under the spiritual, but also political leadership of Archbishop Makarios,, head of the "autocephalous Cypriot Orthodox Church".

During the 1950s there was serious rioting, and frequent bombing attacks were made by the "National Organization of Cypriot Fighters", ENOKA, under the leadership of George Grivas.

After massacres in 1958 things got further out of hand, and the Governments of Greece, Turkey and the United Kingdom began talks on the situation. These led to an agreement between the Heads of Government of Greece and Turkey in Zürich on 11 February 1959, later incorporated in agreements between these Governments and the United Kingdom in London on 19 February, on the principles for the establishment of an independent Republic of Cyprus.[3]

2.2 *Independence*

The London *Memorandum Setting Out The Agreed Foundation For The Final Settlement of The Problem of Cyprus* became the basis for the Constitution of the Republic of Cyprus.

The Constitution set out the fundaments for the structure of the Republic, and provided that:

---

2 Treaty of Peace with Turkey Signed at Lausanne, July 24, 1923. From: The Treaties of Peace 1919-1923, Vol. II (New York: Carnegie Endowment for International Peace, 1924). More specifically Article 20: "Turkey hereby recognizes the annexation of Cyprus by the British Government on the 8th November 1914."

3 The "Zürich-London Agreements" consisted of three separate treaties: an *Agreement on the Basis Structure of the Republic of Cyprus*; a *Treaty of Guarantee* between the United Kingdom, Greece and Turkey; and a *Treaty of Alliance* between the Republic of Cyprus, Greece and Turkey.

> The State of Cyprus shall be a Republic with a presidential regime, the President being Greek and the Vice-President Turkish, elected by universal suffrage by the Greek and Turkish communities of the Island respectively.
>
> The official languages of the Republic of Cyprus shall be Greek and Turkish. Legislative and administrative instruments and documents shall be drawn up and promulgated in the two official languages.
>
> Executive authority shall be vested in the President and the Vice-President. For this purpose they shall have a Council of Ministers composed of seven Greek Ministers and three Turkish Ministers.
>
> Legislative authority shall be vested in a House of Representatives elected for a period of five years by universal suffrage of each community separately in the proportion of 70 percent for the Greek community and 30 percent for the Turkish community, this proportion being fixed independently of statistical data.
>
> The Civil Service shall be composed as to 70 percent of Greeks and as to 30 percent of Turks. It is understood that this quantitative division will be applied as far as practicable in all grades of the Civil Service. In regions or localities where one of the two communities is in a majority approaching 100 per cent. the organs of the local administration responsible to the central administration shall be composed solely of officials belonging to that community.
>
> In the event of agricultural reform, lands shall be redistributed only to persons who are members of the same community as the expropriated owners. Expropriations by the State or the Municipalities shall only be carried out on payment of a just and equitable indemnity fixed, in disputed cases, by the tribunals. An appeal to the tribunals shall have the effect of suspending action. Expropriated property shall only be used for the purpose for which the expropriation was made. Otherwise the property shall be restored to the owners.

Notably, Article 22 of the Agreement specifically prohibits separation: *"It shall be recognised that the total or partial union of Cyprus with any other State, or a separatist independence for Cyprus (i.e. the partition of Cyprus into two independent States), shall be excluded".*

In 1960, British occupation was brought to an end and the Republic of Cyprus was officially founded. Its first President was Archbishop Makarios. Under British rule expelled to the Seychelles Islands, he had succeeded in making a political come-back.

The "Republic of Cyprus" became a member of the United Nations on 20 September 1960.

2.3 *A Troubled Republic*

Almost from the beginning however, difficulties arose with regard to the application of the provisions of the Constitution. A succession of constitutional crises and accumulating tensions followed. Greek Cypriots found the Constitution "unworkable" and the President proposed a series of amendments.

Inter-communal relations broke down, and in December 1963 violent disturbances broke out. The Governments of Greece, Turkey and the United Kingdom offered their joint good offices and their readiness to assist, if invited to do so, in restoring peace and order by means of a joint peacemaking force under British command, composed of British forces already established in Cyprus under the London Treaties.[4]

The parties were to convene in London later to try to reach agreement. The conference met on 15 January, but failed to come to a solution.

2.4 *International Concern, and Action*

The moment had arrived for international concern and action. The Permanent Representative of Cyprus at the United Nations, as well as the Greek, Turkish and United Kingdom representatives demanded urgent action by the Security Council and requested that a peacemaking force was to be put in place on the island, under the control of the United Nations. Meanwhile the Secretary-General appealed to all concerned for restraint, while engaging in intensive consultations on the functioning and organization of such a force.

On 4 March, the Security Council unanimously adopted resolution 186 (1964), by which it noted that the situation in Cyprus posed a threat to international peace and security and recommended the creation of a United Nations peacekeeping force, to be put in place with the consent of the Republic of Cyprus. Ccmposition and size of the force were to be established by the Secretary-General, in consultation with the Governments of Cyprus, Greece, Turkey and the United Kingdom.

Under Article 4 of the Treaty of Alliance of 1960 the Greek government as well as the Turkish government also had been given the right

4 *Supra*, note 2, p. 151.

to maintain an army contingent on the Island, of respectively 950 and 650 officers and men. But when the Turkish government refused for its troops to be put under command of a United Nations Force Commander it was decided that neither these Turkish, nor the Greek troops would form part of the United Nations Force in Cyprus, UNFICYP.

On 13 March, when the last troops from troop-contributing countries had arrived, the Secretary-General could report that the Force was in being, and on March 27 it became operational.[5]

The mandate and functioning of UNFICYP were defined by Security Council resolution 186 in the following terms: "...in the interest of preserving international peace and security, to use its best efforts to prevent a recurrence of fighting [between the Greek Cypriot and Turkish Cypriot communities] and, as necessary, to contribute to the maintenance and restoration of law and order and a return to normal conditions."[6]

Later, as we will see below, the Council had to expand the mandate to be able to meet new challenges.

3 The Concept of Peacekeeping

3.1 *The Early Peacekeeping Operations*

UNFICYP was the sixth in a series of missions that had been established by the United Nations to contain ongoing conflicts. While the responsible UN body would be the Security Council, in charge of questions of peace and security according to the Charter, it proved at that time, in the early sixties, difficult for the Security Council to be able to act.

In major crises, such as the question of the Soviet missiles stationed in Cuba, or other cold war crises of the time such as the Vietnam war, or the Soviet invasion of Czechoslovakia, the great powers had been unwilling to permit the Council, or the Secretary-General, to mediate within their respective spheres of influence. In practice, UN active involvement remained limited to "second- or third-order" conflicts, as the Cyprus question proved to be.

Therefore, when Greece and Turkey threatened to go to war over control of Cyprus, the Council was able to play its role as foreseen in the Charter.

5 *Id.* p. 152.

6 Security Council Resolution 186 (1974) of 4 March; U N Doc. S/5575.

UNFICYP's mandate had no political component: it was designed to give the combatants breathing space to work out the problem. And as in other missions of the period, while a permanent solution could not be found it became "a semi-permanent feature of the landscape as the political situation remained in deadlock."[7]

3.2 *The Concept of Peacekeeping*

Peacekeeping could be characterized as "an invention" of the United Nations. From the first deployment of military observers in the UN Truce Supervision Organization (UNTSO) in 1948, the United Nations' "Blue Helmets" have played a major role in containing conflicts around the world. The peacekeeping concept was formally established in 1957, when then Secretary-General Dag Hammarskjöld submitted a summary report on the handling of the Suez Crisis. At that point it was the General Assembly (the Security Council being unable to act because two of its permanent members were involved) that requested the Secretary-General to submit, within 48 hours, a plan for the setting up, with the consent of the parties concerned, of an *emergency international force to secure and supervise the cessation of hostilities* and invited the Secretary-General "to take such administrative measures as may be necessary for the prompt execution of the actions envisaged in the present resolution."[8]

The United Nations Emergency Force (UNEF) which was set up at that moment has served as a model for peacekeeping operations for the following 60-some years.

The concept of peacekeeping is not foreseen in the Charter. It has been developed to help stabilize a situation where the parties in a conflict have agreed on a cease-fire, but before a final settlement has been reached. In other words: a technique to monitor and support the final stages and the solution of a conflict. For in order to be able to keep the peace, there must first be peace. In the terms of the Charter, peacekeeping could be characterized as a form of "good offices" provided by the international community while the parties to a conflict seek a solution in the framework of Chapter VI.[9]

---

7 James Traub, THE BEST INTENTIONS; KOFI ANNAN AND THE UN IN THE ERA OF AMERICAN POWER p. 17 (Bloomsbury, 2006).

8 G.A. Res. 1000 (ES-1) of 5 November 1956.

9 It consists of a United Nations military presence, bur outside of the terms of an enforcement action as provided in Chapter VII of the Charter; it has been called "action under Chapter Six an a half". *Supra*, note 2, p. 112.

The traditional elements of peacekeeping are: the deployment of UN troops, military contingents, provided to the United Nations by "troop-contributing" Member countries, but put under the command of the Secretary-General.

They are lightly armed and in principle do not use force except in the case of personal self-defence. Military observers are unarmed.

They are deployed by the responsible United Nations bodies (normally the Security Council, in some cases the General Assembly), with the consent of all the parties involved, and maintain a strict impartiality towards the parties in the exercise of their mandate.

While these traditions have evolved in meeting the challenges of a changing international environment, the political, military-strategic and legal prerequisites for the success of peacekeeping operations have basically remained the same.

4 Prerequisites for Success of Peacekeeping Missions

4.1 *Political Conditions*

The main political prerequisites for the success of a peacekeeping mission have traditionally been its impartiality and the non-use of force.

Impartiality means that the military and other personnel of the mission do not regard one of the parties as "the enemy" or "the guilty party". In situations where it has been established that one of the warring parties is the aggressor, and action has to be taken against that party, there can no longer be question of peacekeeping: that would amount to enforcement action under Chapter VII.

A second characteristic has traditionally been the non-use of force by peacekeeping missions. Mandates have in principle not included military force: it used to be said that "it is not a soldier's job, but only a soldier can do it".

This is closely connected with a third prerequisite, and that is the preparedness of the parties to start the process of peace: to stop the fighting, take an active part in negotiations, accept assistance in the form of proposals for a settlement. The presence of a peacekeeping force may be able to further the peace process but it can never replace it. The parties themselves have to make their peace.

Another basic prerequisite is the condition that the force is established by the international community, that is by the United Nations, or at least under the aegis of the UN. A broad international consensus is a necessity. Towards the end of the cold war, and later, peacekeeping missions have sometimes been set up by individual States or by a small coalition of States, acting on their own initiative. In those cases the borderline between peacekeeping and intervention for *raison d'état* becomes dangerously blurred. The initiative and overall responsibility should in principle remain with the United Nations. In principle, it is the Security Council which has the power to establish and deploy a peacekeeping force, to direct and to withdraw it. The executive direction and command rests with the Secretary-General, who of course acts within the limits of the mandate of the Council; he submits regular reports on the progress made. The command in the field is entrusted by the Secretary-General to the chief of mission: the Force Commander.

4.2 *Military-strategic Requirements*

In the interest of the participating forces, military and strategic criteria for the conduct of peacekeeping operations have been formulated and applied. It is considered essential that each operation is carefully prepared, on the basis of the specific local situation. The exact mandate of the mission and the precise area in which the force is operating should be clearly stated on the basis of the enabling resolutions. The question of the use of force, how, and when, and under what circumstances, should be defined in "Rules of Engagement". The chain of command should be well defined.

4.3 *Legal Aspects*

Peacekeeping missions are composed of troops made available by Member States. Agreements are concluded between the United Nations and the troop-contributing countries on the conditions to be applied. With the host country, a *Status of Forces Agreement* (SOFA) is usually concluded, defining the status of the participating military units, their responsibility and liability.

During the cold war, UN peacekeeping operations were largely military in character, and in most cases were deployed after a cease-fire had been reached but before a final settlement had been negotiated. They were a technique, a form of "good offices", to assist the parties in pursuing the resolution of their conflict. Mandates typically included the supervision of a cease-fire agreement, or maintaining a buffer between hostile parties, or defusing local conflicts. The early peacekeeping forces were almost exclusively composed of military units.

This kind of operations is now often referred to as "the first generation of peacekeeping".

Later missions, such as those in Namibia, El Salvador, Mozambique..., with a mandate to supervise negotiated settlements or ceasefires, involved not only a military presence, but also an active political involvement, and wide-ranging civilian tasks such as humanitarian assistance, rebuilding administrative and health- and educational facilities, training of a civilian police force, monitoring human rights, organization and supervision of elections and, most important: economic rehabilitation and reconstruction.[10]

Marrack Goulding, former Under Secretary-General for Peacekeeping, has described the period from 1956 to 1974, during which the United Nations established ten of its thirteen earliest missions, as "the golden age of UN peacekeeping."[11]

On the other hand, it has been pointed out that "much UN peacekeeping during the Cold War, rather than being deliberately planned and properly resourced operations were little more than hastily organized responses to various crises, that often seemed to lack clear objectives, leadership and guidance...."[12]

Over the years, after many lessons learned, the situation has markedly improved. While the earlier missions were operated through the Office of Political Affairs, in 1992 a special *Department of Peacekeeping Operations* (DPKO) was established, manned and active around the clock and supervising all UN operations.[13]

5 The Situation in Cyprus Deteriorating

5.1 *The Turkish Invasion*

In the absence of a political settlement to the Cyprus problem, the mandate of UNFICYP was periodically extended by the Security Council and the Force continued its presence on the Island to supervise ceasefire

---

10 *Id.*, pp. 117-119.

11 Marrack Goulding: The Evolution of UN Peacekeeping in *International Affairs*, Vol. 69, no 3, 1993, pp. 451-464, at p. 452.

12 John Terence O'Neill and Nicholas Rees, UNITED NATIONS PEACEKEEPING IN THE POST-COLD-WAR ERA 24 (2006).

13 www.un.org/about/dpko.

lines, maintain a buffer zone, undertake some humanitarian activities and support the Good Offices mission of the Secretary-General.

However when, in July 1974, the Cyprus National Guard, under the direction of Greek officers, staged a *coup d'état* against the Cyprus Government (at that time still headed by President Makarios), the situation got seriously out of hand.

At that point the Turkish government, invoking the Treaty of Guarantee of 1960, launched an extensive military operation on the north coast of Cyprus for "the protection of Turkish Cypriots in an enclave north of Nicosia". Eventually this resulted in an occupation of the entire enclave, in addition to areas to the north, east and west.

The Security Council immediately called for a ceasefire, for an immediate end to foreign intervention, for the withdrawal of all foreign military personnel, and for continued full cooperation with UNFICYP.[14]

But the situation continued to worsen. In the course of the fighting UNFICYP personnel were being attacked and a number of them were killed or wounded. Also, the Turkish invasion caused an unprecedented flow of refugees of Greek Cypriots living in the north and now forced to leave their homes and possessions and flee to the southern part of the Island. The United Nations High Commissioner for Refugees had to be called in for assistance....

As a consequence of these events, UNFICYP was faced with a situation that had not been foreseen in its mandate. That mandate had been conceived with regard to the inter-communal conflict in Cyprus, not to large-scale hostilities involving action by the armed forces of other states.

The Force was placed on full alert; reinforcements were brought in by the troop-contributing countries; additional observation posts were established. Also, an increasing number of humanitarian tasks were undertaken by a special humanitarian and economics branch.[15]

During this period the Security Council adopted a number of resolutions expanding the mandate and functioning of UNFICYP to include supervising the *de facto* ceasefire which came into effect on August 16 1974, and maintaining a buffer zone between the lines of the Cyprus National Guard on the one side and of the Turkish and Turkish Cypriot

---

14 SC Res. 365 (1974).

15 For a detailed report of the changing mandate of UNFICYP, see: THE BLUE HELMETS; A REVIEW OF UNITED PEACEKEEPING pp. 161-164 (United Nations 2008).

forces on the other. Humanitarian assistance to the population was now to be one of its tasks.

In the absence of a formal ceasefire agreement the *status quo*, as recorded by UNFICYP at the time, became the standard. It was clarified further and adjusted in numerous local agreements between units of the Force and of the sides concerned. An essential feature of these agreements was that neither side may exercise authority or jurisdiction or make any military moves beyond its own forward military lines.

In principle, this expanded mandate still stands.

5.2 *The "Turkish Republic of Northern Cyprus"*

On 15 November 1983 the Turkish Cypriots proclaimed the "Turkish Republic of Northern Cyprus" in the part of Cyprus that had been under Turkish Cypriot control.

This act provoked heavy international criticism, and was condemned as illegal, null and void, and without legal consequences, by the international community. The "TRNC" has never been recognized by any other state than by the Republic of Turkey. It was never admitted to any international or regional organization.

The Security Council spoke in the strongest terms:

> Having heard the statement of the Foreign Minister of the Government Concerned at the declaration by the Turkish Cypriot authorities issued on 15 November 1983 which purports to create an independent state in northern Cyprus,
> Considering that this declaration is incompatible with the 1960 Treaty concerning the establishment of the Republic of Cyprus and the 1960 Treaty of Guarantee,
> Considering therefore that the attempt to create a "Turkish Republic of Northern Cyprus" is invalid, and will contribute to a worsening of the situation in Cyprus, ...
>
> 1. Deplores the declaration of the Turkish Cypriot authorities of the purported secession of part of the Republic of Cyprus;
> 2. Considers the declaration referred to above as legally invalid and calls for its withdrawal;
>
> ...
>
> 6. Calls upon all states to respect the sovereignty, independence, territorial integrity and non-alignment of the Republic of Cyprus;

> 7. Calls upon all states not to recognise any Cypriot state other than the Republic of Cyprus...[16]

As a consequence, the international community has consistently considered Turkish acts and acts of the "TRNC", an illegally occupied territory, as violating international law.

5.3 *Ongoing Efforts to Find Political Solutions*

Although tension has risen periodically, the situation in Cyprus remained relatively calm in the following years. But the Security Council has stated on numerous occasions that the *status quo* is not acceptable, and has requested the Secretary-General to continue his good offices.

Successive Secretaries-General and their Special Representatives have worked towards a political solution. From the establishment of UNFICYP, these "Special Representatives of the Secretary-General" (one of them, from 1975-1977: Xavier Perez de Cuellar) were resident in Cyprus. In 1993, the Secretary-General decided to appoint a senior political

---

16 SC Res. 541 (1983) Adopted by the Security Council on 18 November 1983

"The Security Council,

Having heard the statement of the Foreign Minister of the Government Concerned at the declaration by the Turkish Cypriot authorities issued on 15 November 1983 which purports to create an independent state in northern Cyprus,

Considering that this declaration is incompatible with the 1960 Treaty concerning the establishment of the Republic of Cyprus and the 1960 Treaty of Guarantee,

Considering therefore that the attempt to create a "Turkish Republic of Northern Cyprus" is invalid, and will contribute to a worsening of the situation in Cyprus,

Reaffirming its resolutions 365(1974) and 367(1975),

Taking note of the Secretary-Generals statement of 17 November 1983,

1. Deplores the declaration of the Turkish Cypriot authorities of the purported secession of part of the Republic of Cyprus;

2. Considers the declaration refereed to above as legally invalid and calls for its withdrawal;

...

6. Calls upon all states to respect the sovereignty, independence, territorial integrity and non-alignment of the Republic of Cyprus;

7. Calls upon all states not to recognise any Cypriot state other than the Republic of Cyprus;..."

figure to serve as his Special Representative for Cyprus, but on a non-resident basis, a Deputy Representative being in residence.[17]

Since the 1990s there had been a stepping up of the Secretary-General's good offices , focused on reaching an overall security agreement by way of a "Set of Ideas" and "Confidence Building Measures". However, a breakthrough was not to be expected.

It would take a new challenge, a new sense of urgency, to really begin working towards a final and comprehensive settlement.

Maybe it would take a new "player in the field"?

6 Enter: The European Union

6.1 *Application for Membership by Cyprus*

On 3 July 1990 the Government of Cyprus had submitted to the Council of the European Communities an application for membership of the Communities (the Coal and Steel Community, the European Economic Community and the European Atomic Energy Community). On 17 September, the Council decided to set in motion the procedures as laid down in the Treaties.

Following discussions in Lisbon in June 1992, Edinburgh in December 1992 and in Copenhagen in June 1993 the Council welcomed the intention of the European Commission to present its opinion on the application of Cyprus.

The political situation on the Island had to be taken in consideration:

> Cyprus's geographical position, the deep-lying bonds which, for two thousand years, have located the island at the very fount of European culture and civilization, the intensity of the European influence apparent in the values shared by the people of Cyprus and in the conduct of the cultural, political, economic and social life of its citizens, the wealth of its contacts of every kind with the Community, all these confer on Cyprus, beyond all doubt, its European identity and character and confirm its vocation to belong to the Community.
>
> A political settlement of the Cyprus question would serve only to reinforce this vocation and strengthen the ties which link Cyprus to Europe. At the same time, a settlement would open the way to

17 THE BLUE HELMETS p. 153.

the full restoration of human rights and fundamental freedoms throughout the island and encourage the development of pluralist democracy.
... The Commission is convinced that the result of Cyprus's accession to the Community would be increased security and prosperity and that it would help bring the two communities on the island closer together.
... The government of the Republic of Cyprus shares this conviction. And, even though they object to the conditions under which the application for membership was made, the leaders of the Turkish Cypriot community are also fully conscious of the economic and social benefits that integration with Europe would bring their community.
... This opinion has also shown that Cyprus's integration with the Community implies a peaceful, balanced and lasting settlement of the Cyprus question.
... In view of all the above and in the expectation of significant progress in the talks currently being pursued under the auspices of the Secretary-General of the United Nations, the Commission feels that a positive signal should be sent to the authorities and the people of Cyprus confirming that the Community considers Cyprus as eligible for membership and that as soon as the prospect of a settlement is surer, the Community is ready to start the process with Cyprus that should eventually lead to its accession.
The United Nations Secretary-General is aware that he can count on the Community's support in his continued endeavours to produce a political settlement of the Cyprus question.
Lastly, the Commission must envisage the possibility of the failure of the intercommunal talks to produce a political settlement of the Cyprus question in the foreseeable future, in spite of the endeavours of the United Nations Secretary-General. Should this eventuality arise, the Commission feels that the situation should be reassessed in view of the positions adopted by each party in the talks and that the question of Cyprus's accession to the Community should be reconsidered later.[18]

18 Commission Opinion on the Application of Cyprus for Membership-Extracts; doc/93/5 – June 30, 1993; at http://ec.europa.eu/enlargement/archives/enlargemant_process/past_enlargement/eu10:op_06_93_en.htm.

6.2 *The Impact of Membership*

The application for EC membership was generally thought to going to have an important impact on the "Cyprus issue". For Greek-Cypriots, accession was seen as a "shield" against potential Turkish military action and as a diplomatic advantage, especially given Turkey's interest to join the EU in its turn. At the same time, there was a hope that the benefits of accession would increase the Turkish-Cypriot motivation for resolution.

And they certainly did. Turkish and Turkish Cypriot willingness to enter into negotiations was hugely triggered by the European element. On the one hand, Ankara pushed for a resolution of the dispute, which was an obstacle to Turkey's road towards the EC (Turkey having been a candidate since 1999). On the other hand, the benefits of European integration appealed to the Turkish-Cypriots, who regarded reunification as the only way for them to join the EU, as partners in a federal state with the Greek-Cypriots.

Despite the absence of prospects for a settlement, the European Council of Copenhagen approved a (now) European Union membership for "Cyprus" to enter into force on 1 May, 2004.

6.3 *A New Urgency*

On the UN side (and under political pressure of the United States) it was felt that everything should be done to reach a settlement before that date.

While Turkey and the "TRNC" had always argued that the Greek Cypriot side had no authority to negotiate on behalf of the whole Island, they felt that a solution before 1 May 2004 would be in their interest because it would constitute the only means by which Cyprus, including the territory of the "TRNC", could enter the European Union.

Accordingly, the Secretary General sent letters to the concerned sides and suggested that the negotiations be resumed on 10 February 2004 in New York, on 10-13 February. The talks in New York were successful and paved the way for the resumption of the negotiations in the Island, the main objective being "to bring into being a new state of affairs in Cyprus."

The negotiations were conducted in two parallel tracks – at the political and the technical level. The first phase of the talks was held in the Island between 19 February and 22 March.

At the political level the two sides were not able to reach an agreement although some progress was achieved at technical level. The second phase of the talks began on 24 March 2004 in Bürgenstock, Switzerland with the participation of the two Cypriot parties and the Guarantor powers Greece and Turkey. On 31 March, the UN Secretary-General submitted the final text of the plan to the parties.

As to the European Union: representatives of the EU Commission were also present at the final stage of the negotiations in Switzerland and the EU commitments with regard to the comprehensive settlement were agreed upon between the parties and the EU Commission.

The agreement reached in Switzerland was to be put to separate and simultaneous referenda on 24 April in both parts of the Island.

7 The Annan Plan

7.1 *A New State of Affairs for Cyprus*

The agreement that was put before the population of Cyprus on 26 of April 2004 was about a *New State of Affairs in Cyprus:*

- The Treaty of Establishment, the Treaty of Guarantee, and the Treaty of Alliance were to remain in force and apply *mutatis mutandis* to the new State of Affairs.
- Cyprus would become a full member of the European Union as of 1 May 2004.
- It was to maintain special ties of friendship with Greece and Turkey, respecting the balance in Cyprus established by the Treaty of Guarantee and the Treaty of Alliance and this Agreement, and as a European Union member state would support the accession of Turkey to the Union.
- The United Cyprus Republic would be an independent state in the form of an indissoluble partnership, with a federal government and two equal constituent states, the Greek Cypriot State and the Turkish Cypriot State, being of equal status.
- The Treaty of Guarantee, in applying *mutatis mutandis* to the new state of affairs established in this Agreement and the Constitution, would cover, in addition to the independence, territorial integrity, security and constitutional order of the United Cyprus Republic, the territorial integrity, security and constitutional order of the constituent states.
- *Greek and Turkish contingents* were to be permitted to be stationed under the Treaty of Alliance in the Greek Cypriot State and the Turkish Cypriot State respectively;

> – There was to remain a *United Nations peacekeeping operation* to monitor the implementation of the Agreement and use its best efforts to promote compliance with it and contribute to the maintenance of a secure environment, to remain as long as the federal government, with the concurrence of both constituent states, did not decide otherwise.
>
> The federal government and the constituent states shall cooperate with the United Nations operation...

7.2 *Defeated!*

On 24 April 2004, the Plan was put before the Cypriot Communities in two separate and simultaneous referenda. The Turkish Cypriots approved it with a 64.91 percent majority, the Greek Cypriots rejected it with an overwhelming 75.83 percent majority.

A bitterly disappointed Annan concluded his *Report on his Mission of good offices in Cyprus* with comments on the negotiation process, on the Agreement on a Comprehensive Settlement and on the two referenda as follows:

> **The way ahead**
>
> As for the future of my mission of good offices, the outcome of the referenda has resulted in a stalemate. Mr. Papadopoulos has stated that he is not prepared to submit the plan to referendum once again unless unspecified changes are made. Others on the Greek Cypriot side speak of a second referendum, and look for unspecified additional guarantees on security and implementation. For their part, having approved the plan at referendum, the Turkish Cypriot side is opposed to reopening it for negotiation. Neither of the Cyprus parties has made a proposal to the United Nations or to the other (to my knowledge) to resolve this impasse. I do not see any basis for resuming my good offices as long as this stand-off remains.
>
> Meanwhile, in the aftermath of the watershed vote of 24 April, I believe that a fundamental reassessment of the full range of United Nations peace activities in Cyprus is timely. That reassessment should include the four-decade-old search for peace in Cyprus, and consider how best to address the problem in the future. It should also bear in mind that the implicit central purpose of all peacekeeping operations is to provide an environment conducive to the resolution of conflict. As outlined in my latest report on UNFICYP (S/2004/427), I accordingly intend to conduct a review, to be com-

pleted within three months, of UNFICYPs mandate, force levels and concept of operations, in the light of the developments on the ground, the positions of the parties, and any views the Security Council might have.

I have already indicated my hope that Greek Cypriots will reflect on the outcome of this process in the coming months. In the meantime, I believe that the members of the Council should encourage the Turkish Cypriots, and Turkey, to remain committed to the goal of reunification. In this context and for that purpose and not for the purpose of affording recognition or assisting secession, I would hope they can give a strong lead to all States to cooperate both bilaterally and in international bodies to eliminate unnecessary restrictions and barriers that have the effect of isolating the Turkish Cypriots and impeding their development, deeming such a move as consistent with Security Council resolutions 541 (1983) and 550 (1984).

Conclusion

I wish to thank the Security Council for its strong support of my efforts; the many Member States who provided diplomatic assistance, material resources, technical expertise or conference support; the European Union, including the European Commission, for the truly exemplary assistance and support it provided, in what was a model of European Union/United Nations cooperation; and the many international organizations, including those of the United Nations system, which rolled up their sleeves and joined in this team effort.

I could not close without expressing my warmest thanks to my Special Adviser, Mr. Alvaro de Soto, and his team, for the outstanding dedication which they brought to a difficult task. Their careful and creative peacemaking effort offered the Cypriots the best chance they have ever had to reunify their country.

I know that the failure of this effort, twice now in little over a year, is a source of sadness and confusion for Cypriots, Greek Cypriots and Turkish Cypriots alike, not to mention many in Greece and Turkey, in the European Union, and throughout the international community. Many Cypriots from all walks of life worked with courage and determination to achieve a settlement. I am confident they will continue these efforts. Indeed, they must. The

> prospects for the reunification of their country now rest primarily in their hands.[19]

On May 1st 2004 Cyprus joined the European Union as a divided member nation.

7.3 *Flaws and Criticisms of the Annan Plan*

The 24 April vote was followed by apparent disappointment within the United Nations but also by a surprising level of critical comment from international law experts, politicians and the media.

On the "legalization" of what was considered by all to be an illegal situation it was said:

> One year after the vote, upon a calmer rereading of the Annan plan, the non-committed observer may wonder whether anyone could have reasonably expected the Cypriot population in non-occupied Cyprus to vote in favour of a plan that entailed abandoning positions held by the Security Council and the General Assembly since July 1974, and which seriously undermined fundamental principles of international law contained in numerous universal and regional documents, including the United Nations Charter, General Assembly resolutions, Security Council resolutions, Human Rights instruments...
>
> ... Although the Annan Plan did not go as far as specifically to legalize the Turkish aggression on Cyprus of July 1974, it did throw a mantel of legitimacy over it by virtue of its acceptance of many of the *faits accomplis* that followed the Turkish invasion and occupation of Northern Cyprus, expulsion of part of the Cypriot population, confiscation of their private property, settlement of the occupied Cypriot territory by over 100,000 Turkish colonizers from Anatolia, etc.[20]

---

19 Report of the Secretary General on his Good Offices Mission in Cyprus of 28 May 2004 UN Doc. S/2004/437, § 91-96.

20 Alfred de Zayas, The Annnan Plan and the Implantation of Turkish Settlers in the Occupied Territory of Cyprus in *The Cyprus Yearbook of International Relations*, 2006, 163-178, at p. 8. See also Alfred de Zayas, Self Determination, Turkish Settlers and Cyprus Referenda, in: Andreas Auer and Vasiliki Triga A CONSTITUTIONAL CONVENTION FOR CYPRUS, Berlin, Wissenschaftlicher Verlag, 2009, p. 63-70.

And: "Does the international community really wish to establish a precedent under which a minority may eventually acquire equal status, equal rights and even its own "constituent State" as a consequence of an invasion carried out in breach of international law? If so, why?" And on the complex character of the questions put before the voters: that it had been unwise "to submit to a popular referendum a most complex constitutional, legal, social and economic document, stretching over more than 400 (published) pages and 9000 (unpublished) pages of annexes, including legislation.."[21]

On a possible bias toward the Turkish side of outside negotiators:

> The fact that Turkey's Guarantor Status and its "unilateral right to intervene" was to remain untouched; while the military presence of some 35,000 Turkish military personnel was to be only gradually (over 14 years) to be brought back to the number of 650 as foreseen in 1960 under the Treaty of Guarantee...: demonstrates the inevitable bias towards Turkish needs, dictated at least partially by the needs of "Realpolitik.."[22]

8 The European Court of Human Rights

8.1 *The European Court of Human Rights' Findings on the Issue*

The argument that the Annan Plan violated the international consensus that the creation of the "TRNC" constituted a violation of international law rests for many observers also on a judgment of the European Court of Human Rights of 2001, with regard to an Inter-State application, lodged in 1994 by Cyprus against Turkey, concerning the situation in northern Cyprus since the division of the territory.[23]

---

21 Hubert Faustmann, The Cyprus Question still unsolved: Security concerns and the failure of the Annan Plan; *Südost Europa Mitteilungen*, 06/2004, 44-68, at p. 63.

22 Van Coufoudakis and Klearchos Kyriakides, THE CASE AGAINST THE ANNAN PLAN p. 40 (Lobby for Cyprus, 2004).

23 ECHR Grand Chamber Judgment Cyprus v Turkey; Application no. 25781:942001 on http//hudoc.echr.coe.int/sites/eng/pages/ search=001-59454 paras 14 and 15.

8.2 *On the Question of the Legality of the "TNRC"*

In its judgment the Court found, with regard to the legal status of the "TRNC", that

> A major development in the continuing division of Cyprus occurred in November 1983 with the proclamation of the "Turkish Republic of Northern Cyprus" (the "TRNC") and the subsequent enactment of the "TRNC Constitution" on 7 May 1985.

This development was condemned by the international community. On 18 November 1983 the United Nations Security Council adopted Resolution 541 (1983) declaring the proclamation of the establishment of the "TRNC" legally invalid and calling upon all States not to recognise any Cypriot State other than the Republic of Cyprus. A similar call was made by the Security Council on 11 May 1984 in its Resolution 550 (1984). In November 1983 the Committee of Ministers of the Council of Europe decided that it continued to regard the government of the Republic of Cyprus as the sole legitimate government of Cyprus and called for respect of the sovereignty, independence, territorial integrity and unity of the Republic of Cyprus.

According to the respondent Government, the "TRNC" is a democratic and constitutional State which is politically independent of all other sovereign States including Turkey, and the administration in northern Cyprus has been set up by the Turkish-Cypriot people in the exercise of its right to self-determination and not by Turkey. Notwithstanding this view, it is only the Cypriot government which is recognised internationally as the government of the Republic of Cyprus in the context of diplomatic and treaty relations and the working of international organisations."

8.3 *On the Question of* Locus Standi *for the Republic of Cyprus*

The respondent State, Turkey, had also argued that the applicant, not being the legal representative of the republic of Cyprus, did not have *locus standi* before the Court.

However, in its judgment, the Court found:

> As to the applicant Government's *locus standi*;
> In the proceedings before the Commission, the respondent Government claimed that the applicant Government were not the lawful government of the Republic of Cyprus. Referring to it as the

"Greek-Cypriot administration", they maintained that the applicant Government lacked standing to bring the instant application. The applicant Government refuted this assertion with reference, inter alia, to the Court's conclusions in its Loizidou v. Turkey judgment of 23 March 1995 (preliminary objections) (Series A no. 310) and to the reaction of the international community to the proclamation of the establishment of the "TRNC" in 1983, in particular the two resolutions adopted by the United Nations Security Council and the resolution of the Council of Europe's Committee of Ministers condemning this move in the strongest possible terms.

The Court, like the Commission, finds that the respondent Government's claim cannot be sustained. It notes that it is evident from international practice and the condemnatory tone of the resolutions adopted by the United Nations Security Council and the Council of Europe's Committee of Ministers that the international community does not recognise the "TRNC" as a State under international law. The Court reiterates the conclusion reached in its Loizidou judgment (merits) that the Republic of Cyprus has remained the sole legitimate government of Cyprus and on that account their *locus standi* as the government of a High Contracting Party cannot therefore be in doubt. The Court concludes that the applicant Government have *locus standi* to bring an application under former Article 24 (current Article 33).[24]

---

24 Id. at paras 66 and 67. In this respect it is interesting to also take note of the Court's Grand Chamber judgment of 12 May 2014 on the question of just satisfaction with regard to the same case. In that judgment, the Court held that the passage of time since the delivery of the principal judgment on 10 May 2001 did not preclude it from examining the Cypriot Government's just satisfaction claims. It concluded that Turkey was to pay Cyprus 30,000,000 euros (EUR) in respect of the non-pecuniary damage suffered by the relatives of the missing persons, and EUR 60,000,000 in respect of the non-pecuniary damage suffered by the enclaved Greek-Cypriot residents of the Karpas peninsula. These amounts, said the Court, are to be distributed by the Cypriot Government to the individual victims under the supervision of the Committee of Ministers of the Council of Europe.

9 A New Momentum

9.1 *Negotiations Resumed in 2008*

Following the election of Demetris Christofias as president in February 2008, the parties started preparations for a new round of negotiations to solve their problems. Christofias and his Turkish Cypriot counterpart, Mehmet Ali Talat, met for a first time met on 21 March 2008 under UN auspices and set the stage for further talks.

Progress was slow but steady on a number of problems. However, the core issues: questions of governance, power-sharing, property, citizenship… remained unsolved.

In 2012, the Secretary-General warned: "The time for an agreement is now. The domestic, regional and international context is constantly shifting. The current window of opportunity is not limitless and there is little to suggest that the future will bring more propitious circumstances for a settlement."[25]

9.2 *A Joint Declaration*

The comprehensive settlement negotiations resumed on 11 February 2014. At that point the Secretary-General could report that, after five months of intense discussions, the Greek Cypriot leader, Nicos Anastasiades, and the Turkish Cypriot leader, Derviş Eroğlu, had concluded a *Joint Declaration* marking the official relaunch of high-level negotiations on a comprehensive settlement to the Cyprus problem. The two leaders had agreed to the following:

1. The *status quo* is unacceptable and its prolongation will have negative consequences for the Greek Cypriots and Turkish Cypriots. The leaders affirmed that a settlement would have a positive impact on the entire region, while first and foremost benefiting Turkish Cypriots and Greek Cypriots, respecting democratic principles, human rights and fundamental freedoms, as well as each other's distinct identity and integrity and ensuring their common future in a united Cyprus within the European Union.
2. The leaders expressed their determination to resume structured negotiations in a results-oriented manner. All unre-

---

25 Assessment Report of the Secretary-General on the Status of the Negotiations in Cyprus, 12 March 2012; UN Doc. S/2012/149 at § 23.

solved core issues will be on the table, and will be discussed interdependently. The leaders will aim to reach a settlement as soon as possible, and hold separate simultaneous referenda thereafter.

3. The settlement will be based on a bi-communal, bi-zonal federation with political equality, as set out in the relevant Security Council Resolutions and the High Level Agreements. The united Cyprus, as a member of the United Nations and of the European Union, shall have a single international legal personality and a single sovereignty, which is defined as the sovereignty which is enjoyed by all member States of the United Nations under the UN Charter and which emanates equally from Greek Cypriots and Turkish Cypriots. There will be a single united Cyprus citizenship, regulated by federal law. All citizens of the united Cyprus shall also be citizens of either the Greek-Cypriot constituent state or the Turkish-Cypriot constituent state. This status shall be internal and shall complement, and not substitute in any way, the united Cyprus citizenship...
4. The united Cyprus federation shall result from the settlement following the settlement's approval by separate simultaneous referenda. The Federal constitution shall prescribe that the united Cyprus federation shall be composed of two constituent states of equal status. The bi-zonal, bi-communal nature of the federation and the principles upon which the EU is founded will be safeguarded and respected throughout the island...
5. The negotiations are based on the principle that nothing is agreed until everything is agreed.
6. The appointed representatives are fully empowered to discuss any issue at any time and should enjoy parallel access to all stakeholders and interested parties in the process, as needed. The leaders of the two communities will meet as often as needed. They retain the ultimate decision making power. Only an agreement freely reached by the leaders may be put to separate simultaneous referenda. Any kind of arbitration is excluded.
7. The sides will seek to create a positive atmosphere to ensure the talks succeed. They commit to avoiding blame games or other negative public comments on the negotiations. They also commit to efforts to implement confidence building

> measures that will provide a dynamic impetus to the prospect for a united Cyprus.

9.3 *The Annan Plan Revisited?*

Questions could be raised on why this Declaration would now constitute an opening for further negotiations. Are there elements in this text which make this initiative essentially different from the Annan Plan?

To a certain extent, yes.

While there will be a Cyprian citizenship for all Cypriots, the principle of two "constituent states" remains. The flaws in the Annan Plan and the criticism that this constituted a violation of international law, that it "legitimized the illegitimate", still stand. And many issues remain unsolved.

However, there are new elements.

This time the "Realpolitik"-element is not imposed from outside but the parties themselves are now convinced that the *status quo* is unacceptable.

The text of this Joint Declaration was not drafted by an outside UN Legal Adviser to be put before the parties to take or to reject it.

This time the negotiating process takes place between the parties themselves where, of course, elections have been held and new leaders are in power since 2004.

This time, the negotiations and an eventual settlement will be Cypriot-led and Cypriot-made.

This time there will be no reason for the leaders of the opposing parties to call upon their people to reject the proposals put before them, as had been the case in 2004.

In any case, the tone of this Joint Declaration is positive and the approach realistic.

9.4 *The United Nations Point of View*

The newly appointed Adviser to the Secretary-General on Cyprus, Espen Barth Eide, appears positive on the progress and positive climate in the negotiations. He noted that the international community is looking forward to a solution:

> It is interesting that the Cyprus issue, while is is very divisive on the Island, is quite uniting in New York in the sense that the Security Council has one opinion namely that there should be a process

towards a settlement; and that they consider settlement the reunification of the island.

That is quite important because we are living in times where there is big disagreement on issues like Ukraine, Syria. But on the Cyprus issue the P5 countries are perfectly aligned.[26]

9.5 *UNFICYP to Remain in Place*

In any case, the support of the Secretary-General, and the presence of the peacekeeping force will be necessary for some time to come. Most recently, the Security Council authorized the Force until 31 January 2015.

As UNFICYP marked the fiftieth year of its continued presence in Cyprus since its establishment on 4 March 1964, the situation along the ceasefire lines has remained calm and stable. Minor incidents and challenges remain a regular occurrence. In that context, the Force's regular patrolling and liaison with the opposing forces and the respective authorities continue to play a critical role in preventing the escalation of tensions.

Of course, UNFICYP continues to maintain close collaboration with the United Nations Secretary-General's Mission of good offices and other United Nations actors on the island.

At this moment (2014) the Force comprises 912 total uniformed personnel, including 854 troops and 58 police; supported by 38 international civilian personnel and 112 local civilian staff. They are from the following countries: Argentina, Austria, Brazil, Canada, Chile, Hungary, Paraguay, Serbia, Slovakia, Ukraine and the United Kingdom.

Its Headquarters are in Nikosia.

Force Commander is, since 14 August 2014, Major General Kristin Lund of Norway.

UNFICYP's budget amounts to some $ 60 million.[27]

---

26 From the website of the Mission of Good Offices of the Secretary-General in Cyprus <www.uncyprustalks.org/nqcontent.cfm?a_id=2466>.

27 UNFICYP's website (supra, note 1) provides information on the Mandate, the structure and the working of the Force. It has links to relevant UN documents, such as the various Security Council Resolutions, the Reports of the Secretary General, the Reports of the Secretary-General on his mission of Good Offices in Cyprus, etc.

10 Conclusions

Having followed the various stages, the up and downs, in UNFICYP's history, and its actions in support of the United Nations efforts to facilitate a definite and comprehensive settlement in the Cyprus question, the outcome of that process remains uncertain and may be far away.

Meanwhile, the presence of the Force remains a necessary element in keeping the situation under control; indeed, it seems to have become "semi-permanent feature", however necessary, of the Cyprus problem.

The balance of operations such as the one on Cyprus, the "first generation peacekeeping operations" appears, at first sight, to be a positive one. One achievement is that at least further escalation of the situation was stopped and a direct involvement of the Big Powers could be avoided. On the other hand, many of the situations where these operations were deployed still remain a source of unrest and the United Nations does not really succeed in contributing towards a final solution of the conflict at hand.

While the goal was to further a stabilization of the situation and to create a climate for negotiations and a final settlement, in practice the presence of UN-peacekeeping operations has not really contributed to a solution. On the contrary, they seem to help prolong the situation and to confirm the *status quo*. The fact that some of these operations, such as in South Lebanon, the Golan Heights and Cyprus, after 60 or 50 years are still operative, provides food for thought.[28]

Nevertheless, a future final settlement of the Cyprus question is now in the hand of the Cypriots themselves. They might keep in mind what Dag Hammarskjöld had to say:

> The pursuit of peace and progress cannot end in a few years in either victory or defeat. The pursuit of peace and progress, with its trials and its errors, its successes and its setbacks, can never be relaxed and never abandoned.[29]

---

28 Francis Baert, Ann Pauwels and Stefaan Smis (red.), LANGS DE VUURLIJN; DE VN EN GEWAPENDE CONFLICTEN p. 21 (Acco 2010).

29 *United Nations Bulletin* Vol. XVI, No. 4 (15 February 1954).

CHAPTER 6

The International Court of Justice, Back to the Future: Keeping the Dream Alive

*Karel Wellens**

1 Introduction

In 2016 the Court will celebrate its 70th anniversary, which undoubtedly will give rise to an abundance of in-depth and detailed analyses of the Court's performance. 'The (seventy) years of the Court's life could certainly be divided into several periods; each period could be given a specific label depending on the issues dealt with and the personalities which dominated the scene'.[1] That is not the purpose of this contribution, rather to modestly formulate a few remarks on some of the old and new challenges the ICJ (still) has to face in the years to come. These reflections find their origin in the profound changes having taken place in triple closely interconnected areas: the legal landscape, the judicial landscape and the judicial function in general. The Court's judicial functions have to be approached from both an internal (the Court's own perception) and an external perspective (the impact of the general changes on the Court's judicial function).

The general changes are bound to have a substantial impact on the Court's own perception of its functions and on its way of reasoning, on relaxing the policy of judicial economy, the interpretation and use of its inherent powers, its approach towards third party participation, the regime and scope of its provisional measures, the non-involvement in even merely monitoring the compliance with and the implementation of its judgments.

It has been a matter of the Court's judicial policy not to align itself with the 'early 20th century conceptions of the aims of international

* Emeritus Professor of International Law, Nijmegen University.

1 Manfred Lachs, *Thoughts on the Recent Jurisprudence of the International Court of Justice*, 4 Emory International Law Review, 77 (1990) (adaptation of a speech delivered on the occasion of the Court's 40th anniversary in 1986).

Karel Wellens (ed.), International Law in Silver Perspective: Challenges Ahead.
 ISBN 978-90-04-27167-8. pp. 137-206.

adjudication'.[2] Time has come not so much to restyle the Respected Old Lady to use Cassese's expression[3] but to move it away from a judicial policy which on too many occasions was characterized by caution, restraint and hesitation towards a more pro-active judicial policy in both procedural questions and matters of substance. This will enable the Court to perform the various judicial functions each international court or tribunal is nowadays expected to perform.

One should recall that the 'answer to a question of procedure may be of no less importance than the reply to a question of substance'.[4] Indeed, an 'answer – if acted upon – to a question of procedure may in substantial respects affect the outcome of the dispute'.[5]

2 The International Legal Landscape Has Changed

Since the end of the Cold War international law underwent profound and irreversible changes. Although the various categories of actors on the international plane may have different opinions on the extent and impact of these changes no one can seriously doubt that they actually have occurred although in various forms, depending on the areas concerned and on the involvement and responses by those actors.

The *institutionalisation of international law,* although of course manifesting itself long before the 1990's, has in the last two and a half decades become more pronounced. International organisations have become major players, both in the decisional and operational field; not surprisingly a satisfactory regime of their accountability still has to be worked out. At the same time the interplay between substantive and institutional law has rightly so attracted incisive doctrinal attention.[6]

---

2 Ian Scobbie, *'All Right, Mr. DeMille, I'm ready for my close-up'; Some Critical Reflections on Professor Cassese's 'The International Court of Justice: It is High Time to Restyle the Respected Old Lady',* 23 E.J.I.L. 1071 (2012).

3 For a list of a 'highly varied range of proposals for reform' which have been put forward see *inter alia* ROBERT KOLB, THE INTERNATIONAL COURT OF JUSTICE, 1205-1207 (2013): we will only occasionally touch upon them.

4 SIR HERSCH LAUTERPACHT, THE DEVELOPMENT of INTERNATIONAL LAW by the INTERNATIONAL COURT 109 (1982).

5 *Id.* at 353.

6 See most recently M.RUPPERT & C.WALTER, INSTITUTIONALISATION OF INTERNATIONAL LAW (2014) and E.LAGRANGE & J.M.SOREL, (Eds.), DROIT DES ORGANISATIONS INTERNATIONALES (2013).

The *judicialisation of international law* testifying of the international legal order's growing maturity has in the same period given rise not only to a proliferation of international courts and tribunals which no one could have foreseen but in the process has become deeply rooted in the legal system itself; perhaps it is even a mixed blessing.[7]

The *humanisation of international law* undoubtedly constitutes the most profound change. Its most early manifestation can be traced back to the coming into being of the law of armed conflict in the middle of the nineteenth century transforming itself into international humanitarian law after the Second World War The protection of fundamental human rights, until recently considered to be kept separate from international humanitarian law, can be traced back to the minorities protection regime established during the interbellum and came to full growth and expansion once the United Nations entered the scene. 'The feeling of *humanness* permeates the whole *corpus juris* of contemporary international law'. It is 'a historical process of a *true humanisation* of International Law'.[8] The principle of humanity as a general principle of law 'confer(s) an ineluctable axiological dimension to the international legal order'.[9]

The *constitutionalisation of international law* is the least uncontroversial change one has to acknowledge. It directly flows from the two changes mentioned previously. The humanisation of international law inevitably brought about a foundational paradigm shift away from the State-centric approach which in turn was bound to lead to the recognition, interpretation and application of superior norms of a humanitarian character. This substantive reorientation was accompanied by the judicialisation of international law thereby providing the instrumental tools for putting into operation the now not merely embryonic features of an international constitutional legal order.

7 *The Judicialization of International Law – A Mixed Blessing?*, ESIL Annual Conference, Oslo, September 2015.

8 *Application of the Convention on the Prevention and Punishment of the Crime of Genocide (Croatia v. Serbia), I.C.J. Reports 2015*, Dissenting Opinion of Judge Cançado Trindade, para. 83.

9 *Id.* para. 546.

3 The Judicial Landscape Has Changed

The various changes in the international legal landscape have entailed the well-known proliferation of international courts, tribunals and quasi-judicial bodies across numerous branches of international law. The phenomenon has raised concerns about the fragmentation and unity of the international legal order but such concerns have in the meantime persuasively been put to rest as judicial dialogue and cross-fertilisation – admittedly to varying degrees between the various international judicial actors – have become more and more a matter of course.

When entering the judicial stage these new international judicial actors although not immediately warmly welcomed by those who for so long were used to play a dominant role had to find their way, with trial and error of course, but gradually made their mark not only within their specialized 'champ opératoire' but more importantly and in a rather decisive way on the judicial functions as they perceive and perform them and as they increasingly came to be approached by the major non-judicial actors on the international scene, the individual human person, States, international organisations, NGOs and in appropriate areas multinational corporations.

4 The Judicial Function Has Changed

The changes in the international legal and judicial landscape are so profound and irreversible that the perception, the expectations and the performance of the judicial function inevitably had to undergo similar changes as well, as 'one's vision of the international judicial function is a reflection of one's specific vision of the international legal order.'[10] The most notably fact in this regard is that the one-sided concept of the international judicial function – an instrument to settle in a binding and final way an inter-state dispute – had to be reviewed, reconsidered and in many ways to be overhauled.

10 GLEIDER HERNANDEZ, THE INTERNATIONAL COURT OF JUSTICE AND THE JUDICIAL FUNCTION 284 (2014).

It is common ground that courts 'and their role within international law have also been a persistent part of the theoretical debates about the nature of international law'.[11]

In 1958 Lauterpacht rightly described the 'problems of the judicial function in general and of international tribunals in particular' as 'persistent ones'.[12]

More than 20 years ago President Bedjaoui rightly observed that '(U)ne relance authentique de la justice internationale appelle' à part d' une *nouvelle définition des sujets* du droit international susceptibles d'ouvrir plus largement au contentieux les portes du prétoire international' également 'de nouveaux *efforts conceptuels*...'[13]

Within that context there 'is an active debate about the functions of international adjudication, and two main schools of thought can be distinguished'.[14] One view considers the future of the ICJ to be a 'private function: to settle the dispute brought before' it. Another view considers the future of the ICJ also to be a 'public function': to contribute to 'the positive creation of norms which can generate obedience among members' of the international community.[15]

In the past decade or so one has witnessed an unprecedented expansion of the literature dealing with the judicial function either with a focus on a particular actor or more recently on a more comprehensive attempt to identify and assess the various aspects of a *multiplicity of functions* of international courts and tribunals.

---

11 Mary Ellen O 'Connell & Leonore Vanderzee, *The History of International Adjudication* in THE OXFORD HANDBOOK OF INTERNATIONAL ADJUDICATION, 41 (Cesare Romano et al. eds., 2014).

12 LAUTERPACHT, *supra* note 4, at XIII. On the permanent tension between the sovereignty of States and procedures of international adjudication see for instance Hélène GELAS, PROCEDURE CONTENTIEUSE INTERNATONALE ET SOUVERAINETE ETATIQUE, (2004), mimeographed copy of doctoral thesis, Université Panthéon-Assas (Paris II).

13 Mohammed Bedjaoui, *L'Avenir de la Cour internationale de justice,* 53, Annales de Droit de Louvain 503, 512 (1993).

14 Chester Brown, *Inherent Powers in International Adjudication,* in THE OXFORD HANDBOOK OF INTERNATIONAL ADJUDICATION 842 (Cesare Romano et al. eds., 2014).

15 *Id.* at 842-843.

5 The Plurality of Judicial Functions

It is highly relevant to acknowledge and agree that the judicial function has become multifaceted and much less static than it traditionally used to be, although in several of his opinions Judge Trindade has skilfully and persuasively recalled how the multiplicity of the Court's functions was already present in the minds of the members of the International Committee of Jurists.

Broadly speaking and without any need to go into more detail neither to present a more complete picture in this regard the *plural judicial functions* have been described as comprising the following elements and aspects, although not every single one them neither all of them have to be found and performed by every international court and tribunal at all times.

Apart from the promotion and compliance with primary specialised or general rules within the context of the cases before them – their dispute settlement function as such – they also have to ensure compliance with the rule of law in the international society[16] they have a fact-finding function, a law-making function and a governance function.[17] They establish precedents and give rise to a general practice (the *erga omnes* effect of their decisions) and they contribute to the operation and legitimisation of related legal regimes and institutions.[18]

Others have described the main functions as enforcement, dispute settlement, constitutional and administrative review.[19]

These various functions may have been explicitly attributed to a judicial body, they may be implicit or assumed and it goes without saying that there are bound to emerge tensions between the various functions

16 Geir Ulfstein during the meeting of the ESIL Interest Group on International Courts and Tribunals at the 2014 Vienna ESIL Conference, September, (on file with the author).

17 José Alvarez, *What are International Judges for? The Main Functions of International Adjudication,* in THE OXFORD HANDBOOK OF INTERNATIONAL ADJUDICATION 166, 168, 170 (Cesare Romano et al. eds., 2014).

18 Geir Ulfstein during the meeting of the ESIL Interest Group on International Courts and Tribunals at the 2014 Vienna ESIL Conference, September (on file with the author).

19 KJ Alter, *The Multiple Roles of International Courts and Tribunals: Enforcement, Dispute Settlement, Constitutional and Administrative Review,* in INTERNATIONAL LAW AND INTERATIONAL RELATIONS: SYNTHETIZING INSIGHTS FROM INTERDISCIPLINARY SCHOLARSHIP (J.Dunoff & M.Pollacks eds., 2012).

and it is up to the international courts and tribunals to balance these various functions.

Moreover 'international courts and tribunals should be seen *beyond* those functions' as 'multinational actors exercising public authority'[20] thus raising the question of their accountability the most relevant forms of which are 'process accountability (for procedures)' and 'content accountability (for individual judgments)', both forms directly linked to 'the question of legitimate or illegitimate judicial activism.'[21]

6 The Court's Judicial Functions

6.1 *The Original Approach towards the Court's Judicial Functions*

'The task of clarifying and developing international law by the highest international tribunal was an object which was present in the minds of those who, at the close of the First World War, urged the establishment of a permanent court of international justice'.[22]

The Council of the League of Nations has made it clear that it was 'one *of the Court's important tasks* to contribute, through its jurisprudence, to the development of international law'.[23] This statement should be noted not only because of the intrinsic linkage between the dispute settlement function and the developmental one (a linkage to which we return shortly) but above all since the Council considered the *plurality* of the Court's functions. The 'general expectation that the Court would pay a pivotal role in the development of international law was apparent from its inception', a view that 'was also current in contemporary doctrine'.[24]

Recently the views of Hersch Lauterpacht, one of the leading authorities after the Permanent Court had come into existence, were referred to as 'situating the Court as an 'arbiter of the common interest' speaking to the community as a whole', charging the Court 'with upholding the very existence and the common values of the international communi-

20 Von Bogdandy and Venzke as cited by G. HERNANDEZ, *supra* note 10, at 94.

21 Paul Mahoney, *The International Judiciary – Independence and Accountability*, 7 L.P.I.C.T. 314, 339 and 340 (2008).

22 LAUTERPACHT, *supra* note 4, at 5. On the most relevant pars of the debate during that period see *inter alia* Ian Scobbie, *supra* note 2, at 1073-1077.

23 As cited by HERNZANDEZ, *supra* note 10, at 33 (emphasis added).

24 Ian Scobbie, *supra* note 2, at 1077.

ty, rather than acting as a mere mediator between disputing parties',[25] views put forward well ahead of the conceptual debate about the Court's private and public functions. It has rightly so also been acknowledged that Lauterpacht's view on the judicial function has been endorsed by several of the Court's judges; 'although they are but a small cross-section, they are testament to the fact that the idea retains some purchases on the bench';[26] one should add, to the present day.

6.2 *The Court's Own Perception of Its Judicial Function*

The way international judicial bodies are performing their tasks is of course in the first instance circumscribed by their statutory texts but in addition and to a rather significant extent by any judicial body's own perception of its mandate and the ICJ is no exception in that regard. The 'way in which it carries out its function is dependent upon the conceptualisation of its task'.[27]

The Court's judgments and advisory opinions are of course the first source to turn to in order to discern, to detect the ICJ's perception of its judicial function and this throughout its activities spreading over almost seven decades.

The Court's perception plays an important role in the way it carries out its judicial function, and it is basically shaped and reshaped certainly by its collegiate nature but also and quite certainly by the personal views of the individual Court members. While indeed individual 'judges may and do clearly differ in their view of the judicial function' it is also true that the ICJ 'as any single court might engage with different philosophies at different times'.[28]

Separate and dissenting opinions – voicing differences of opinion or disagreement with the Court's majority views on both procedural and substantive matters but also expressing their personal views on the Court's functions – are a regular source of challenges for the Court, although even 'at the jurisdictional or merits stage of a case, the Court does not always feel called upon to reply specifically in its decisions to arguments presented by dissenting judges; still less is this considered a

25 HERNANDEZ, *supra* note 10, at 204.

26 *Id.* at 89.

27 P.Kooijmans, *The ICJ in the 21st Century: judicial restraint, judicial activism, or proactive judicial policy*, 56 I.C.L.Q. 741, 742 (2007).

28 F.Zarbiyev, *Judicial Activism in International Law – A Conceptual Framework for Analysis*, 3 J.I.D.S. 247, 258 (2012).

requirement under the pressure of time normal in provisional measures proceedings'.[29]

'Ultimately, the outcome of many of its cases has depended on the vision which particular judges have had of the role the Court should play in the development of international law'.[30]

Addresses delivered since the early 1990's by the Court's President to the General Assembly of the United Nations and to the Sixth Committee and/ or Security Council also provide an interesting insight into the President's views on the matter. So do contributions delivered and written by judges in their extra-judicial capacity.

Skilfully using this amount of material in his 2014 monograph Gleider Hernandez has persuasively developed and applied 'a meaningful conceptual framework to understand properly the Court's understanding of the judicial function in international law'.[31] The Court's perception not only *co-determines* how the Court makes its choices but as Hernandez has aptly demonstrated is crucial in understanding *why* and *how* such choices are being made.

However, the question is whether these changes in the international and judicial landscape will allow the Court to continue its current judicial policy.

6.3 *Impact of the General Changes on the Court's Functions*

The *institutionalisation of international law* has fully left untouched the *access of* international organisations to the Court's contentious jurisdiction that is to say the Court 'remains trapped by Article 34 (1) in the notions about international law structure of the 1920s'.[32] Lauterpacht pointed out that if Article 34, – 'in important senses a judicial anach-

29 Hugh Thirlway, *Peace, Justice, and Provisional Measures* in ENHANCING THE RULE OF LAW THROUGH THE INTERNATIONAL COURT OF JUSTICE 82, note 29 (GIORGIO GAJA & JENNY GROTE STOUTENBURG eds., 2014).

30 Vera Gowlland-Debbas, *The Role of the International Court of Justice in the Development of the Contemporary Law of Treaties,* in THE DEVELOPMENT OF INTERNATIONAL LAW BY THE INTERNATIONAL COURT OF JUSTICE 26 (Christian Tams & James Sloan eds., 2013), the spectrum including Judges Alvarez, Weeramantry, Guillaume, Jennings and Higgins.

31 HERNANDEZ, *supra* note 10, at 6.

32 Sir Robert Jennings, *The International Court of Justice after Fifty Years,* 89 A.J.I.L. 493, 504 (1996).

ronism'[33] – 'is allowed to remain unaltered, the result will be that although the United Nations is entitled to bring a claim it is not entitled to do so before its own principal judicial organ even if the State concerned agrees to such a course'.[34]

The Court's role *towards* international organisations has always been characterized by the duality of protection and control.[35]

Requests for information pursuant to Article 34, 2 of the Statute have been barely made[36] and have not led to a regular supply of information, neither have international organisations shown any tendency to actively make use of the possibility provided to them under article 69, 2 of the Rules of Court or to submit their observations when their constitutive instrument or a convention adopted thereunder is in question in a case before the Court pursuant to Article 34, 3 of the Statute.

The Court's advisory jurisdiction has largely been underutilized, the responses given to the Court's opinions have been on several occasions lukewarm or sometimes rather almost non-existent.

Some minor and rather indirect impact of the institutionalisation may be detected in the recent practice and surrounding debate when the Court has to give judicial weight to intra-institutional fact-finding.[37]

The *humanisation of international law* – which in itself testifies to its 'progressive' evolution away from a purely State-centered order, requiring as it was argued in the early 1990s a complete overhaul and rethinking of all fundamental concepts, notions and principles of international law – although the 'dynamics of international relations 'had already

33 Sir Robert Jennings, *The Role of the International Court of Justice,* LVIII B.Y.I.L., 1, 58 (1997).

34 LAUTERPACHT, *supra* note 4, at 181, note 14. The same observation had also been made by Gerald Fitzmaurice in 1973 and referred to by Jennings, *supra* note 32, at 505. There is no need to elaborate on this here, see for instance the 2004 ILA Committee on Accountability of International Organisations, Final Report, annex.

35 See for instance T. Furukawa, *Dual Role of the ICJ towards International Organisations: Protection and Control,* in Mélanges offerts à Paul Reuter. Le Droit International: Unité et Diversité 293-314 (D.Bardonnet, ed., 1981).

36 For some examples see for instance Ian Scobbie, *supra* note 2, at 1085.

37 K. del Mar, *Weight of Evidence Generated through Intra-Institutional Fact-finding before the ICJ,* 2, J.I.D.S. 393-415 (2011).

back in 1974 'long surpassed the anachronistic inter-State dimension'[38] – undoubtedly poses the greatest challenge for the ICJ.

Because of its exclusive inter-state jurisdiction and the ensuing lack of *locus standi* for non-state entities in contentious proceedings there seems to be at first glance an inherent and constitutional limit to the impact of the humanisation on the ICJ's functions and its potential involvement in and contribution to that humanisation. However, the Court's docket has provided it with opportunities to *directly* touch upon, refer to, and deal with for instance the protection and violations of international human rights. Still the Court will continue to face difficulties when invited upon, called upon, compelled to by the subject-matter of the disputes, the arguments of the Parties, to address *more or less indirect* implications of this irreversible humanisation. It has to be acknowledged that not only a State's exercise of diplomatic protection or claims for respect of its state immunity are a challenge for the Court in this respect. Indeed humanisation permeates the whole of the international legal order and hence also of the Court's potential 'champ opératoire'.

The *constitutionalisation of international law* poses another major difficulty for the Court. Not only had it been unwilling to overcome its fear when the opportunity was there to conduct a judicial review – the *operational aspect of a constitutional role* – of Security Council resolutions but moreover when after its *obiter dictum* on *obligations erga omnes* its long overdue recognition of superior norms of *ius cogens* as *a matter of substantive international law* was not followed by removing the ultimate jurisdictional obstacle.

The *judicialisation of international law* has not yet had a significant impact on the Court's overall perception of its judicial functions but at least it has brought about in recent years a notable, gradually increasing tendency of the Court to embark upon a *formal judicial dialogue* through a more frequent use of cross-references to the jurisprudence of other international courts and tribunals and quasi-judicial bodies, although this had already occurred more often in separate and dissenting opinions.

38 Cançado Trindade, *Reflections on a Century of International Justice and Prospects for the Future*, in ENHANCING THE RULE OF LAW THROUGH THE INTERNATIONAL COURT OF JUSTICE, 7 (G. Gaja & J. Grote Stoutenburg, eds., 2014).

7 Finding a New Balance between the Court's *Institutional* and *Systemic* Role

Time has come first to find a new balance between the dispute-settlement function and the progressive development of international law before revisiting judicial economy.

No active participant in international adjudication nor external observer has ever seriously contested that an international judicial body when dealing with a case before it is mandated to settle the dispute as submitted and argued by the parties through its interpretation – 'the role of determining the meaning of a norm'[39] and application – 'that of attributing consequences of a norm to a given fact'[40] – of international law and in the process of doing so contributes to its development, which is 'in the long run, one of the important conditions of (its) continued successful functioning and of (its)jurisdiction'.[41]

The distinction between the Court's *institutional* role as the principal judicial organ of the UN 'whose function is to decide in accordance with international law such disputes as are submitted to it' and its *systemic* role in the development of international law as the principal judicial organ of the international community are certainly not mutually exclusive rather complementary. Whether a dispute 'is not an opportunity to set the world right on particular issues of international law' is a matter for debate; one certainly has no difficulty in agreeing that the 'Court's decisions are of course valued for their contribution to the development of international law; but that is not their *primary* function'.[42] On the other hand its dispute settlement function is important but insufficient.[43]

At present and at least for a considerable period in the past the Court clearly 'emphasizes its 'private' – or transactional – function and perhaps does not recognize expressly any systemic role for itself, at least in contentious cases',[44] whereas in contrast the Court has a 'tradition

39 M.Papadaki, *Compromissory Clauses as the Gatekeepers of the Law to be "Used" in the ICJ and the PCIJ*, 5, J.I.D.S. 560, 571 (2014).

40 *Ibidem.*

41 LAUTERPACHT, *supra* note 4, at 6-7.

42 Hugh Thirlway as cited by HERNANDEZ, *supra* note 10, at 86 (emphasis added).

43 Alvarez, *supra* note 17, at 159.

44 HERNANDEZ, *supra* note 10, at 93.

of using advisory opinions as an opportunity to elaborate and develop international law'.[45]

However, it has rightly been observed that 'the more the advisory procedure is seen as the vehicle through which the Court can indeed exert a conscious and abstract influence on the 'progressive development' of international law, the more consistently will questions arise as to the judicial propriety of the process'.[46]

In 1947 the UN General Assembly considered it of 'paramount importance that the Court should be utilized to the greatest possible extent in the progressive development of international law'.[47] This progressive development is not limited to the 'curative judicial function within a legal system'[48] but has to be assessed in light of the pre-existing international law, as *curia novit ius.*

'A judgment of the Court does not simply decide a particular dispute, but inevitably also contributes to the development of international law. Fully aware of this, the Court takes account of these two objectives in preparing and drafting its judgments'.[49] It is among other things the extent to which the Court actually takes account which is a matter for debate and to which we return shortly.

Divergent views have always been held as to the relative interaction between the two judicial functions and with regard to the *progressive nature of the development* to which a court's jurisprudence may/ has to contribute. In this latter regard it does make a major difference whether one considers the adherence to the principle of non-regression in international law as the pre-condition for the chances and perspectives of international law's *progressive* development, as the present writer does, or when one is of the view that the 'deepening understanding of (international law's) conceptual foundations and rules *ipso facto* entails

45 Judge Higgins in the *Wall Opinion* as cited by HERNANDEZ, *supra* note 10, at 119, note 163. The contribution to the progressive development by the PCIJ was more extensive than by the ICJ: Cançado Trindade, *supra* note 38, at 14.

46 Sir Franklin Berman, *The International Court of Justice as an 'Agent' of Legal Development?* in THE DEVELOPMENT OF INTERNATIONAL LAW BY THE INTERNATIONAL COURT OF JUSTICE, 16 (Tams & Sloan, eds. 2013).

47 United Nations General Assembly Resolution 171(II), A, adopted on November 14, 1947, fourth preambular paragraph.

48 HERNANDEZ, *supra* note 10, at 241.

49 THE ICJ HANDBOOK, 2014, 77 (published under the responsibility of the Registrar, available on the Court's website).

progress'.[50] Both approaches correspond to the larger conception of the exercise of the judicial function i.e. to say what the law is: *juris dicere.*

It is clear that the call for progressive development of international law by the Court does not mean that the Court should 'give judgments according to what in its opinion *should* be the rule of international law' as suggested in one of 'the early draft schemes presented to the 1920 Advisory Committee'.[51]

Hernandez has explored 'whether the Court's vision of international law rests upon a faith that law is by nature a progressive force and that the Court should actively participate in its development'.[52] That law is 'by its nature a conservative force' as argued by James Brierly[53] is nowadays seriously challenged and strongly being eroded by both the humanisation and constitutionalisation of international law. Hence, progressive development of international law has to be understood in light of these two fundamental changes of international law, which are irreversible, closely interlinked and together determine the direction for any development: they do constitute the ultimate benchmarks for any assessment of international law's progressive development, through judicial activity or otherwise.

Given the two main functions of the Court its effectiveness has to be assessed *inter alia* through the prism of a final settlement of the dispute but also in terms of norm-development.[54] Indeed, 'a court that encourages litigants to settle their disputes may receive high-marks for case-specific effectiveness but be less effective in developing international law'.[55]

Sir Robert Jennings' observation twenty years ago 'that international law may now be getting beyond the stage when one hoped for more cases before the Court simply to get the law authoritatively stated and developed'[56] may perhaps still be valid, given the constant elaboration and refinement of primary rules since 1995, but it does not detract from

50 HERNANDEZ, *supra* note 10, at 4.

51 *Id.* at 32.

52 *Id.* at 281.

53 As cited by HERNANDEZ, at 281.

54 Laurence Helfer, *The Effectiveness of International Adjudicators,* in THE OXFORD HANDBOOK OF INTERNATIONAL ADJUDICATION 466 (Cesare Romano et al. eds., 2014).

55 *Id.* at 481.

56 Jennings, *supra* note 32, at 498.

the fact that developing the law is an *inherent part* of the Court's judicial functions.[57]

Indeed, international courts and tribunals 'contribute to the making of international law by weaving a web of precedents, imbuing treaties with meaning, and generally, by establishing new reference points for legal argument. Judicial decisions frequently amount to influential arguments in later legal discourse'.[58]

Whether the Court's policy is merely 'reactive' is a question to which we turn later. Obviously it is for the parties to 'decide whether to submit a dispute to it, how that dispute will be framed and defined, and what arguments will (and will not) be presented in support of their claims. The Court's contribution to the development of the law is constrained and shaped to a greater or lesser extent by these variables, as well as by other factors, such as the relative clarity of the substantive and procedural law involved, the prevailing political climate, and the expected consequences of the Court's decision'.[59] That is certainly a correct picture of how things are but it still leaves out the inevitable judicial choices to be made by the Court as part of its judicial policy. The Court is not fully bound by the parties' submissions in developing its own legal reasoning to reach its decision responding to the submissions while respecting the principle of *non ultra petita*.[60]

---

57 An incisive and paramount judicial textbook provides 'a general account of the ICJ's influence on the development 'of international law 'in broadly defined areas' (Christian Tams and James Sloan, *General Introduction,* in THE DEVELOPMENT OF INTERNATIONAL LAW BY THE INTERNATIONAL COURT OF JUSTICE 5 (Christian Tams & James Sloan eds., 2013). We will return to several aspects of this analysis shortly. With regard to the Court's influence on private international law see most recently J. van Loon and S. De Dycker, *The Role of the International Court of Justice in the Development of Private International Law,* in ONE CENTURY PEACE PALACE, FROM PAST TO PRESENT, (Royal Dutch Society of International Law, Asser Press, 2013).

58 Cesare Romano, *Litigating international disputes: Where to?,* in LITIGATING INTERNATIONAL DISPUTES. WEIGHING THE OPTIONS 469 (Natalie Klein, ed., 2014).

59 Vaughan Lowe and Antonios Tzanakopoulos, *The Development of the Law of the Sea by the International Court of Justice* in THE DEVELOPMENT OF INTERNATIONAL LAW BY THE INTERNATIONAL COURT OF JUSTICE 179 (Christian Tams & James Sloan eds., 2013).

60 KOLB, *supra* note 3, at 923.

8 Revisiting Judicial Economy: *'There is No Need for the Court to Consider…'*

8.1 *The Policy of Judicial Economy*

Time has come to revisit the policy of judicial economy – recently identified by Judge Donoghue as one of the greatest challenges for the Court[61] – which 'belongs to the fundamental canons of international procedure' and requires international judges 'to obtain the best result in the management of a controversy with the most rational and efficient use possible of his or her powers'.[62] However, in the present writer's view it would be go too far to consider judicial economy as belonging to *fundamental interests* for whose protection 'international courts may resort to certain non-enumerated powers' i.e. inherent powers.[63] It is 'working like a benchmark or measure of rationalization for the judge's discretionary activities'.[64] It may be considered part of the inevitable accountability regime for international judicial bodies *vis-à-vis* their various constituencies.

A fine distinction can be made between judicial economy *sensu lato* which is aiming at the use of the 'resources' at the Court's disposal – bringing the Court to join proceedings[65] or allowing intervention , an institution 'intended to ensure economy of justice by avoiding repetitive litigation and contradictory judgments'[66] – indeed, the Court 'always strives to ensure that the disputes submitted to it are settled promptly,

61 Interview conducted by Sheila Ward on January 28, 2015 for the ASIL Forum (available on the ASIL website): 'When should it decline to decide difficult issues that can be avoided (e.g. by deciding a case on other grounds) and when should it make pronouncements that are not strictly necessary.'

62 Fulvio Palombino, *Judicial Economy and Limitation of the Scope of the Decision in International Adjudication*, 23 L.J.I.L. 909, 909 (2010).

63 Yuval Shany, *Jurisdiction and Admissibility*, in THE OXFORD HANDBOOK OF INTERNATIONAL ADJUDICATION 797 (Cesare Romano et al. eds., 2014).

64 Palombino, *supra* note 62, at 912.

65 *Construction of a Road in Costa Rica along the San Juan River (Nicaragua v. Costa Rica), Joinder of Proceedings, Order of 17 April 2013, I.C.J. Reports 2013*, p. 184, at p. 188, para. 18 and at p. 187, para. 12: 'consonant not only with the principle of the sound administration of justice, but also with the *need for judicial economy*'. (emphasis added).

66 Inna Uchkunova, *The Minotaur's Labyrinth: Third State Intervention before the International Court of Justice*, *13* L.P.I.C.T. 178, 179 (2014).

in order to reduce its judicial backlog, or even eliminate it entirely'[67] – and judicial economy *sensu stricto* manifesting itself in the scope of the Court's reasoning; we concentrate on judicial economy *sensu stricto*.

'Broadly, it may be said that the Court as a whole has tended to adopt the approach of judicial economy' meaning that 'if there are two lines of argument leading to the same result, (it) should adopt one or another and not follow up both' while 'individual judges have urged a more activist policy and have followed it themselves'.[68]

The judicial limitation *sensu stricto* of the scope of the decision implies 'the presence of an issue which, as a matter of logic, should be analysed before the others; if the decision as to the former is able to settle the dispute by itself' then it 'either precludes or implies a solution to the latter…'.

The judicial limitation *sensu lato* 'takes place where a judge does not wish to enter into a particular question raised in the proceeding' and decides the issue which 'enables the dispute to be settled and the resolution of that question to be precluded or implied'.[69]

In the first variant the judge 'deems that (he) does not need to address a given issue to resolve the dispute. In the second, in addition to judicial economy, there is also judicial avoidance…'. [70]

As far as the first scenario is concerned, with regard to the relationship between two or more merits issues it is well-known that the Court is 'free to base its pronouncement on the ground which is more 'direct and conclusive' as it made clear in 1957.[71]

When the relationship between two or more competence or admissibility issues has to be decided, once the question 'is decided in the light of one of the grounds raised in the trial (i.e. the one which generally is more direct and conclusive), the Court is inclined not to enter into the others'.[72]

67 Speech delivered by the Court's President Judge Tomka before the UN General Assembly October 30, 2014 (text available on the Court's website).

68 Hugh Thirlway, *Judicial Activism and the International Court of Justice,* in LIBER AMICORUM JUDGE SHIGERU ODA 90and 91 (Nisuke Anod *et al.*eds., 2002).

69 Palombino, *supra* note 62, at 913.

70 *Ibidem.*

71 *Id.* at 914 referring to the *Norwegian Loans case.*

72 *Id.* at 915.

As the 'principle of judicial economy has to be applied keeping in mind the aim of the dispute settlement system'[73] it is immediately clear that the conceptual approach to the judicial functions as mentioned earlier is of crucial importance here. Indeed, if international judges are merely dispute settlers then the 'main judicial philosophy which must guide judicial economy 'is that 'whenever a case can be decided on multiple grounds, judges must, in this account, give preference to the least disputed grounds'.[74]

As far as the second scenario is concerned the Court has made use of it several times[75] attracting the criticism of judicial avoidance, a notion to be distinguished from related concepts such as judicial activism/ judicial hesitation/ judicial restraint and judicial caution. Palombino – using a 'broad notion of judicial activism, one which includes all acts carried out by the judge in disagreement with the *petitum*' – discerns its manifestations 'not only in the case where some issues are decided using general solutions that go beyond the dispute, but also where *some issues – exactly for reasons of judicial economy – are not decided at all*'.[76]

8.2 *Relaxing the Policy of Judicial Economy*

Various reasons for the use by the Court of judicial economy in both of its variations have been put forward; time has come to reassess their continuous validity in light of the changes of the legal and judicial landscape and to *gradually* abandon the straightjacket the Court has imposed upon itself and to do so in light of the reactions by states.

Relaxing the policy of judicial economy should not be postponed any longer in order not to offend and to lose the Court's clientele; given its current docket there seems to be no real risk at the moment.

Relaxing the policy of judicial economy should not be postponed any longer either to guarantee and maintain the Court's legitimacy which after seven decades is well-established and is at present not facing any serious threats or criticism.

Relaxing the policy of judicial economy should not be postponed any longer either out of fear to endanger or jeopardize parties' compliance with the Court's judgments as the record is reasonably good.

---

73 *Id.* at 920.

74 Zarbiyev, *supra* note 28, at 257.

75 For several examples up to 2010 see Palombino, *supra* note 62, at 922-924.

76 *Id.* at 932.

Relaxing the policy of judicial economy should not be postponed any longer either out of fear for the impact on acceptance by States of the Court's jurisdiction given the fact that the optional clause system has been relatively stable for a longer period of time and there is no prospect of a sudden and drastic change in that situation, while the same goes for compromissory clauses.[77]

Relaxing the policy of judicial economy should not be postponed any longer because it maintains and extends the margin of appreciation for states in the implementation of international law due to the continuing uncertainty flowing from the resistance of the Court to deal with some controversial questions it did not consider necessary to clarify in order to settle the dispute before it.

Relaxing the policy of judicial economy should not be postponed any longer because in adapting 'certain rules to the specific circumstances of a given case in an attempt to reach a result without addressing fundamental issues (the Court) runs the risk of undermining even further the normativity of the already somewhat shaky rules…'.[78]

Relaxing the policy of judicial economy should not be postponed because third party submissions influencing judicial decision-making and judicial reasoning may indicate considerable disagreement on particular issues[79] given the relatively limited current revival of intervention and the Court's refusal to accept *amicus curiae.*

Relaxing the policy of judicial economy may have a positive impact on the external dimension of the interaction between national and international courts when the former would less be inclined to 'ground a decision on a norm that should have been followed' by the ICJ.[80]

---

77 Christian Tams, *The Continued Relevance of Compromissory Clauses as a Source of ICJ Jurisdiction,* in A WISER CENTURY? JUDICIAL DISPUTE SETTLEMENY, DISARMAMENT AND THE LAWS OF WAR 100 YEARS AFTER THE SECOND HAGUE PEACE CONFERENCE 476 (Thomas Giegerich ed., 2009).

78 Andreas Zimmermann, *The International Court of Justice and State Succession to Treaties: Avoiding Principled Answers to Questions of Principle,* in THE DEVELOPMENT OF INTERNATIONAL LAW BY THE INTERNATIONAL COURT OF JUSTICE 68 (Christian Tams & James Sloan eds., 2013).

79 Armin von Bogdandy and Ingo Venzke, *The Spell of Precedents. Lawmaking by International Courts and Tribunals,* in THE OXFORD HANDBOOK OF INTERNATIONAL ADJUDICATION 518 (Cesare Romano et al. eds., 2014).

80 André Nollkaemper, *Conversations among Courts. Domestic and International Adjudicators,* in THE OXFORD HANDBOOK OF INTERNATIONAL ADJUDICATION 536 (Cesare Romano et al. eds., 2014).

Finally the Court 'may have sound reasons not to rule on issues which are not strictly necessary for the determination of the *petitum*. One may wonder, however, whether this is the most meritorious attitude for a court which is the principal judicial organ of the international community…'.[81]

In some cases the Court has demonstrated 'une économie judiciaire qui frôle la radinerie' undoubtedly the price to be paid to obtain almost unanimity.[82]

It is clear that the Court's policy of judicial economy inevitably and substantially reduces its potential to contribute to the progressive development of international law, although this is to some extent counterbalanced by the separate and dissenting opinions attached to its judgments.

On the other hand the Court's policy of judicial economy co-determines the scope and most likely also the persuasive quality of its judicial reasoning.

9 The Scope and Persuasive Quality of Judicial Reasoning

As 'consent remains an abiding preoccupation of the Court' it is bound to colour 'many aspects of its reasoning on a wide range of questions in contentious cases'[83] and this includes the scope and persuasive quality of its judicial reasoning.

On the other hand the 'very obligation to give reasons has evolved into an 'incontrovertible' judicial power to influence international law'.[84] In this respect the 'real life of a decision should be found in the reasoning rather than in the conclusion'.[85] As trustee of the international community we expect the Court 'to give reasoned opinions that have expansive potential'.[86]

In some instances a question 'needs closer examination by the Court, so that the legal world is provided with legal reasoning rather worthier

81 Kooijmans, *supra* note 27, at 753.

82 Luigi Condorelli, *La Cour internationale de justice: 50 ans et (pour l'heure) pas une ride*, 6 E.J.I.L., 388, 389 (1995) (referring to the *Libya Chad case*).

83 HERNANDEZ, *supra* note 10, at 46 referring to Lauterpacht.

84 *Id.* at p. 101, note 40 referring to Emmanelle Jouannet.

85 *Id.* at 103 citing Judge Tanaka in the *Barcelona Traction case.*

86 Alvarez, *supra* note 17, at 167 referring to Karin Alter.

of the name'. It is clear that throughout its jurisprudence the Court 'has not so far stepped up the mark in the way it ought to'.[87]

With regard to the persuasiveness of judicial reasoning Hernandez has introduced the distinction between *rational persuasiveness* – 'able to persuade on the merits of its reasoning' and comprising 'a certain degree of discretion' – and *normative persuasiveness* – 'convincing in a manner notwithstanding the merits of the assessment itself' and confining the judge discretion.[88] The authority of a judgment combines both.[89] The persuasive quality of the Court's reasoning co-determines the so-called compliance pull for its judgments; this is important as 'the fate of pronouncements 'by the ICJ 'will depend in large part on their acceptance and recognition by other actors'.[90]

While the Court itself has recalled that 'consistency is the essence of judicial reasoning',[91] the scope of that reasoning is a different matter altogether.

Lauterpacht's passionate call for a full measure of exhaustiveness of judicial reasoning is well-known[92] and it may very well be that judges 'do not, by and large, adhere to 'his call[93] but the main question is whether the reasons underling Lauterpacht's call still hold today. It is my view that the 'compelling considerations of international justice and of development of international law' are still present today and perhaps more compelling than ever before, although they should not necessarily entail 'a *full measure of exhaustiveness*'.[94]

We do not have to dwell anymore on the consideration of the development of international law as we consider that to be an essential part of the Court's judicial functions. Suffice it to recall that if 'such reasons are 'exhaustive', in that they clarify any ambiguities and make clear the wider legal principles on which the decision is based, their contribution to the development of international law can be potent'.[95]

87 KOLB, *supra* note 3, at 427 on the Court's handling of Rwanda's reservation to Article IX of the Genocide Convention.

88 HERNANDEZ, *supra* note 10, at 183.

89 *Id.* at 185.

90 Nollkaemper, *supra* note 80, at 538.

91 HERNANDEZ, *supra* note 10, at 161 citing the *Legality of Use of Force cases.*

92 LAUTERPACHT, *supra* note 4, at 37-43.

93 HERNANDEZ, *supra* note 10, at 88.

94 LAUTERPACHT, *supra* note 4, at 37.

95 HERNANDEZ, *supra* note 10, at 124: one could not agree more.

As to considerations of international justice there is no reason to assume that States attitude have changed in a drastic way since 1958: when the case has not been successful a State is still willing to reconcile itself with that fact 'provided the defeat is accompanied by the conviction that (its) argument was considered in all its relevant aspects'. The record of compliance with the Court's judgments should not obscure the fact that the losing party may still 'not find it easy to accept it as expressive of justice – or of law – if (it) feel(s) that (its) argument was treated summarily, that it was misunderstood, or that dialectic have usurped the place of judicial reasoning'.[96] More than ever before any 'such impression, if lasting, is bound to adversely affect the cause of international justice'.[97] Separate and dissenting opinions can only marginally and for that particular case alleviate the international community's and the States' concerns.

Lauterpacht's call clearly implied a rather limited policy of judicial economy as well since procedural and substantive objections should be examined by the Court 'in all cases in which it finds it necessary to reject all of them… (and the) decision on every point adduced by the defendant State forms an essential part of the final decision'.[98]

Although it is fair to say that the Court's judicial impartiality is beyond reproach, it is from a perspective of judicial accountability not just towards the parties before it but *vis-à-vis* the international community at large still important that 'the fullest possible completeness of judicial reasoning' renders 'it practicable for everyone to know and to assess the value of the grounds of the decisions.' This 'must in itself constitute a factor of compelling cogency in discouraging any semblance of deliberate brevity'.[99]

The present writer fails to see why the reasons put forward by Lauterpacht in 1958 would have lost their persuasive power in modern times as no neutral observer would certainly have difficulty, with all due respect, to identify examples where the brevity of the Court's reasoning could easily led to the suggestion that 'it gave the impression that on account of a clerical error entire pages have been omitted in the crucial part of the Court's pronouncement'.[100]

96 LAUTERPACHT, *supra* note 4, at 39.

97 *Ibidem.*

98 *Id.* at 37.

99 *Id.* at 40.

100 *Id.* at 48, note 30 referring to Brierly's comments on the *Customs Union case.*

It is quite certain to put it mildly 'that the Court's statements of its reasons are often designed in a relatively narrow manner'.[101]

As Lauterpacht sharply observed the 'legal and moral authority of a judicial pronouncement acquires an important accession of strength if it bears the visible hallmark of comprehensive effort and of a studious avoidance of short-cuts of reasoning'.[102]

For instance with regard to the law of armed conflict there are 'a significant number of more or less controversial legal statements, some of which the Court made without much or even any legal reasoning'.[103] For instance with regard to the question 'whether the threat or use of nuclear weapons is generally unlawful by reference to 'the principles and norms of the law of armed conflict, the Court 'reaches the conclusions without the benefit of detailed analysis. An essential step in the judicial process – that of legal reasoning – has been omitted'.[104]

A pronouncement purely based on the Court's own authority without further explanation or elaboration may amount to a '*petitio principii* militating against the proper exercise of the international judicial function'.[105]

The sector-specific 'influence' of the Court on the development of international law and which has been classified as 'significant contribution' or 'targeted influence on specific issues within a broader area' and 'with a particular focus on linkages between a particular area and general international law'[106] can very well be traced back to Lauterpacht's visible hallmark.

It may be true that recent research not suggested a difference in 'influence' depending on the quality of the judicial reasoning – whether it is poorly or cogently reasoned – and that 'fullness and cogency would

101 KOLB, *supra note* 3, at 1158. For a short list of savage criticism of the Court's reasoning see *inter alia* HERNANDEZ, *supra* note 10, at 108.

102 LAUTERPACHT, *supra* note 4, at 40-41.

103 Claus Kress, *The International Court of Justice and the Law of Armed Conflicts,* in THE DEVELOPMENT OF INTERNATIONAL LAW BY THE INTERNATIONAL COURT OF JUSTICE 280 (Christian Tams & James Sloan eds., 2013).

104 *Id.,* at 283-284 citing Judge Higgins in the *Nuclear Weapons case.*

105 *Application of the Convention on the Prevention and Punishment of the Crime of Genocide (Croatia v. Serbia), I.C.J. Reports 2015,* Dissenting Opinion of Judge Cançado Trindade, para. 468.

106 Christian Tams, *The ICJ as a 'Law-Formative Agency': Summary and Synthesis,* in THE DEVELOPMENT OF INTERNATIONAL LAW BY THE INTERNATIONAL COURT OF JUSTICE 380 (Christian Tams & James Sloan eds., 2013).

seem to be too subjective to determine the long-term impact of ICJ pronouncements'[107] but that does not take care of the considerations of international justice mentioned earlier both from the perspective of litigant States and of the international community at large.

Lauterpacht has convincingly argued that 'considerations of judicial caution 'have brought the Court 'to refrain from indulging in academic disquisitions and redundant expressions of opinions on controversial matters' but these' considerations have not prevented it, in numerous cases, from examining with thoroughness the pleadings of the parties and thus fulfilling at the same time a task of an importance transcending the issue directly before it'.[108]

Both the *rational* and *normative persuasiveness* demand that 'the learning and the effort which have shaped 'the Court's decisions 'ought not merely to be assumed but must find clear expression in the content of the decision'.[109] Moreover, transparency 'in the reasoning of judgments will help them to stand up to scrutiny…'.[110]

Given the 'essentially dispute-settling, transactional character of a judgment' the *rationes decidendi* 'are already most difficult to identify in judgments'.[111] Moreover "essential" reasons 'are those on which the *dispositif* is based. They may sustain the operative part of the judgment even if this is self-standing'.[112] In contrast reasons 'are "inseparable" when the operative part of the Judgment is not self-standing and contains an express or implicit reference to these reasons'.[113]

A tendency over the last 25 years or so and which 'has become more marked as the Court's docket has expanded' is to 'settle for terse logical formalism which may or may not have weakened the overall legal reasoning but has quite often left an unreasoned gap between the terminal point of the detailed argument and the Court's final conclusions'.[114]

---

107 *Id.*, at 391.

108 LAUTERPACHT, *supra* note 4, at 61.

109 *Id.*, at 42.

110 C.Foster, *New Clothes for the Emperor? Consultation of Experts by the ICJ*, 5 J.I.D.S. 139, 161(2014).

111 HERNANDEZ, *supra* note 10, at 173.

112 *Request for Interpretation of the Judgment of 15 June 1962 in the Case concerning the* Temple of Preah Vihear (Cambodia v. Thailand) (*Cambodia v. Thailand*), *Judgment, I.C.J. Reports 2013*, p. 281, Joint Declaration of Judges Owada, Bennouna and Gaja, at pp. 320-321, paras. 1-2.

113 *Ibidem.*

114 Berman, *supra* note 46, at 11.

This tendency is regrettable as is the use by the Court of more explicit language in its reasoning, expressions which then have tendency to become less direct in the *dispositif*, as part of a policy of 'deliberate omission'[115] whereas the Court should take a bolder approach by including in its *dispositif* those pronouncements and rulings which actually do constitute part of its final decision instead of merely enclosing them in its judicial reasoning.

In its reasoning the Court may include obiter *dicta* – which 'could have been omitted without affecting the Judgement of the Court'[116] – without 'substantially' weakening the authority of 'part of a judgment'; quite to the contrary the fact of expressing 'a view on a general and controversial issue, although it (is) not strictly necessary for it to do so, adds weight to its pronouncement'.[117] An argument 'based on an *obiter dictum* does not add a new argument to settle a legal question, but restates the argument on another level of generality, and in some respects, commits the court to abide by its *obiter dicta* in future decisions'.[118]

For purposes of legal development extensive research covering a wide range of broadly-defined areas of international law does not suggest 'that a judicial pronouncement should be more likely influential if it was a *ratio decidendi* – or that merely being an *obiter dictum* would weaken it'.[119]

10 The Role of Separate and Dissenting Opinions

Generally speaking judicial and doctrinal views on the role and function of separate and dissenting opinions are not unreservedly positive.

If and when in its own perception of its judicial functions the Court feels no need 'to pronounce on all legal issues' put before it by the parties or otherwise calling for treatment as part of its judicial reasoning in

115 Christine Gray, *The International Court of Justice and the Use of Force*, in THE DEVELOPMENT OF INTERNATIONAL LAW BY THE INTERNATIONAL COURT OF JUSTICE 240 (Christian Tams & James Sloan eds., 2013) citing Judge Simma in the *DRC Uganda case*. See also *ibidem* on the *Corfu Channel case* and the *Oil Platforms case*.

116 LAUTERPACHT, *supra* note 4, at 361.

117 *Id.*, at 307.

118 HERNANDEZ, *supra* note 10, at 102.

119 Tams, *supra* note 106, at 389.

order to reach its decision, 'it seems desirable that one of the judges, at least should examine them'.[120]

Thirlway considers 'individual opinions a 'luxury' for individual judges, allowing them to point out the missed opportunities for clarification or development of the law,' a risk which the Court as a body would not be wise to take'.[121]

'A separate or dissenting opinion is in principle an indication of what its author considers ought to have been stated in the judgment'[122] and this is done 'in the hope of thus contributing to the clarification of the issues raised and to *the progressive development of international law*'.[123]

Views are divergent on the further question whether they can be assessed '*authority* qua *judicial pronouncement, or mere doctrine*?'[124]

A rather nuanced approach was taken by Lauterpacht when he wrote that 'the collective method of formulating the pronouncements of the Court provides a means of reconciling legitimate diversities of judicial outlook' while individual opinions 'greatly facilitate the fulfilment of the indirect purpose of the Court, which is to develop and clarify international law'.[125]

Separate and dissenting opinions are not just a reflection, to an extent unknown to external observers, of the debate which has been going on during the Court's deliberations on procedural questions and matters of substance. It has been authoritatively observed that 'the fact that certain ideas only appear in a separate opinion does not mean that the Court as a whole rejected them. Its significance is that the Court did not find it necessary to base its decision on them – quite different'.[126]

Those opinions also give expression to the individual judges' own perception of the Court's functions as described earlier and by the same token of course to their views on the role of international law.

They 'can influence the development of international law ... '(as they) make it possible to go deeper into the corpus of law and facts thrown

120 HERNANDEZ , *supra* note 10, at 114 citing Judge Alvarez in the *Corfu Channel case*.

121 HERNANDEZ, *supra* note 10, at 116, note 143 citing Thirlway.

122 Thirlway, *supra* note 68, at 94.

123 *Application of the Convention on the Prevention and Punishment of the Crime of Genocide (Croatia v. Serbia), I.C.J. Reports 2015*, Dissenting Opinion of Judge Cançado Trindade, para. 2 (emphasis added).

124 HERNANDEZ, *supra* note 10, at 121 and 121-123.

125 LAUTERPACHT, *supra* note 4, at 65and 66.

126 HERNANDEZ, *supra* note 10, at 97, note 12 citing Rosenne.

up by the particular case, shedding light on them, and on the outcome, from a multiplicity of angles. They can operate like marker buoys in uncharted or even hostile waters, so that the positive law can sail onwards in greater confidence'.[127] In this sense they 'can offer a sort of 'first airing' of possible new legal rules that the majority might not yet be prepared to recognize; these can contribute to the progressive development of international law'.[128]

No more should be said about the functional role of individual and dissenting opinions, a role the potential of which is largely dependent upon the degree of judicial caution/restraint or activism the Court as a collegiate body is prepared to exercise.

The International Court of Justice because of both its institutional and systemic role cannot afford to disregard the changes in the international legal and judicial landscape which have taken place in recent years. As a result the policy of judicial economy *sensu stricto* has to be gradually relaxed and the scope of its judicial reasoning has to return to some mitigated form of exhaustiveness in order to fully respond to both the considerations of international justice, as presently understood, and the need for further progressive development of international law. This should be part and parcel of a decisive move by the Court towards a more pro-active judicial policy in procedural as well as in matters of substance.

11 Judicial Policy

In a seminal article published twenty years ago Pierre-Marie Dupuy made a most useful distinction. Judicial policy *sensu stricto* '*calls attention to the general orientations which underlie the jurisprudence of the Court with some basic legal issues connected with the way the Court understands its judicial function*' whereas judicial policy *sensu lato* refers to' *the way by which the Court tends to apply international law, in order to adapt the interpretation and contents of the applicable rules to the necessities which it considers to be implied by the general evolution of the international legal order*'.[129]

127 KOLB, *supra* note 3, at 1014.

128 HERNANDEZ, *supra* note 10, at 119.

129 Pierre-Marie Dupuy, *The Judicial Policy of the International Court of Justice*, in IL RUOLO DEL GIUDICE INTERNAZIONALE NELL'EVOLUZIONE DEL DIRITTO INTERNAZIONALE E COMUNITARIO 62 (Francesco Salerno, 1995).

Judicial policy *sensu stricto* has to be placed within the context of the general debate about the Court's judicial functions and finds expression in the Court's own perception of its function as indicated earlier.

Judicial policy *sensu lato* 'deals with the way it applies international law to the cases which it has to settle' [130] and as such is related to the Court's role in the development of international law.

Judicial policy in both senses is influenced by 'elements' – some 'permanent structural data' namely the Court's institutional position within the UN and the differentiation between 'the exercise by the Court of its *jurisdiction* and the mere resolution of the dispute' – and by 'factors' – 'being of quite a temporary or changing nature, as for instance, the composition of the Court at a certain time, or the nature of the legal problems which are to be solved'.[131]

It would be a fair assessment to note that the Court's judicial policy has in a slow but decisive way , moved towards an almost exclusive settlement-of-dispute approach to the detriment of its inherent developmental role which in a now rather distant past has led to important breakthroughs in important areas of institutional and/or substantive international law. The fact and the view that the Court's 'assumption of a systematically, yet essentially *reactive* posture with regard to the current international legal order makes it a vessel ill-suited for channelling such pretensions 'as the ones put forward by Lauterpacht about the 'progressive potential judicial reasoning may have, over time,...'[132] can only be the result of the Court's deliberate judicial policy.

11.1 *Judicial Policy Has Many Faces*

The Court's judicial policy – 'oû s'enchevêtrent les percées audacieuses et les prudents coups de frein'[133] – may find expression through various forms and manifestations such as have been masterfully distinguished in an almost surgical way by Lauterpacht: judicial caution; judicial restraint; judicial hesitation and appearance of judicial indecision.[134]

Judicial caution – 'an enduring and legitimate characteristic of the judicial process' is 'an attitude of mind'[135] in itself 'not incompatible

130 *Id.*, at 63.
131 *Id.*, at 64 and 66.
132 HERNANDEZ, *supra* note 10, at 286 (emphasis added).
133 Condorelli , *supra* note 82, at 388.
134 LAUTERPACHT, *supra* note 4, Part Two, at 75-152.
135 *Id.* at 75.

with a positive contribution to the development of the law'[136] becoming *judicial restraint* when exercised to an extreme degree[137] and 'closely connected 'with 'what may be described as *judicial hesitation*'[138] which may be caused 'by the undoubted complexities of the issue'[139] before the Court. Also nowadays '*appearance of judicial indecision*' may be found in 'isolated instances in which superficial examination may create the impression of reluctance , on the part of the Court, to face a clear decision on the issue with which it was confronted'.[140] On the other hand, the *Nuclear Weapons* advisory opinion is a clear example of *deliberate judicial indecision.*

Judicial avoidance as a manifestation of judicial policy may be found in the *Nicaragua* and *DRC Uganda cases* where the Court has 'expressly chosen to avoid two divisive issues in its judgments: anticipatory self-defence and self-defence against attacks by non-state actors in the absence of state complicity in those attacks'.[141]

Admittedly one 'need not be terribly audacious to assume that the formulation of every reasonably difficult decision the Court has had to render has involved an element of *judicial diplomacy*'.[142]

The overall picture is 'that, in handling the ebb and flow of contentious cases brought before it, the ICJ has been essentially conservative. It has seen its task as being to produce a fair and objective *reasoned* solution to the particular dispute in front of it, constructed in such a way as to maximize the prospects of its judgments being complied with, rather than as being to seize the opportunity to shape or develop the law'.[143] The case-law 'reveals a court more attracted by a transactional judicial approach than by large-scheme purposes'.[144]

The Court's judicial policy consists in deciding 'the underlying issues on a case-by-case basis, be it for reasons of judicial expediency or due to lack of consensus among the members of the bench.'[145]

---

136 *Id.* at 84.
137 *Id.* at 91.
138 *Id.* at 116 (emphasis added).
139 *Id.* at 140.
140 *Id.* at 142 (emphasis added).
141 Gray, *supra* note 115, at 257.
142 Kress, *supra* note 103, at 292 (emphasis added).
143 Berman, *supra* note 46, at 11.
144 Zarbiyev, *supra* note 28, at 259.
145 Zimmermann, *supra* note 78, at 54.

Judge Kooijmans' observation, writing in an extra-judicial capacity in 2007, that judicial restraint 'seems to characterize the Court's judgments of the last 10 years' is still valid today.[146]

11.2 *Judicial Activism*

Caution, restraint and hesitation may still constitute 'a necessary and often unavoidable characteristic' of the work of the Court as observed by Lauterpacht[147] and the 'degree of sensitivity to state sovereignty is obviously bound to produce an impact upon the way the judicial function is carried out'[148] but the changes in the legal and judicial landscape and the ensuing paradigm shift with regard to the Court's judicial functions, have brought to the fore the pressing need for a *certain degree* of judicial activism, which 'can only be defined in a highly contextualized way'[149] and is a 'term of art to characterize a course of action that goes beyond the boundaries of what is deemed appropriate for the judiciary in a given context'.[150]

Among the variables co-determining the resort to and the extent of judicial activism which may be displayed, the conception of the judicial function, discussed earlier and the societal demands[151] may be considered to be rather decisive.

There is a constant interaction between the Court's *institutional role* towards the parties and its *systemic role vis-à-vis* the international community. In exercising both of its roles the Court does possess a variable but considerable judicial discretion as an inherent instrument to conduct and carry out its judicial policy. The 'degree of determinacy in the 'international legal system and 'the modern interpretive regime... leaves room for a great deal of discretion, facilitating judicial activism'.[152]

According to Thirlway 'formal judicial activism' takes place where a judge 'deals with legal issues... other than those which could suffice to constitute logical structure leading up to his ruling' in order to contribute to what the judge conceives to be the development of the law.[153]

---

146 Kooijmans, *supra* note 27, at 751.

147 LAUTERPACHT, *supra* note 3, at 142.

148 Zarbiyev, *supra* note 28, at 261.

149 *Id.* at 251.

150 *Id.* at 252.

151 *Id.* at 254-257 for an overview of those variables.

152 *Id.* at 254 and 263.

153 *Id.* at 250 citing Thirlway.

'Substantive judicial activism' on the other hand, manifests itself when the judge being 'unsatisfied with existing law or what he sees as lacunae in the existing law' decides 'to indulge in something close to open law-creation in order to base his decision.'[154] Zarbiyev rightly pointed out that the qualification of judicial activism 'is not perceived to be the same as judicial law-making.'[155]

One should also not forget that 'States can also seek to limit law-making by promoting an attitude of *judicial passivity* on the part of judges'.[156]

Clear demonstrations of judicial policy namely *judicial eagerness* are well-known and may be found for instance in the *Nicaragua* and *Oil Platforms cases* where 'it was not strictly necessary for the Court to consider (necessity and proportionality) criteria of the legality of self-defence; they were additional grounds of wrongfulness' and in the *DRC Uganda case* where 'it said that there was no need for it to inquiry into necessity and proportionality' but it still 'nevertheless observed that' certain actions 'did not seem proportionate… or necessary…'.[157]

There is room to distinguish between 'judicial activism pur sang' in order to respond to 'the legitimate needs and aspirations of the international community'[158] and a *pro-active* approach provided 'the "extras" given by the Court rest on a solid legal basis'.[159]

We will now review various ways the Court could and should conduct such a pro-active policy.

12 As Guardian of the International Community the Court Should Adopt a (More) Pro-Active Judicial Policy

The fundamental changes in the international legal land-scape provide compelling reasons for the Court to abandon its reluctance to perform its judicial functions also as guardian of the international communi-

---

154 Thirlway, *supra* note 68, at 76.

155 Zarbiyev, *supra* note 28, at 253.

156 Tom Ginsburg, *Political Constraints on International Courts,* in THE OXFORD HANDBOOK OF INTERNATIONAL ADJUDICATION 491 (Cesare Romano et al. eds., 2014) (emphasis added).

157 Gray, *supra* note 115, at 255.

158 Kooijmans, *supra* note 27, at 743 referring to Judge Weeramantry in the *Lockerbie cases.*

159 *Id.* at 750.

ty.[160] That 'content-based conceptions of international community conflict with the classical positivist view of the international legal system' [161] is hardly surprising but in the current state of the international legal order the Court's *systemic role* is self-evident.

It may be recalled that Lauterpacht has charged 'the Court with upholding the very existence and the common values of the international community, rather than acting as a mere meditator between disputing parties'.[162]

That is no to say that this more international community-oriented aspect of the Court's judicial function(s) has been completely absent in the past – traces and indications could be found in *obiter dicta* or cautiously formulated recommendations or observations concerning and addressed to non-parties to the case, states or non-state entities alike- although until now 'it has never been relied upon (by the Court) to generate even the semblance of a legal effect'.[163]

As far as the concepts of *obligations erga omnes* and *ius cogens* are concerned – which 'would constitute the vector through which the international community of *States* becomes legally effective'[164] – the case-law[165] demonstrates an evolution from the notions playing 'little to no part in the legal reasoning'[166] over setting 'clearly *erga omnes* obligations within the traditional State-centric framework'[167] to the 'belated recognition of *ius cogens* and the 'hollowing out' of the concept'[168] and its final *merely judicial* 'recognition'.[169] The *DRC Rwanda case* has amply demonstrated 'the tension within the contemporary Court as to accommodate the classical view of its judicial function with *ius cogens* norms and *erga omnes* obligations'.[170] The Court has been unwilling to draw the judicial consequences from the restructuring of the international legal order.

---

160 Terminology taken from HERNANDEZ, *supra* note 10, at 194: 'A Reluctant Guardian: The Court and the Concept of 'International Community'.

161 *Id.* at 202.

162 *Id.* at 204.

163 *Id.* at 207.

164 *Id.* at 217.

165 *Id.* at 224-236.

166 *Id.* at 225.

167 *Id.* at 227.

168 *Id.* at 229.

169 *Id.* at 230.

170 *Id.* at 231.

It may be true that no 'amendment to the Court's Statute will lead to a paradigm shift in the Court's function'[171] but its case-law has clearly demonstrated that it is essentially a matter of deliberate choice for a particular judicial policy. 'The mere process of thinking and understanding the law requires synchronizing the law with the dynamics of international life'.[172] It seems fair to say that the Court most regrettably has frequently failed to deliver.

Reviewing the Court's case law in 1958 Lauterpacht was right in pointing out that the Court was 'applying the law in a constructive spirit with its eyes on the practical necessities of international life and the efficacy of the *vincula juris* by which the governments profess to have bound themselves'.[173] Since that period the Court seems to have lost the first part of its attention and it urgently needs to reconnect with the complex realities of current international relations and international law.

Time has come for the Court, not only to 'arrogate for itself (a) central role in *sketching the contours of the notion of 'international community'*, a concept that has already resulted in the 'basic transformation of international law'[174] but to fully integrate community interests in the way it deals with questions of its jurisdiction and the admissibility of the claims, and in the manner in which it exercises its inherent powers. Those interests which in the past may have 'animated' a Court pronouncement without having constituted 'the legal justification upon which it relied'[175] should be included in the 'material part of the Court's reasoning',[176] they should affect the settlement of the dispute before it and accordingly find their proper place in the operative clauses of its judgments, instead of merely coming close 'to actually basing its judgment (although *sub silentio*...) on the enforcement of a community interest'.[177] In other words the Court has to move decisively well beyond 'any superficial communitarian sensibility... denuded of legal force'.[178]

As part of its '*governance function*' the Court has to more fully and as a matter of course take into account, when elaborating its reasoning and

171 *Id.* at 291.
172 *Id.* at 90 citing Judge Lachs.
173 LAUTERPACHT, *supra* note 3, at 282.
174 HERNANDEZ, *supra* note 10, at 237 (emphasis added).
175 *Id.* at 212.
176 *Id.* at 208.
177 *Id.* at 213.
178 *Id.* at 215 referring to Judge Higgins in the *Wall Opinion*.

taking its operative decision, a wider range of interests than just those of the parties before it.

A more proper and less ambiguous stance by the Court would certainly underscore that the cases before it cannot be seen as completely dissociated from their wider conceptual background but it would also firmly reposition the Court within the larger international legal community, the guardianship of whose interests and values is part and parcel of the Court's overall even 'constitutional' task and mandate, as it belongs to the multiple judicial institutions exercising public authority.[179]

The Court clearly 'advances a claim to normative authority'[180] but there is no reason to assume that this normative authority would in any way be jeopardized, diminished or otherwise negatively affected by the Court adopting a more pro-active judicial policy in the various matters to be reviewed shortly and this apart from the side-effect of securing 'institutional and legal space' for itself 'in a busy and competitive legal playing field'.[181]

It is perfectly plausible and easily understandable, as indicated earlier, that 'consent remains an abiding preoccupation for the Court, one that colours many aspects of its reasoning on a wide range of issues in contentious cases'[182] and that 'consent shapes the judicial reasoning of the Court'[183] but the consent-based nature of its jurisdiction cannot continue to be invoked as the ultimate justification for the Court's conservative and too formalistic approach to questions of both procedural and substantive nature and still should certainly not prevent the Court from exploring more often and in pro-active way the outer limits of that consent.

179 Armin von Bogdandy during the meeting of the ESIL Interest Group on International Courts and Tribunals at the 2014 Vienna ESIL Conference, September (on file with the author).

180 HERNANDEZ, *supra* note 10, at 192.

181 Antoine Vauchez, *Communities of International Litigators*, in THE OXFORD HANDBOOK OF INTERNATIONAL ADJUDICATION 659 (Cesare Romano et al. eds., 2014) (emphasis added).

182 HERNANDEZ, *supra* note 10, at 46, referring to Lauterpacht.

183 *Id.* at 50.

13 A More Pro-Active Judicial Policy *Sensu Stricto*

Judicial policy *sensu stricto* according to Pierre-Marie Dupuy to be found in general orientations underlying the Court's jurisprudence on basic legal issues related to the way the Court sees its judicial function[184] manifests itself mainly albeit not exclusively in the manner the Court deals with questions of jurisdiction and admissibility. Indeed , 'procedural and jurisdictional objections can often serve as a convenient way for a court to avoid adjudication on politically difficult issues 'as a mere comparison between the *Nauru and East Timor cases* aptly illustrates.[185] On the other hand, confidence 'in the jurisdictional competence of the relevant court or tribunal' is a 'critical factor in litigation strategy'.[186]

On a general level it has been observed that 'qualifying an issue as jurisdictional may imply control over the business of the court by the member states or sponsoring IGO, whereas qualifying it as one of admissibility may suggest control by the court over its docket'.[187] As far as the Court's case-law is concerned the distinction between questions of jurisdiction and admissibility is not always clear-cut.

Decisions on jurisdictional issues 'inevitably have been influenced by policy considerations. Courts hungry for cases or eager to advance a certain normative agenda may read jurisdictional powers in an expansive manner, while conservative courts whose approach to state sovereignty is deferential or those facing a heavy case load may construe their jurisdiction rather narrowly'.[188] Given the changes in the international legal land-scape the Court's 'normative agenda' should include, as argued before, the progressive development of international law while it is also clear to the present writer that for the same reason the Court's deference to state sovereignty is certainly reaching its outer limits. The Court should not anymore 'engage in an ad hoc case selection when construing general jurisdictional standards (as there) is no room... for

184 Dupuy, *supra* note 129, at 62.

185 Henry Burmeister, *Australia's experience in international litigation,* in LITIGATING INTERNATIONAL DISPUTES. WEIGHING THE OPTIONS 70 and 72 (Natalie Klein, ed., 2014).

186 MD. Saiful Karim, *Litigating law of the sea disputes using the UNCLOS dispute settlement,* in LITIGATING INTERNATIONAL DISPUTES. WEIGHING THE OPTIONS 266 (Natalie Klein, ed., 2014).

187 Shany, *supra* note 63, at 786.

188 *Id.* at 798-799.

treating differently similar cases that raise essentially identical jurisdictional problems'[189] as the criticism voiced against the judgments involving Yugoslavia (*Legality use of force*) and Serbia (*Bosnia-Herzegovina and Croatia genocide cases*) made clear.

An issue which the Court as a matter of its judicial policy *sensu stricto* has so far and on several occasions has always declined to consider is the validity of the 1928 General Act for the Pacific Settlement of International Disputes.

13.1 *The Court's Foundational Jurisdiction*

One of the reasons adduced in favour of a restrictive jurisprudence to exercise its *foundational jurisdiction* [190] through the invocation and use of the *Monetary Gold rule* is 'the growing interdependence of legal interests and of the developing multilateralism characteristic of the modern world',[191] a reason which in light of the changed international legal land-scape would evenly persuasively justify abandoning the rule in appropriate circumstances when for instance fundamental values of the international community are involved and have been protected by applicable intransgressible principles and norms.

Although the Court 'has been instrumental in elaborating the concept of treaties with a collective interest'[192] it has, until recently with regard to *erga omnes parties* failed to draw the jurisdictional consequences.

The Court should abandon when the occasion next arises 'the narrowest possible interpretation to the scope of rights of protection based on violations of obligations *erga omnes*, situating them purely within a treaty regime'[193] and to settle 'the argument that the right to claim for such violations can exist without a special written empowerment'[194] instead of 'holding consistently that whatever the nature of the substantive primary rules in issue, the applicable secondary rules on jurisdiction, remain unaffected'.[195]

On the other hand it has been rightly been pointed out as result of the Court's judgment in the *Belgium Senegal case* and given 'the large num-

---

189 Shany, *supra* note 63, at 800.

190 *Id.* at 782.

191 KOLB, *supra* note 3, at 574-575.

192 Gowlland-Debbas, *supra* note 30, at 35.

193 As the Court did in the *Belgium Senegal case:* HERNANDEZ, *supra* note 10, at 228.

194 *Ibidem.*

195 *Id.* at 229.

ber of treaties containing 'erga *omnes* obligations 'and, at the same time, containing compromissory clauses', that this case 'has thus significantly broadened the possibility of seizing the Court with a whole category of cases, namely in the field of human rights'.[196] However, the 'hesitation by states to pursue community interests and enforce compliance with obligations *erga omnes*, particularly those flowing from human rights norms, by judicial means is not specific for the ICJ'.[197]

It remains to be seen whether 'other States will follow the trend towards the invocation of 'community concerns' as such cases 'raise difficult issues not only of standing, but also of availability of remedies, of coordination between different state parties sharing an interest in treaty compliance, and ... of the relationship between the Court and treaty mechanisms',[198] the last point connected with the change of the international judicial land-scape.

13.2 *The Court's Specific Jurisdiction*

As far as its *specific jurisdiction*[199] is concerned the Court should not miss another opportunity 'to clarify one of the most doubtful concepts in the law on reservations, namely the legal configuration of the 'object and purpose' of a convention'.[200]

In several contentious cases 'directly concerning the legality of the use of force 'and in which the Court 'found that it had no jurisdiction', the 'dissenting opinions suggested that the Court could conceivably have come to a different conclusion and found jurisdiction by adopting a more radical approach'.[201] This way the Court should more properly exercise its responsibility as one of the UN's principal organs in the maintenance of international peace and security.

---

196 Andreas Zimmermann, *Between the Quest for Universality and its Limited Jurisdiction: The Role of the International Court of Justice in Enhancing the International Rule of Law,* in ENHANCING THE RULE OF LAW THROUGH THE INTERNATIONAL COURT OF JUSTICE 43 (GIORGIO GAJA & JENNY GROTE STOUTENBURG eds., 2014).

197 Bruno Simma, *Human Rights Before the International Court of Justice: Community Interest Coming to Life?,* in THE DEVELOPMENT OF INTERNATIONAL LAW BY THE INTERNATIONAL COURT OF JUSTICE 321 (Christian Tams & James Sloan eds., 2013).

198 Zimmermann, *supra* note 195, at 44.

199 Shany, *supra* note 63, at 782.

200 KOLB, *supra* note 3, at 117.

201 Gray, *supra* note 115, at 318 and a list of cases in notes 59 and 60.

Whereas it is clear that if on the one hand in several contentious cases the Court 'has not gone out of its way to assert jurisdiction in cases concerning the use of force'[202] its jurisprudence also provides us with examples of controversial assertions of jurisdiction in similar cases[203] notably *Nicaragua* and *Oil Platforms cases* where 'the Court seemed keen to pronounce on the legality of the use of force over the objections of the United States'.[204]

The fact that 'at least some States have excluded issues related to the use of force from the ambit of their declarations ... has the problematic effect of excluding litigation about a rule that forms the bedrock of international law'.[205]

As far as advisory proceedings are concerned the end result of the *Legality of Nuclear Weapons* opinion – the General Assembly having been 'deeply divided whether to ask for an opinion'[206] and States challenging the propriety of the Court replying to the request – 'may have made it less likely that states would seek advisory opinions on such general questions on the use of force in the future'.[207] A similar divisive situation presented itself with regard to the *Wall* Opinion.

The question of admissibility allows the Court 'to engage in some degree of case selection in response to (its) internal policy preferences and external expectations';[208] a re-occurrence of the CERD saga certainly should be avoided at all costs.

14 A More Pro-Active Judicial Policy *Sensu Lato*

Judicial policy *sensu lato* according to Pierre-Marie Dupuy consists in the Court's application of international law as it is oriented towards its adaptation to the necessities implied by the general evolution of the international legal order.[209]

202 *Id.* at 319.
203 *Id.* at 319-323.
204 *Id.* at 319-320.
205 Zimmermann, *supra* note 195, at 38-39.
206 Gray, *supra* note 115, at 326.
207 *Ibidem.*
208 Shany, *supra* note 63, at 780.
209 Dupuy, *supra* note 129, at 62.

'Each judgment is either a step forward or a step backward in the development of law'[210] in this first sense the Court should use the opportunity to 'defreeze' particular interpretations of a rule or principle.[211]

Whereas decisions 'given by a Court show what *in all probability* the Court will in future treat as law'[212] it is also important to recall that subject 'to the overriding principle of *res judicata*, the Court is free at any time to reconsider the substance of the law as embodied in a previous decision'.[213]

In the process of skilfully performing an almost comprehensive 'judicial impact assessment'[214] of the Court's 'influence' – 'in its widest possible connotation, one which is not synonymous with 'development' because it goes wider'[215] – on the development of substantive international law – as compared 'to other law-development processes'[216] – recent research has also and inevitably identified the Court's missed opportunities – some of which have been referred to earlier – and a large number of questions left open by the Court as result of its judicial policy of restraint, hesitation and indecision and which a more pro-active judicial policy should be able to redress and clarify.

Admittedly the Court's 'significant role in 'thickening' at least some fields and questions of international law is today beyond dispute'[217] and it has 'left its mark 'across the board' of contemporary international law'.[218] There is also certainly the possibility that 'the ICJ may be an institution that in some circumstances effectively *blocks the development of the law*, at least for a period of time'.[219] On other occasions the Court

---

210 Lachs, *supra* note 1, at 80.

211 HERNANDEZ, *supra* note 10, at 190 in contrast to the 'freezing effect' described by President Guillaume.

212 Thirlway, *supra* note 68, at 104, citing Lauterpacht (emphasis added by the present writer).

213 LAUTERPACHT, *supra* note 4, at 19.

214 Christian Tams and James Sloan, *Preface*, in THE DEVELOPMENT OF INTERNATIONAL LAW BY THE INTERNATIONAL COURT OF JUSTICE (Christian Tams & James Sloan eds., 2013).

215 Berman, *supra* note 46, at 7.

216 Tams and Sloan, *supra* note 57, at 6.

217 Von Bogdandy and Venzke, *supra* note 79, at 504.

218 Tams, *supra* note 106, at 379.

219 Lowe and Tzanakopoulos, *supra* note 59, at 177 (emphasis added).

'has usefully *opened the door for future legal developments,* but wisely without foreshadowing them in detail'.[220]

Arguably while 'still avoiding to discuss the topic of universal jurisdiction' in the *Belgium Senegal case*[221] the Court's 'commitment to formalism enabled it to avoid the risk of being forced to advance a reasoning that could be counter-productive to the process of developing a customary obligation to exercise universal jurisdiction over crimes against humanity'.[222]

The Court's role goes well beyond a 'contextual approach' – a plausible and generally justified example may be found in a delimitation case such as between Cameroon and Nigeria where the Court has avoided 'a decision on the legality on the use of force'[223] as arguably such an 'approach would make the eventual resolution of boundaries more difficult'[224] while 'adding an award of damages ... could have been harmful[225] – and stretches into 'safeguarding of the coherence of the international legal system'.[226] A more systematic use of Article 31, 3 (c) of the Vienna Convention on the Law of Treaties would be most welcome.

Furthermore, the fact that the 'occasional and adventitious nature of the ICJ's caseload has the almost automatic consequence that the Court is unlikely to be given the opportunity to revisit successively particular areas of substantive international law'[227] does not only render the range of missed opportunities the more regrettable but provides even more reason for the Court to use every single opportunity to elaborate and clarify remaining grey areas. There are of course branches of international law where cases being brought before the Court are rather unlikely to arise and hence the opportunities for a pro-active judicial policy are almost non-existent and where other actors take over such as space law, the law of natural disasters and the law on humanitarian assistance.

220 Kress, *supra* note 103, at 283 (emphasis added).

221 Jessica Almqvist, *Searching for Common Ground on Universal Jurisdiction: The Clash between Formalism and Soft Law,* 15 I.C.L.R. 437, 440. (2013).

222 *Id.* at 443.

223 Gray, *supra* note 115, at 309.

224 *Id.* at 319.

225 James Crawford, *The International Law of State Responsibility,* in THE DEVELOPMENT OF INTERNATIONAL LAW BY THE INTERNATIONAL COURT OF JUSTICE 82 (Christian Tams & James Sloan eds., 2013).

226 HERNANDEZ, *supra* note 10, at 1.

227 Berman, *supra* note 46, at 20.

A brief reference to some recently missed opportunities might suffice at this stage.

Although at some moment in time the Court arguably wished 'to avoid the controversies associated with the decolonisation process',[228] and later on the 'legal nature of the principle (self-determination) was no longer questioned',[229] it recently in *Kosovo* 'did not examine whether a right to unilaterally declare independence applied' and limited itself to mention 'widely divergent views exist' on this point and with regard to remedial secession.[230]

With regard to international environmental law the Court followed an evasive judicial policy by concentrating on procedural aspects of international obligations.

In *Gabcikovo* the Court 'effectively adopted a *procedural* approach to sustainable development' but it avoided 'debates as to its substantive content'[231] whereas 'a fuller engagement might have helped clarify the status and implications of the principle'.[232]

Whereas in *Gabcikovo* the Court 'stopped short of embracing EIA as a rule of customary international law and did not specifically mention EIA in its judgment'[233] it did derive such requirement from general international law[234] in Pulp *Mills* but it 'left open how much information states would have to provide in their transboundary EIA documentation'[235] and 'challenges remain for the effective linking of procedural and substantive obligations'.[236]

---

228 Shany, *supra* note 63, at 789 and 803.

229 Marcelo Kohen, *The Court's Contribution to Determining the Content of Fundamental Principles of International Law,* in ENHANCING THE RULE OF LAW THROUGH THE INTERNATIONAL COURT OF JUSTICE 142 (GIORGIO GAJA & JENNY GROTE STOUTENBURG eds., 2014).

230 *Id.* at 143.

231 Tim Stephens, *International environmental disputes: to sue or not to sue?, in* LITIGATING INTERNATIONAL DISPUTES. WEIGHING THE OPTIONS 298 (Natalie Klein, ed., 2014).

232 Malgosia Fitzmaurice, *The International Court of Justice and International Environmental Law,* in THE DEVELOPMENT OF INTERNATIONAL LAW BY THE INTERNATIONAL COURT OF JUSTICE 369 (Christian Tams & James Sloan eds., 2013).

233 Stephens, *supra* note 231, at 297-298.

234 Fitzmaurice, *supra* note 232, at 371.

235 *Id.* at 372.

236 Stephens, *supra* note 231, at 300.

In the *Whaling case* parties and the intervener 'addressed the principle of prevention and the precautionary principle' but the Court did not dwell upon them.[237]

14.1 *The Perspective of the Humanisation of International Law*

Although 'international law is a law primarily between States, it regulates and protects the interests of the individual, who is the ultimate unit of the law of nations as indeed of all law'.[238]

From *the perspective of the humanisation of international law* it has to be recognised that the ICJ 'despite its anachronistic inter-State mechanism of operation has been attentive to developments in the domains of the international law of human rights and of international humanitarian law'.[239]

'More recently, the contentious cases wherein the Court's concerns have *had to go* beyond the strict inter-State outlook have further increased in frequency'.[240]

Whereas in the *Burkina Faso Niger case* 'the *principle of humanity*' – which permeates the whole *corpus juris* of protection of the human person'[241] and has been properly acknowledged in the case-law of contemporary international tribunals[242] – 'seemed to have permeated the handling of the case by the ICJ',[243] in the *Lagrand* and *Avena cases* the Court did not want to examine the human rights arguments with regard to the individual entitlements under the Consular Relations Convention.[244]

In contrast in the *Diallo case* the 'ICJ has opened the entire body of international human rights law as a basis for an international claim, beyond the traditional categories of injury subject to diplomatic

237 *Application of the Convention on the Prevention and Punishment of the Crime of Genocide (Croatia v. Serbia), I.C.J. Reports 2015*, Dissenting Opinion of Judge Cançado Trindade, paras. 60 and 70.

238 LAUTERPACHT, *supra* note 4, at 32.

239 Trindade, *supra* note 38, at 26.

240 *Application of the Convention on the Prevention and Punishment of the Crime of Genocide (Croatia v. Serbia), I.C.J. Reports 2015*, Dissenting Opinion of Judge Cançado Trindade, para. 495 (emphasis added).

241 *Id.* at para. 64.

242 *Id.* at para. 77.

243 *Id.* at para. 72.

244 Simma, *supra* note 197, at 307.

protection'.[245] The 'human rights aspects rose like a phoenix from the ashes of the case' – after the 2007 judgment on preliminary objections – and the Curt did engage 'in straightforward assessments of breaches of human rights treaty provisions as such …',[246] thus making 'an important contribution to reconciling these two areas of the law in a progressive sense'.[247] However, bringing the international law of human rights within the mainstream of international law may have been done 'at the cost of curtailing the substance of international human rights law'.[248]

On the other hand, in the *Diallo case* , the Court 'missed a chance to bring into line the standard of protection of investors … with the standard now found in jurisprudence emanating from regional courts and arbitral tribunals'.[249] The Court took 'restrictive approaches both to the question of standing to bringing claims for injuries to rights of shareholders and to the question of the substance of those direct rights of shareholders'.[250]

Given the Yugoslavia-related cases, the Court's jurisprudence, until now, 'does not support a particular approach to the contested question of automatic succession to human rights'[251] as it avoided 'principled answers to questions of principle'.[252] Although the special nature of human rights treaties 'requires their continuing applicability, irrespective of the uncertainties of state succession'[253] and UN supervisory organs have expressed their 'firm support' for 'automatic succession'[254] which 'is an *imperative of humaneness*'[255] and the Court considers the Geno-

245 Ivan Shearer, *Human rights as a subject of international litigation,* in LITIGATING INTERNATIONAL DISPUTES. WEIGHING THE OPTIONS 356-357 (Natalie Klein, ed., 2014).

246 Simma, *supra* note 197, at 311.

247 *Id.* at 312.

248 *Id.* at 322.

249 Gowlland-Debbas, *supra* note 30, at 44.

250 Kate Parlett, *Diplomatic Protection and the International Court of Justice,* in THE DEVELOPMENT OF INTERNATIONAL LAW BY THE INTERNATIONAL COURT OF JUSTICE 106 (Christian Tams & James Sloan eds., 2013).

251 Zimmermann, *supra* note 78, at 63.

252 *Id.* at 53.

253 *Application of the Convention on the Prevention and Punishment of the Crime of Genocide* (*Croatia v. Serbia*), *I.C.J. Reports 2015*, Dissenting Opinion of Judge Cançado Trindade, para. 45.

254 *Id.* at para. 42.

255 *Id.* at para. 64

cide Convention to be a human rights treaty it still 'has ... to extract the legal consequences therefrom'.[256] The Court saw no need to rule on the question.[257]

In the same case the Court 'missed a prime opportunity to improve the clarity and authority of this area of international law'[258] namely what constitutes genocidal intent[259] neither did it fully nor properly canvas 'the current jurisprudential standard of genocidal intent emanating 'from international criminal tribunals.[260]

In the *German Italy case* the Court 'failed to answer the question of how immunity from suit can be reconciled with the right of the individual to access to justice',[261] a decision 'adopted by a great majority' and which 'gravely disappointed human rights circles and at the same time put concerns in Foreign Offices to rest'.[262]

As far as international humanitarian law is concerned, 'the readiness of states to voluntarily submit contentious cases of *jus in bello* to impartial third-party adjudication ranges close to zero ...'.[263] On the other hand when occasionally given the opportunity the Court considers it for instance 'not the task of the Court' to rule on the relationship between international humanitarian law and the Genocide Convention.[264]

In the *DRC Uganda case* the Court 'missed the opportunity to confirm that the protective scope of the law of armed conflicts ... extends to persons irrespective of their nationality'.[265] In the *Belgium Senegal case* the Court 'declined to deal with the question whether Senegal had

256 *Id.* at para. 29.

257 *Application of the Convention on the Prevention and Punishment of the Crime of Genocide (Croatia v. Serbia), I.C.J. Reports 2015,* Judgment, para.117.

258 *Application of the Convention on the Prevention and Punishment of the Crime of Genocide (Croatia v. Serbia), I.C.J. Reports 2015,*Separate opinion of Judge Bhandari, para. 37.

259 *Id.* at para. 6

260 *Id.* at para. 14.

261 Mohammed Bennouna, *The International Court of Justice: Bestriding Past and Present,* in ENHANCING THE RULE OF LAW THROUGH THE INTERNATIONAL COURT OF JUSTICE 153 (GIORGIO GAJA & JENNY GROTE STOUTENBURG eds., 2014.

262 Simma, *supra* note 197, at 316.

263 *Id.* at 319.

264 *Application of the Convention on the Prevention and Punishment of the Crime of Genocide (Croatia v. Serbia), I.C.J. Reports 2015,* Judgment, para. 474.

265 Kress, *supra* note 103, at 289.

violated a customary law duty to prosecute or extradite a non-national alleged to have committed a war crime in a non-international armed conflict abroad'.[266]

Turning now to advisory proceedings, in its *Nuclear Weapons Opinion* the Court 'avoided the more fundamental question whether nuclear weapons are by their nature incapable of being proportionate'.[267] Neither did the Court find it 'necessary to inquiry into the question whether certain tactical nuclear weapons existed which were sufficiently precise to limit' the risk of devastation[268] and it avoided 'the controversial question whether Additional Protocol I applies to the use of nuclear weapons' and it 'also explicitly declined to decide on the customary nature of the prohibition on recourse to reprisals under Article 51, paragraph § 6' of the Protocol.[269]

In its *Wall opinion* the Court 'took the opportunity to condemn the Israeli settlements in the occupied territories as illegal despite the fact that the question of the legality of the settlements was not directly before it'.[270] This 'is readily understandable from a legal policy perspective'.[271] The Court choose to ignore the legal issue 'whether it is legally conceivable that a (non-international) armed conflict can take place within an occupied territory'.[272] The Court failed 'to genuinely address 'the Israeli central argument of military necessity'.[273] The Court took a progressive stand on the interpretation of Common Article 1 of the Geneva Conventions but 'it refrained from elaborating too much on the precise contours of the duty of third states to act …'.[274]

14.2 *The Perspective of the Constitutionalisation of International Law*

From *the perspective of the constitutionalisation of international* law the late judicial recognition of the concept of *ius cogens* and the Court's position that 'even the character of substantive obligations' of a multilat-

---

266 *Id.* at 290.

267 Gray, *supra* note 115, at 255.

268 *Ibidem.*

269 Kress, *supra* note 103, at 289.

270 *Id.* at 287.

271 *Ibidem.*

272 *Id.* at 288.

273 *Id.* at 291.

274 *Id.* at 281.

eral convention such as the Genocide Convention 'as ius cogens could not compensate for, or replace, the lack of consent'[275] have already been mentioned.

Within a time span of less than six months in the *DRC Uganda case* the Court 'finally qualified the prohibition of the crime of genocide as a norm of *ius cogens*'[276] and it did the same in the *Belgium Senegal case* for the prohibition of torture.[277]

On the other hand in the *Germany Italy case* the Court 'merely *supposed'* a *ius cogens* nature 'for the sake of argument' with regard to 'the prohibition to kill civilians in an occupied territory, or to deport them for use as force labour'.[278]

The Court went for a 'outright rejection' of 'an exception to immunity *ratione personae* from foreign criminal jurisdiction in relation to war crimes and crimes against humanity, even where, as in relation to the grave breaches of the Geneva Conventions at issue' in the *Arrest Warrant case,* 'states parties to a treaty are obliged both to extend extraterritorial jurisdiction over a specified offence and to submit to their authorities for the purpose of prosecution or to extradite persons suspected of its commission'.[279] The Court went for an 'implicit rejection' of an exception in respect of either international crimes generally or the crime of torture pursuant to the Torture Convention to the immunity *ratione materiae* from foreign criminal proceedings of a serving or former state official' in the *Germany Italy case.*[280] Both cases reflect the Court's 'attempt to close the door to future customary developments'[281] on these controversial points.

The main problem with the above demonstrations of judicial policy *sensu lato* when they involve judicial passivity in one form or another is whether and how the Court's broad deference to the traditional law-creating processes and actors within the international community could possibly be reconciled with the Court's fundamental role as guardian of

---

275 Simma, *supra* note 197, at 309.

276 Kohen, *supra* note 229, at 149 (emphasis added).

277 *Ibidem.*

278 *Ibidem.*

279 Roger O'Keefe, *Jurisdictional Immunities,* in THE DEVELOPMENT OF INTERNATIONAL LAW BY THE INTERNATIONAL COURT OF JUSTICE 122 (Christian Tams & James Sloan eds., 2013).

280 *Id.* at 128.

281 *Id.* at 115.

the fundamental and other values of that same international community keeping in mind that not every manifestation of judicial restraint, hesitation or indecision may be interpreted as the Court's invitation to those actors 'to embark by common effort upon such modifications of the law as appear necessary'.[282]

15 Transcending the Bilateral Nature of the Disputes: Towards More Third-party Participation

The unprecedented interdependence of political, economic and legal interests in international relations and the ensuing multilateralization of inter-state relations are posing a serious challenge to the mostly bilateral nature of the disputes giving rise to proceedings before the Court.

The challenge manifests itself most prominently albeit not exclusively in the area of maritime delimitation of the Court's 'champ opératoire', where admittedly the Court takes into account the interests of third States both in the determination of the relevant area and the tripoint.

In addressing the challenge the Court should perhaps explore more often the outer limits of the impact of the consent of States even when its broad acceptance of 'applications or interventions by states 'other than injured states' might 'come as a rather unpleasant surprise to many of its clients…'.[283]

The increasing role of non-state actors is a permanent, additional complicating factor because the Court 'whose jurisdiction is based on consent' is not 'able to accommodate the voices of non-state actors, which are today important vehicles of the 'dictates of the public conscience', nor international organisations in contentious cases, despite the important place they occupy today'.[284]

On a general level the Court should take into account the 'regional' aspects of a dispute or a situation and this should be done to a larger extent and in a more consistent way than for instance in the *DRC Uganda case* and in the *Wall Opinion*.

---

282 LAUTERPACHT, *supra* note 4, at 221. Lauterpacht's proposed addition of a third paragraph to Article 38 of the Statute has to be seen in the same perspective: HERNANDEZ, *supra* note 10, at 278, note 238 reproducing the text of the proposal.

283 Simma, *supra* note 197, at 323.

284 Zimmermann, *supra* note 78, at 52.

As part of its governance function the Court 'must generally(or at least sometimes) consider the impact of (its) rulings on, states, persons, or entities not directly represented in the case before' it. [285]

The 'old bilateralist bias that permeates dispute-settlement under the procedure' before the Court 'should be surmounted.' Therefore, 'it is about time to overcome such dogmatisms of the past, with their characteristic immobilization, remnant of the old arbitral practice'.[286]

The complex phenomenon of shared responsibility has certainly exacerbated the challenges for the ICJ *vis-à-vis* third States. Indeed, 'one might say that an intervention by, evaluation of evidence regarding and indication of provisional measures against a co-responsible party are located along the spectrum of progressively increasing impact against the absent party'.[287] There is no doubt that shared responsibility 'does raise certain particular challenges and one hopes that future development will display greater sensitivity to these matters'.[288]

Third-party participation 'brings to the fore the tension between two views of the international 'judicial process: 'as a means for comprehensive conflict prevention and development of international law, and a party-driven mechanism for dispute resolution'.[289]

The tendency towards various forms and modes of third-participation as it can be found in the jurisprudence of several international judicial and quasi-judicial bodies provides the Court, in addition to the tools available pursuant to its Statute and Rules with a useful source of inspiration to face the challenge.

Third-party participation in its *direct form*, through intervention, 'is serving a personal interest in the case or in the law that emerges from the case'.[290]

---

285 Alvarez, *supra* note 17, at 171.

286 *Whaling in the Antarctic (Australia v. Japan), Declaration of Intervention of New Zealand, Order of 6 February 2013,I.C.J.Reports 2013*, p. 3, Separate opinion of Judge Cançado Trindade, at p. 38, para. 71.

287 Martins Paparinskis, *Procedural Aspects of Shared Responsibility in the International Court of Justice*, 4 J.I.D.S. 295, 306 (2013).

288 *Id.* at 318.

289 Yaël Ronen and Yael Naggan, *Third Parties*, in THE OXFORD HANDBOOK OF INTERNATIONAL ADJUDICATION 807 (Cesare Romano et al. eds., 2014).

290 *Ibidem.*

Third-party participation in its *more indirect form*, through the channel of *amicus curiae*, is rather 'participation in pursuit of public interest'.[291]

'The phenomenon of third-party participation' is 'an acknowledgment of the power of reality over formality'[292] and as such constitutes a major challenge for the Court. This was abundantly clear in the *East Timor case* where 'the East Timorese people had no *locus standi* to request intervention in the proceedings, not even to present an *amicus curiae* brief, although the crucial point under consideration was that of sovereignty over their territory'.[293] The criticism did not go unnoticed as the Court in the *Wall* and *Kosovo advisory* proceedings provided an opportunity for the non-state actors involved to participate.[294]

15.1 *Direct Third-party Participation*

'As the organ of the international community of States, the Court must concern itself with justice for that community. In this context, the interests of third States, who are member of the community have obviously to be seen in a very different light'.[295]

The 'law and practice of intervention is slowly evolving and being consolidated' although there 'are quite a number of grey areas outstanding'.[296]

The object and purpose of intervention under both Article 62 and 63 of the Statute 'was to seek to overcome the bilateralisation of the controversy at stake, thus widening dispute-settlement, when it could be of direct interest or concern to other States'.[297] As such, intervention 'has at last seen the light of the day' in 'domains of concern to the international community at large'.[298]

---

291 *Ibidem.*

292 *Id.* at 808.

293 Trindade, *supra* note 38, at 9.

294 Writing in an extra-judicial capacity President Higgins noted that it 'would have been inconceivable to exclude Palestine': Rosalyn Higgins, *Some misconceptions about the judicial settlement of international disputes,* 20 Hague Yearbook of International Law, 13, 15 (2007).

295 KOLB, *supra* note 3, at 696.

296 *Id.* at 697 and 698.

297 *Whaling in the Antarctic (Australia v. Japan), Declaration of Intervention of New Zealand, Order of 6 February 2013, I.C.J. Reports 2013,* p.3, Separate opinion of Judge Cançado Trindade, at p. 27, para. 34.

298 *Id.* at p. 37, para. 66.

Hence, this would call 'for a more proactive attitude as to the institute of intervention in international judicial proceedings'.[299]

As part of its judicial policy *sensu stricto* the Court 'sets limits to the nature of the 'legal interest qualifying for protection under Article 62. Indeed, 'the limits will be relatively wide if the jurisprudence seeks to multilateralise the process by which justice is administered, but relatively narrow if the concern is to maintain the primarily bilateral nature of the principal case'.[300] Only the first option will enable the Court to rise to the challenge of the growing multilateralization of inter-State disputes.

In this respect the *Monetary Gold* rule – which should be gradually relaxed – 'does not belong to the realm of the *prima principia*, being nothing more than a concession to State consent, within an outdated State voluntarist framework'.[301]

The question whether the Court does have 'any discretion' under Article 62 has been answered in the negative by Judge Abraham in 2011: 'there is a right to intervene under Article 62, subject to conditions the satisfaction of which the Court has to verify'[302] – a verification it has to perform with regard to Article 63 as well.[303] 'The mere possibility of the third State's legal interests to be affected is sufficient' for the request under Article 62.[304] It is clear that this approach toward intervention, if it would be taken up by the Court, would substantially reduce parties' control over the 'bilateral' nature of the proceedings.

The extent as to which a legal interest advanced by a would-be intervener is 'sufficient' as to justify intervention still has be worked out by

299 *Id.* at p. 27, para. 34 and at p. 32, para. 51.

300 KOLB, *supra* note 3, at 695.

301 *Application of the Convention on the Prevention and Punishment of the Crime of Genocide (Croatia v. Serbia), I.C.J. Reports 2015*, Dissenting Opinion of Judge Cançado Trindade, para. 519.

302 KAREL WELLENS, NEGOTIATIONS IN THE CASE LAW OF THE INTERNATIONAL COURT OF JUSTICE, 237 (2014) referring to Judge Abraham: *Territorial and Maritime Dispute (Nicaragua v. Colombia), Application by Honduras for Permission to Intervene, Judgment, I.C.J. Reports 2011*, p. 348, Dissenting Opinion by Judge Abraham, at p. 448, para. 8 and at p. 450, para. 12.

303 *Whaling in the Antarctic (Australia v. Japan), Declaration of Intervention of New Zealand, Order of 6 February 2013, I.C.J. Reports 2013*, p. 3, at p. 6, para. 8.

304 WELLENS, *supra* note 302, at 237 referring to Judge Abraham's Dissenting opinion in the 2011 judgment, at p. 455, para. 30.

the Court[305] which still refuses 'to treat an intervener's legal interest in the interpretation and application of general law as sufficient...'[306] as it considers itself too much and to exclusively as an 'agent 'for state principals'[307] A change in judicial policy appears to be long overdue. Moreover it should be noted that this function of intervention would be correspondingly reduced to the extent the Court's perception of its own function would include more significantly and as a matter of fact the contribution to the development of international law.

As a practical matter it 'would be useful if, with a view to avoiding further difficulties, the Court would in future specifically indicate' that the contents of its decision 'in so far as it relates to 'the subject-matter of the intervention is binding upon the intervener' in 'the operative part of its judgment'.[308]

With regard to Article 63 States should not be congratulated for having failed to frequently use it as they could significantly contribute to the (progressive) development of international law through providing the Court with their views on the evolutive interpretation of the treaties concerned also based on their subsequent practice as States Parties to those conventions. Such an attitude could perhaps have convinced the Court in the *CERD case* to adopt a less formalistic approach towards the conditional jurisdictional clause.

That 'States Parties to multilateral treaties are committed to contribute to their proper interpretation' is 'even more compelling when such treaties embody matters of *collective interest*, and are endowed with *collective guarantee* of the observance of the obligations contracted by the States Parties'.[309]

15.2 *Indirect Third-party Participation*

Amicus curiae participation 'demonstrates the transformation of the judicial process from bilateral to a public one' as its goal 'is to introduce public interest considerations into the decision... rather than to affect

305 KOLB, *supra* note 3, at 708.

306 *Id.* at 712.

307 Alvarez, *supra* note 17, at 161.

308 KOLB, *supra* note 3, at 720.

309 *Whaling in the Antarctic (Australia v. Japan), Declaration of Intervention of New Zealand, Order of 6 February 2013, I.C.J.Reports 2013*, p. 3, Separate opinion of Judge Cançado Trindade, at p. 33, para. 53.

the outcome of the case'.[310] This goal also explains 'the resistance by some States to the introduction of *amicus* briefs'.[311]

The fact that there 'has been practically no *amicus curiae participation* in the ICJ finds its explanation in the Court's judicial policy *sensu stricto* of reluctance 'to expand the dispute beyond the limits proscribed by the parties'.[312]

Judge Gaja has poignantly proposed that the Court 'should establish a new procedural mechanism short of intervention that would allow third States to submit information which they consider useful in order to protect their interests of a legal nature'.[313]

16 Towards a More Frequent Exercise of Inherent Powers

As any judicial body the Court has at its disposal 'certain non-enumerated powers'[314] namely its inherent powers in order to properly and fully carry out and to protect its judicial functions – which 'define which powers 'it may 'exercise as inherent powers, and where any limitations lie'[315] – as part and parcel of the proper administration of justice. The fact that those powers are explicitly referred to in the Court's constituent instruments does not remove their inherent nature.

'An international tribunal such as the ICJ has the "inherent power" to take *motu proprio* the measures necessary to secure the sound administration of justice',[316] comprising *inter alia* the equality of the Parties in the proceedings before the Court. Examining these matters in con-

310 Ronen and Naggan, *supra* note 289, at 822 and 821.

311 Natalie Klein, *Who litigates and why*, in THE OXFORD HANDBOOK OF INTERNATIONAL ADJUDICATION 589 (Cesare Romano et al. eds., 2014).

312 Ronen and Naggan, *supra* note 289, at 823. In advisory proceedings NGO's may submit a written statement or document on their own initiative but it will not be considered as part of the case file and shall be treated as publications readily available: Court's Practice Direction XII.

313 *Territorial and Maritime Dispute* (*Nicaragua v. Colombia*), *Application for Permission to Intervene, Judgment, I.C.J. Reports 2011*, p. 348, Declaration of Judge *Ad Hoc* Gaja, at pp. 417-418, para. 5.

314 Shany, *supra* note 63, at 797.

315 Brown, *supra* note 14, at 842.

316 *Construction of a Road in Costa Rica along the San Juan River* (*Nicaragua v. Costa Rica*), *Joinder of Proceedings, Order of 17 April 2013, I.C.J. Reports 2013*, p. 184, Separate opinion of Judge Cançado Trindade, at p. 195, para. 18.

sidering for instance the admissibility of intervention under Article 63 'is inherent in the judicial function of the Court as a court of justice'.[317]

The changes in the international legal and judicial landscape as described earlier will require revisiting the relationship between the ICJ and the sovereign States appearing before it and this in turn has 'an impact on the likelihood of 'the Court 'exercising powers that are not expressly conferred upon it'.[318]

Within the context of a more pro-active judicial policy *sensu stricto* the Court should – in addition to its powers under the Statute – more frequently utilise those inherent powers with regard to matters such as fact-finding and handling of evidence, the indication of provisional measures and the monitoring of parties' compliance with its orders and judgments.

16.1 *Fact-finding and Handling of Evidence*

The Court's fact-finding function is 'as essential as identifying the law'[319] and has recently been described as 'one of the Court's greatest challenges'.[320] Although 'the legal rules applicable to the fact-finding function are almost entirely judicially created' still the Court 'is often accused of being insufficiently pro-active in deploying its powers to find facts'.[321]

'In many ways, the production and management of evidence constitute the most crucial building blocks in ensuring a just and well-reasoned judicial outcome in a dispute between sovereign States'.[322]

The Court is reticent 'to fully use its powers of instruction or investigation, which exist in theory by virtue of Articles 48 to 51 of the Statute

317 *Whaling in the Antarctic (Australia v. Japan: New Zealand intervening), Order of 6 February 2013, I.C.J. Reports*, 2013, p. 3, Declaration of Judge Owada, at p. 11, para. 1.

318 Brown, *supra* note 14, at 847.

319 Alvarez, *supra* note 17, at 166.

320 John Crook, *Adjudicating armed conflict,* in LITIGATING INTERNATIONAL DISPUTES. WEIGHING THE OPTIONS 341 (Natalie Klein, ed., 2014).

321 Alvarez, *supra* note 17, at 167. When most recently parties disagreed on the number and ethnicity of disappeared persons the Court took the view that it was not for the Court 'to determine their precise number and ethnicity': *Application of the Convention on the Prevention and Punishment of the Crime of Genocide* (*Croatia v. Serbia*), *I.C.J. Reports 2015*, Judgment, para. 357.

322 Speech delivered by the Court's President Judge Tomka before the Sixth Committee of the UN General Assembly on October 31 , 2014 (text available on the Court's website).

and 61 and 62 of the Rules'.[323] The Court should abandon its policy of 'non-interventionism'.[324] Alain Pellet's position is a step further away from President Higgins' view expressed 15 years ago that there are things that 'can be *requested* of (States), but *not demanded* of them'[325] admittedly a fine line indeed.

The principle *actori incumbit probation* applies to the burden of proof and the provision of evidence but the other party has to co-operate 'in the provision of such evidence as may be in its possession that could assist the Court in resolving the dispute submitted to it'.[326]

Although 'the issue was addressed by the contending Parties' recent jurisprudential developments by other international courts and tribunals such as proceeding from 'factual presumptions and inferences' to 'the reversal of the burden of proof'[327] and inferring the genocidal intent 'on the basis of circumstantial evidence' were not taken into account by the ICJ in the recent *Croatian Genocide case*.[328]

Time has come now for the Court to abandon its reluctance 'to exercise its powers to appoint its own fact-finders'.[329] This is the more pressing given the 'absence of enforcement or subpoena powers to compel the production of evidence or secure witnesses'.[330]

In contentious cases involving armed conflict 'the primary – and perhaps only – sources of evidence available to either party may be those that the ICJ discounts'.[331] This has brought the Court 'to rely heavily on evidence developed by others…' (such as the GA, the SC or the SG of the

323 Alain Pellet, *The Anatomy of International Courts and Tribunals,* 7 L.P.I.C.T. 275, 283 (2008). On the way the Court has so far exercised the most obvious of its inherent powers see Anna Riddell, *Evidence, Fact-Finding, and Experts,* in THE OXFORD HANDBOOK OF INTERNATIONAL ADJUDICATION (Cesare Romano et al. eds., 2014): 853-855, the power to request the production of evidence; 855-856, the power to make investigations *motu proprio*, and the power to engage experts, 856-858.

324 Pellet, *supra* note 323, at 283.

325 Rosalyn Higgins, *Respecting Sovereign States and Running a Tight Courtroom,* 50 I.C.L.Q. 121, 124 (2001) (emphasis added).

326 *Application of the Convention on the Prevention and Punishment of the Crime of Genocide (Croatia v. Serbia), I.C.J. Reports 2015*, Judgment, para. 173.

327 *Id.* Dissenting opinion Judge Cançado Trindade, para. 123.

328 *Id.* paras. 123, 124 and 142.

329 Alvarez, *supra* note 17, at 161.

330 *Id.* at 168.

331 Crook, *supra* note 320, at 342.

UN) notwithstanding 'its limited ability to assess the quality of information others assemble, the collector's biases, or the integrity or accuracy of the collection process'.[332] It has been rightly observed that 'the Court should attribute *prima facie* evidentiary weight to' the qualifications made in such reports,[333] evidentiary value which 'can of course be countered by evidence to the contrary that meets a high standard of proof'.[334]

A general 'difficulty faced with any analysis of the weight attributed by the Court to items of evidence before it is the sparse reasoning provided by the Court in many cases',[335] a problem raised earlier. It is quite certain that in these as in other matters '(T)ransparency in the reasoning of judgments will help them to stand up to scrutiny…'.[336]

In advisory proceedings – without real parties and no real burden of proof – there clearly has been a positive evolution in the Court's handling of this problem. Whereas in its *Nuclear Weapons Opinion* the Court merely noted that 'it lacked the factual information' necessary for it to give a full answer to the question put to it[337] in the *Wall* and *Kosovo* proceedings the Court has interpreted Article 66, paragraph 2 of its Statute 'as giving it broad powers to seek information from those who might be in a position to provide it'.[338]

16.2 *Dealing with Technical and Scientific Evidence*

In recent cases the Court has been confronted with the growing use of *technical and scientific evidence* adduced by the parties.[339]

Although pursuant to Article 1 of the Resolution on its Internal judicial Procedure the Court had held a deliberation prior to the oral proceedings in both the *Pulp Mills case and Whaling case*, enabling it 'to

---

332 *Id.* at 343.

333 K. del Mar, *supra* note 37, at 395.

334 *Id.* at 396.

335 *Id.* at 403.

336 Foster, *supra* note 110, at 161.

337 Christopher Greenwood, *Judicial Integrity and the Advisory Jurisdiction of the International Court of Justice,* in ENHANCING THE RULE OF LAW THROUGH THE INTERNATIONAL COURT OF JUSTICE 69 (GIORGIO GAJA & JENNY GROTE STOUTENBURG eds., 2014.

338 *Id.* at 68.

339 On a more general level see the thematic issue of the Journal of International Dispute Settlement on the treatment by international courts and tribunals of scientific issues: Volume 3, issue 3 (2012).

identify any issue on which it would like further explanation or clarification' – and 'which is particularly useful in cases with a high scientific content, or where the factual background is a particularly complex one',[340] – individual judges have criticised the way the Court has been addressing this issue in the *Pulp Mills case* – where 'the Court should have appointed independent experts to assist' it.[341] In the *Whaling case* the Court held the view that it was 'not called upon to resolve matters of scientific or whaling policy' about which 'members of the international community hold divergent views'.[342]

The Court's President was of the view that the *Whaling case* proves 'that the Court can deal vast amounts of highly technical scientific evidence in a cogent and methodological fashion'.[343] In contrast some individual judges considered the Court's approach somewhat 'impressionistic'[344] and its reasoning regarding alleged violations risking to lack 'some coherence'.[345]

The more pro-active approach followed in the recent *Whaling case* has been referred to as the best way forward.[346] Indeed, the 'procedure followed in the hearings in the *Whaling case* constitutes a step ahead. It is likely to contribute to enhancing the confidence of the international community in the Court's capacity to settle disputes characterized by complex scientific questions'.[347]

'The Court is recommended to consult experts in an *individual* capacity rather than as a *group*, and to consider adopting an *interactive* con-

340 Speech delivered by the Court's President Judge Tomka before the UN General Assembly on October 30, 2014 (text available on the Court's website).

341 Foster, *supra* note 110, at 164.

342 *Whaling in the Antarctic (Australia v. Japan: New Zealand intervening), Judgment, I.C.J. Reports 2014*, para. 69.

343 Speech delivered by the Court's President Judge Tomka before the Sixth Committee of the UN General Assembly on October 31, 2014 (text available on the Court's website).

344 *Whaling in the Antarctic (Australia v. Japan: New Zealand intervening), Judgment, I.C.J. Reports 2014*, Dissenting opinion by Judge Bennouna, at p. 1.

345 *Id.* Separate opinion by judge Xue, para. 2.

346 Judge James Crawford during the interview conducted by Sheila Ward on January 28, 2015 for the ASIL Forum (available on the ASIL website).

347 Fernando Lusa Bordin, *Procedural Developments at the International Court of Justice*, 13 L.P.I.C.T. 223, 241 (2014).

sultation process (with the parties) in order to benefit more fully from their expertise'.[348]

16.3 *Towards an Autonomous Legal Regime for Provisional Measures*

The fact that Article 41 of the Statute is explicitly endowing the Court with the power to indicate provisional measures does not exclude the inherent character of that power.

A more frequent use of the Court's power to indicate provisional measures *motu proprio*, independently from a request by (one of) the parties would certainly be welcomed as an important manifestation of a more pro-active judicial policy.

Provisional measures are 'of increasing importance' in a situation where the requesting party's 'own interests were not prejudiced *per se*', but the request aims' to protect the interests of the international community' in cases concerning the preservation of rights *erga omnes*'.[349] In those situations the Court should not wait for such a request to be submitted but act motu *proprio*.

In other more traditional bilateral situations the Court may be of the view that the circumstances of the case do not require it to order provisional measures *motu proprio* notwithstanding a request to that effect by an Applicant.[350]

The 'diplomatic aspect of the Court's activities and the necessary tact to be used with the sovereign States before it, make it desirable for the Court to behave with great circumspection 'with regard to provisional measures.[351] Although the recent introduction by the Court of a 'plausibility test' may be considered an example of a small degree of a more pro-active judicial approach and also 'a marked example of a legal doctrine progressing from the separate opinion of judges into the view of the majority'[352] there is 'certainly 'room 'for the development of clearer

---

348 Foster, *supra* note 110, at 139.

349 Cameron Miles, *The Origins of the Law of Provisional Measures before International Courts and Tribunals*, 73 ZAöRV 615, 670 (2013).

350 *Certain Activities Carried out by Nicaragua in the Border Area* (*Costa Rica v. Nicaragua*)*; Construction of a Road in Costa Rica along the San Juan River* (*Nicaragua v. Costa Rica*)*, Order of 16 July 2013, Provisional Measures, I.C.J. Reports 2013*, p. 230, at p. 232, para. 7.

351 KOLB, *supra* note 3, at 632.

352 HERNANDEZ, *supra* note 10, at 58, note 107.

jurisprudence on this condition relating to the chances of success on the merits'.[353]

The *humanisation of international law* makes it necessary for the Court to 'contribute to the confirmation of an *autonomous legal regime* of those measures, beyond the traditional inter-Sate dimension, in the proper exercise of its judicial function'[354] because their object is different from that of an application, the rights to be protected 'are not necessarily the same', the obligations flowing from the measures are not the same as those on the merits, and the legal consequences of non-compliance are clearly distinct.[355] The Court 'still has before it the task of elaborating on the *legal consequences* of non-compliance…'.[356]

Admittedly over the last three decades the Court 'has gradually overcome the strictly inter-State outlook in the acknowledgment of the rights to be protected'.[357]

Moreover , the 'combination of enduring Article 60 jurisdiction and binding provisional measures' may be welcomed 'as a new-found tool whereby the Court can protect human lives and property'.[358]

---

353 KOLB, *supra* note 3, at 633. For the latest application of the plausibility test see *Questions relating to the Seizure and Detention of Certain Documents and Data (Timor-Leste v. Australia), Request for the Indication of Provisional Measures, Order of 3 March 2014, I.C.J. Reports 2014,* paras. 25, 26 and 28. One could also note in passing that the Court in a departure from its previous practice did not request a compliance report in this Order, an issue to which we will turn shortly: *Id.* para. 55.

354 Trindade, *supra* note 38, at 30.

355 *Questions relating to the Seizure and Detention of Certain Documents and Data (Timor-Leste v. Australia), Request for the Indication of Provisional Measures, Order of 3 March 2014, I.C.J. Reports 2014,* Separate opinion of Judge Cançado Trindade, paras. 60 and 70. For a contrary view see *Id.* Dissenting opinion of Judge Greenwood, para. 6.

356 *Certain Activities Carried out by Nicaragua in the Border Area (Costa Rica v. Nicaragua); Construction of a Road in Costa Rica along the San Juan River (Nicaragua v. Costa Rica), Order of 16 July 2013, Provisional Measures, I.C.J. Reports 2013,* p. 230, at p. 267, para. 70.

357 *Id.* at p. 261, para. 49.

358 *Request for Interpretation of the Judgment of 15 June 1962 in the Case concerning the* Temple of Preah Vihear (Cambodia v. Thailand) (*Cambodia v. Thailand*), *Provisional Measures, Order of 18 July 2011, I.C.J. Reports 2011,* p. 537, Dissenting Opinion of Judge Donoghue, at pp. 623-624, para. 2 as cited by Thirlway, *supra* note 29, at 85.

Binding provisional measures are limited to the parties to the case before the Court and cannot be addressed to other States or non-state entities as the Court made clear in September 1993 because they 'would not be bound by the eventual judgment to recognize and respect 'the rights the measures are aiming to preserve.[359]

Prior to its *Lagrand* decision, 'the Court might have felt more free to go, in the interests of peace, beyond the narrow confines of the rights asserted'.[360] The now binding nature of its orders containing provisional measures does not exclude that the Court may deem it wise, in its *facilitative role*, to include recommendations of such a nature and scope and addressed to the parties.

16.4 *Monitoring the Compliance with Orders and Judgments*

16.4.1 Provisional Measures

Prior to its *Lagrand* decision 'the provisional measures indicated by the Court in the past have usually not been implemented'[361] In its *LaGrand* decision the Court reaffirmed that 'its jurisdiction to decide a case' also includes 'jurisdiction to deal with submissions requesting it to declare than an order' indicating provisional measures 'has not been complied with'.[362] Indeed, the question of compliance may be considered by the Court 'in the principal proceedings, irrespective of whether or not the respondent State raised the issue by way of a counter-claim'.[363]

In proceedings for interpretation of a judgment under Article 60 of the Statute the Court has 'incidental jurisdiction to make findings about alleged breaches of the Order indicating provisional measures'.[364] Kolb's

---

359 *Application of the Convention on the Prevention and Punishment of the Crime of Genocide, Provisional Measures, Order of 13 September 1993, I.C.J. Reports 1993*, p. 325, at p. 344, para. 40.

360 Thirlway, *supra* note 29, at 83.

361 Sigheru Oda, *Provisional measures. The Practice of the International Court of Justice*, in FIFTY YEARS OF THE INTERNATIONAL COURT OF JUSTICE 555 (Vaughan Lowe & Malgosia Fitzmaurice eds., 1996).

362 *LaGrand (Germany v. United States of America), Judgment, I.C.J. Reports 2001*, p. 466, at p. 484, para. 45.

363 *Certain Activities Carried out by Nicaragua in the Border Area (Costa Rica v. Nicaragua); Construction of a Road in Costa Rica along the San Juan River (Nicaragua v. Costa Rica),Counter-Claims, Order of 18 April 2013, I.C.J. Reports 2013*, p. 200, at p. 215, para. 40.

364 *Request for Interpretation of the Judgment of 31 March 2004 in the Case concerning* Avena and Other Mexican Nationals (Mexico v. United States of America)

observation that this 'jurisprudence might operate as an incitement to States to seek the Court's aid in implementing existing judgments, using provisional measures which, in truth, are less "protective" than "executive" in nature...'[365] did materialize in the *Temple of Preah Vihear interpretation case.*

The Court should not 'encourage this practice, assuming it views it as unwelcome, because it would suck the Court into directly concerning itself with the manner in which its own judgments are implemented'.[366] One has no difficulty to agree that *(I)n principle,* that is not the Court's job under the Statute'[367] but it does not say anything about such monitoring being an inherent power of international courts and tribunals.

The Court may respond to any request for clarification of a particular Order by issuing a subsequent one *motu proprio* unless particular reasons would make it necessary to follow formal proceedings under Article 60 of the Statute.[368]

Once the Court has indicated provisional measures the Parties concerned may always request the Court to modify its Order in light of changed circumstances on the ground. A refusal to modify may be considered as 'judicial self-restraint' and if without adequate justification as an exercise of "unfortunate formalism".'[369]

Moreover, a negative reply to a request for modification of an existing order 'is without prejudice as to any finding on the merits concerning the Parties' compliance with that Order'.[370]

Although the ICJ 'has been extremely cautious in changing the rules laid down by its predecessor'[371] a pro-active judicial policy would in our

---

(Mexico v. United States of America), Judgment, I.C.J. Reports 2009, p. 3, at p. 19, para. 51 (emphasis added).

365 KOLB, *supra* note 3, at 798.

366 *Id.* at 796.

367 *Ibidem,* (emphasis added).

368 *Id.* at 786.

369 *Certain Activities Carried out by Nicaragua in the Border Area* (*Costa Rica v. Nicaragua*)*; Construction of a Road in Costa Rica along the San Juan River* (*Nicaragua v. Costa Rica*)*, Order of 16 July 2013, Provisional Measures, I.C.J. Reports 2013,* p. 230, Dissenting opinion of Judge Cançado Trindade, at p. 265, paras. 64 and 65.

370 *Certain Activities Carried out by Nicaragua in the Border Area* (*Costa Rica v. Nicaragua*)*; Construction of a Road in Costa Rica along the San Juan River* (*Nicaragua v. Costa Rica*)*, Order of 16 July 2013, Provisional Measures, I.C.J. Reports 2013,* p. 230, at p. 240, para. 39.

371 ICJ YEARBOOK, *supra* note 49, at 49.

view require bringing back to life Article 61, paragraph 7 of the 1946 Rules of Court allowing the Court to modify *motu proprio* existing Orders. By the same token the consistency within an emerging autonomous legal regime of provisional measures would be restored as under Article 75 of the Rules the Court has the power to order *motu proprio* such measures. The fact that the Court has so far never used this power does not change the argument.

With regard to *assurances given* by one of the parties concerning conduct which may be covered by provisional measures, the Court confirms its *jurisprudence constante* at a general level that once a State has made a commitment to act in a particular way or to abstain from a particular action, it is not for the Court to speculate about future conduct as a State's good faith always has to be presumed.[372] The Court has seen no reason to depart from this policy of deference once assurances are being given during oral proceedings at the provisional measures stage.

Clearly the Court 'disclosed its unwillingness to learn lessons to be extracted from its own experience in recent cases'.[373] As a matter of judicial policy the Court, while *taking note* of such assurances should not take such a promise 'at its face value' nor 'take such 'unilateral acts 'as the basis for the reasoning of its own decisions'.[374] The Court should, in such situations, as it did, indeed order its own provisional measures partly independently from a request by the other party.[375]

In case of failure to comply with provisional measures the Court can 'declare , in an operative part of a decision, that the State concerned is responsible for the failure.' but it 'cannot *sanction* non-compliance... either at a *procedural or at a substantive level*'.[376] In the Temple *of Preah Vihear interpretation case* it 'was not argued, as it had been 'in *Avena II* 'that there had been breaches of the order and that the Court should sanction

---

372 *Questions relating to the Seizure and Detention of Certain Documents and Data (Timor-Leste v. Australia), Request for the Indication of Provisional Measures, Order of 3 March 2014, I.C.J. Reports 2014*, para. 44.

373 *Questions relating to the Seizure and Detention of Certain Documents and Data (Timor-Leste v. Australia), Request for the Indication of Provisional Measures, Order of 3 March 2014, I.C.J. Reports 2014*, Separate opinion of Judge Cançado Trindade, para. 17.

374 *Id.* at paras. 56, 22 and 58.

375 For a contrary view see the dissenting opinion of Judge Greenwood, at para. 28.

376 KOLB, *supra* note 3, at 848 (emphasis added).

these in its judgment'.[377] In fact the Court 'has never made a Separate Order consequential upon a breach of a Provisional Measure'.[378]

However, when the question of compensation for the injury caused by the breach of an Order merges with the question of compensation for the injury suffered from the violation of corresponding treaty obligations, the Court 'does not therefore find it appropriate to give effect' to a request for 'an order for symbolic compensation.' The Court will then include in its operative clause 'by way of satisfaction, a declaration' of failure to comply with the Order.[379]

In case of non-compliance recourse by any of the parties to the Security Council pursuant to Article 41, paragraph 2 of the Statute could provide a possible additional avenue.[380]

In case of compliance it is worth considering that the Court could mention this in the operative part of its judgment. Alternatively there' is no reason why a State that is complying in good faith should not allow the Court to publish' compliance reports on its website[381] which as a matter of course are communicated to the Court.[382] This implies that the Court remains seized of the matters which form the subject of the Order although occasionally the Court may feel the need to explicitly state this.[383] The Court seems to consider the monitoring of compliance as belonging to is inherent powers to be exercised *ex office,* thus irrespective of arguments or request having been put forward by a party.

---

377 Thirlway, *supra* note 29, at 84.

378 KOLB, *supra* note 3, at 649.

379 *Application of the Convention on the Prevention and Punishment of the Crime of Genocide (Bosnia and Herzegovina v. Serbia and Montenegro), Judgment, I.C.J. Reports 2007,* p. 43, at p. 236, para. 469.

380 KOLB, *supra* note 3, at 848.

381 E. Leonhardsen, *Trials of Ordeal in the International Court of Justice. Why States Seek Provisional Measures when non-Compliance Is to be Expected,* 5 Journal of International Dispute Settlement 343 (2014).

382 *Certain Activities Carried out by Nicaragua in the Border Area* (*Costa Rica v. Nicaragua*), *Provisional Measures, Order of 8 March 2011, I.CJ. Reports 2011,* p. 6, at p. 28, para. 86 (4).

383 *Request for Interpretation of the Judgment of 15 June 1962 in the Case concerning the* Temple of Preah Vihear (Cambodia v. Thailand) (*Cambodia v. Thailand*), *Provisional Measures, Order of 18 July 2011, I.C.J.Reports 2011,* p. 537, at p. 556, para. 69 (C).

16.4.2 Judgments

In terms of the protection of its judicial functions it is rather difficult to understand why the Court has the possibility 'at any time to require previous compliance with the terms of the judgment the revision of which is sought, before it admits proceedings in revision'[384] – under Article 61, paragraph 3 of the Statute and Article 99, paragraph 5 of the Rules of Court – clearly reflecting an inherent interest of the Court in such compliance , and why such an interest cannot be accepted and put into operation with regard to *any* judgment. Moreover, the Court has never applied that provision upon request nor *motu proprio,*[385] the last option certainly being a manifestation of a pro-active judicial policy.

With regard to the remedial aspect of the Court's dispute settlement function[386] its policy may be characterized as too deferential both in 'cases where the Court avoided damages despite findings of responsibility'[387] as with regard to assurances and guarantees provided by (one of) the parties. 'Increasingly, the Court has done everything to avoid not requiring assurances'.[388]

A more pro-active judicial policy instead of judicial passivity would be most welcome, as judicial deference at the expense of proper performance of its judicial functions can seriously jeopardize the implementation of its decisions.

International courts and tribunals have 'recognized that they possess inherent powers which relate to the post-adjudication phase, such as the power of rectification, interpretation and revision'[389] why then do these inherent powers not stretch into compliance with judgments? In 1957 Lauterpacht, commenting on the *Monetary Gold case,* raised 'the interesting question, which was not considered by the Court, to what extent

384 *Application for Revision of the Judgment of 11 September 1992 in the Case concerning the* Land, Island and Maritime Frontier Dispute (El Salvador/Honduras: Nicaragua intervening) *(El Salvador v. Honduras), Judgment, I.C.J. Reports 2003,* p. 392, at p. 399, para. 22.

385 KOLB, *supra* note 3, at 822.

386 For a recent overview of remedies by the ICJ see *inter alia* Christine Gray, *Remedies* in THE OXFORD HANDBOOK OF INTERNATIONAL ADJUDICATION 873-883(Cesare Romano et al. eds., 2014).

387 Crawford, *supra* note 225, at 72, note 4.

388 *Id.* at 82.

389 Brown, *supra* note 14, at 837.

a State which has failed to comply with a previous judgment of the Court can appear before it by consent'.[390]

There can be no doubt that 'faithful compliance with, or execution, of their judgments is a *legitimate concern* of all contemporary international tribunals'.[391] There is no reason to assume that the situation would be different for the ICJ. It is equally true that 'each international tribunal counts on a mechanism of its own; yet all of them are susceptible of improvement'.[392]

An international court such as the IACtHR 'has interpreted its mandate to allow it to remain seized of a case until it deems there is compliance and to demand states to report on their efforts toward compliance'.[393] Of course the IACtHR operates in a completely different framework as constitutional court of a regional human rights regime but it is still a manifestation of pro-active judicial policy.

The move by the IACtHR 'to incorporate compliance hearings in which judges act as mediators'[394] could find its place in a different format such as post-adjudicative meetings with the President, representing the Court 'more as an administrative organ, for its judicial function is limited to declaring the law between the parties'.[395]

Whether 'the Court is not in some way responsible for the good sense and practical effects of its pronouncements' is a reasonable question to ask. 'The principle of the good and proper administration of justice, and value of precedent, may be seen as compelling reasons for the Court to take these matters' such as the effect in domestic and regional legal orders into account.[396]

The fact that the Court in the *Avena II case* 'made it clear that it did not see a particular role for itself in supervising (non)implementation of its judgments by national courts'[397] is a manifestation of the ultimate judicial deference towards the parties as far as the post-adjudicative phase

390 LAUTERPACHT, *supra* note 4, at 343, note 21.

391 Trindade, *supra* note 38, at 32 (emphasis added).

392 Trindade, *supra* note 38, at 30-31.

393 Alexaandra Huneeus, *Compliance with Judgments and Decisions*, in THE OXFORD HANDBOOK OF INTERNATIONAL ADJUDICATION 451 (Cesare Romano et al. eds., 2014).

394 *Id.* at 452.

395 SHABTAI ROSENNE, THE LAW AND PRACTICE OF THE INTERNATIONAL COURT OF JUSTICE 1920-2005, 198 (2006).

396 KOLB, *supra* note 3, at 431.

397 Alvarez, *supra* note 17, at 545.

is concerned. However, it does not have to be the final word on this question and it certainly does not necessarily mean the end to any prospect of a pro-active judicial policy.

Looking at the *Namibia* and *Wall Opinions* the Court could have followed a more pro-active judicial policy *sensu lato*, instead of the large degree of deference, by elaborating in more detail the legal consequences for the State concerned, as well as for the non-state actors and the UN organs involved flowing from its judicial assessment of the illegality at hand, whereas in its *Nuclear Weapons Opinion* the Court could have indeed while noting divergent views on particular issues, have given the international community clearer signals to work on them. On the other hand , whether the Court in its *Kosovo Opinion* 'by denying any legal effect to that resolution (1244), thus resolving a situation that had been left open by the Council' may have embarked 'upon the beginning of a break with the Court's heretofore deferential posture towards the principal organs'[398] remains indeed to be seen.

17 Final Observations

It may be fairly said that the Court should more duly take into account the background of the disputes submitted to it in addition to a closer examination of the facts. Indeed, there is a growing feeling that the Court is not really paying due attention to the history of the disputes as has been observed by Judge Kooijmans in the *Wall opinion* and most recently by Judge Trindade in the *Croatian Genocide case* where 'both contending Parties dwelt upon the issue in their arguments before the Court, and *expected* the Court to address it'[399] but where the Court 'flatly dismissed an examination of the historical origins of the onslaught in the Balkans'.[400]

---

398 James Sloan and Gleider Hernandez, *The Role of the International Court of Justice in the Development of the Institutional Law of the United Nations*, in THE DEVELOPMENT OF INTERNATIONAL LAW BY THE INTERNATIONAL COURT OF JUSTICE 232 (Christian Tams & James Sloan eds., 2013).

399 *Application of the Convention on the Prevention and Punishment of the Crime of Genocide (Croatia v. Serbia), I.C.J. Reports 2015*, Dissenting of Judge Cançado Trindade, para. 349 (emphasis added).

400 *Id.* at para. 348.

'In the interpretation – or even in the search – of the applicable law, there is space for judicial creativity: each international tribunal is free to find the applicable law, independently of the arguments of the contending parties (*jura novit curia*)'.[401]

Pursuant to Article 49 of the Statute the Court may 'even before the hearing begins, call upon the agents… to supply any explanations. Formal note shall be taken of any refusal.'

The Court has the right, prior to the written or oral pleadings, to identify in an order issues to be dealt with by the parties during the early stage of the proceedings.

It 'must always be open to the Court to order a second round of written pleadings if the Court decides that this is necessary, for example because the Court considers it does not have sufficient information on a particular matter'.[402]

Moreover questions from the Bench could also be instrumental in this regard.

Conversely it has been proposed that if the Court 'after all decides on the basis of a reason of its own, that reason should have been brought to the attention of the parties who should have had the opportunity arguing the point if they wished to do so'.[403]

On the other hand ignoring several of the parties' arguments might amount to a violation of the principle of fairness of the proceedings and the handling of a case as component elements of good administration of justice.

That the change of judicial policy 'might only strengthen (States') general reluctance to litigate'[404] seems rather unlikely to the present writer.

One major challenge for the Court in the years to come certainly is a proper and thorough reassessment of the scope and use of its various judicial functions, – as 'settling disputes has just become one of the several functions that international adjudication fulfils'[405] – more in particu-

401 Trindade, *supra* note 38, at 18.

402 *Whaling in the Antarctic (Australia v. Japan: New Zealand intervening), Judgment, I.C.J. Reports 2014*, Separate opinion of Judge Greenwood, para. 34 and *Maritime Dispute (Peru v. Chile), Judgment, I.C.J. Reports 2014*, Declaration of Judge Donoghue.

403 Jennings, *supra* note 33, at 43.

404 Scobbie, *supra* note 2, at 1087.

405 Romano, Alter and Shany, *Mapping International Adjudicative Bodies, The Issues, and Players*, in THE OXFORD HANDBOOK OF INTERNATIONAL ADJUDICATION 6 (Cesare Romano et al. eds., 2014).

lar its role as guardian of the fundamental values of the international community, in light of the changed international legal and judicial landscape. The Court has to interpret its own Statute and Rules by reference to the concept of 'institutional effectiveness',[406] an effectiveness, that 'would embrace 'the larger needs of the international community',[407] an international community in which the Court should be more clearly embedded.

Unless the Court consciously would like to take the risk of becoming increasingly marginalised and irrelevant – 'd'entrer dans une phase de vieillissement rapide' – the Court should take its future in its hands – 'par des choix appropriés de politique judiciaire'.[408]

As an expression of the Court's accountability to the public – 'through a pro-active policy of neutral communication on the work of the Court'[409] – and to increase its embeddedness in the international community regular statements made by the President to the media after the delivery of a judgment or the rendering of an advisory opinion would certainly be welcomed.[410]

'We can study when international judges become activists, and when they remain conservative legal formalists'.[411] 'The field of judicial behaviour studies *why* judges make the choices they make' and 'examines the factors that (co-)determine how judges use' their discretion'.[412]

---

406 Gowlland-Debbas, *supra* note 30, at 40.

407 Alvarez, *supra* note 17, at 164 citing Lauterpacht.

408 Condorelli, *supra* note 82, at 399, writing on the occasion of the Court's 50th anniversary.

409 Mahoney, *supra* note 21, at 346.

410 President Higgins did so after the judgments in the *Bosnian Genocide case* and the *Pulp Mills case* : Stéphanie Cartier and Cristina Hoss, *The Role of Registries and Legal Secretariats in International Judicial Institutions,* in THE OXFORD HANDBOOK OF INTERNATIONAL ADJUDICATION 719, note 21 (Cesare Romano et al. eds., 2014).

411 Karen Alter, *The Multiplication of International Courts and Tribunals after the End of the Cold War,* in THE OXFORD HANDBOOK OF INTERNATIONAL ADJUDICATION 88 (Cesare Romano et al. eds., 2014).

412 Erik Voeten, *International Judicial Behaviour,* in THE OXFORD HANDBOOK OF INTERNATIONAL ADJUDICATION 550 and 551 (Cesare Romano et al. eds., 2014).

'Judicial law acts precisely as modulator of morality into the legal order: it transposes and specifies moral principles or moral values in an institutional context by making normative choices'.[413]

Because 'the importance of the interests at stake' – those of the parties, of third States, of non-state actors, of the individual as ultimate beneficiary of international law, and of the international community at large – the Court should not put 'excessive or decisive reliance upon formal or technical rules'.[414]

The humanisation and constitutionalisation of international law reflect 'hierarchies of value or systems of prioritisation that would suggest when one of the main (judicial) functions should give to another'.[415]

The Court's belief 'in the need to sustain the welfare of the international legal system as a whole'[416] continues to be part and parcel of its general background in developing its judicial reasoning and reaching a decision.

The Court's role as principal judicial organ of the UN is of 'systemic importance (also) because of the possibility of its judgments being enforced by the UN Security Council'.[417]

'Since time and again, the ICJ has proven to be impervious to reform – bar a few cosmetic retouches – it is, and will remain, a forum where states can now and then turn to for the settlement of certain kinds of disputes'.[418] This may be so, but even 'if the *mechanism* of dispute-settlement by the ICJ remains strictly or exclusively inter-State, the *substance* of those disputes or issues brought before the Court pertains also to the human person'.[419] It cannot be denied that 'the strictly inter-State outlook has an ideological content, is a product of its time, a time long past 'although in its most recent decisions, 'the ICJ has at times rightly endeavoured to overcome that outlook…'.[420]

413 Samantha Besson, *Legal Philosophical Issues of International Adjudication,* in THE OXFORD HANDBOOK OF INTERNATIONAL ADJUDICATION 426 (Cesare Romano et al. eds., 2014).

414 LAUTERPACHT, *supra* note 4, at 366.

415 Alvarez, *supra* note 17, at 168.

416 Shany, *supra* note 63, at 798.

417 Shirley Scott, *Litigation versus dispute resolution though political processes,* in LITIGATING INTERNATIONAL DISPUTES. WEIGHING THE OPTIONS 28 (Natalie Klein, ed., 2014).

418 Romano, *supra* note 58, at 464.

419 Trindade, *supra* note 38, at 10 (first emphasis added).

420 *Ibidem.*

States apparently have no difficulty or hesitation to accept or to utilise international litigation by other international judicial and quasi-judicial bodies, which they have endowed with specialist and/ or regional jurisdiction, and which have chosen to follow a pro-active judicial policy. There is no real, compelling reason to expect that States will turn away from the ICJ if it would take a similar pro-active course of action. In fact and in retrospect the 1966 judgment is a clear indication that 'judicial passivity' may exactly produce that kind of effect.

States will continue to provide the opportunity to the Court to develop international law in the process of settling disputes before it. For instance 'Latin American States remain faithful clients of the Court and have largely given it the opportunity to further clarify and *develop* the law of the sea and related aspects such as maritime delimitation'.[421]

The overall picture of the Court's performance of its judicial functions over the last seven decades of its existence shows a clear lack of pro-active judicial policy with regard to matters of both procedure and substance, but to qualify it as pure stagnation[422] seems to be rather unfair, although it is equally clear that 'formalism continues to inform the role of the Court'[423] and its approach might be characterized' for good and for bad' as 'benign conservatism'.[424]

We hope to have demonstrated that the fundamental changes of the international legal and judicial landscape require the Court to return to its judicial functions as originally envisaged and to follow a (more) pro-active judicial policy *sensu stricto* and *sensu lato.*

It is our role as members of the 'epistemic community of international lawyers'[425] to continue critically observing the Court's performance.

The judicial and doctrinal debate about the role of the Court in the constantly changing contemporary world will of course continue, and

421 Speech delivered by the Court's President Judge Tomka before the International Law Commission July 27, 2014 (text available on the Court's website) (emphasis added).

422 Mark Pollack, *Political Science and International Adjudication,* in THE OXFORD HANDBOOK OF INTERNATIONAL ADJUDICATION 379 (Cesare Romano et al. eds., 2014).

423 Rusell Buchan and Duncan French, *Introduction. The International Court and Restatement of Fundamental Principles,* 15 International community Law Review 411, 412 (2013).

424 Andreas Zimmermann, *Business as Usual? The ICJ's 2012 Judicial Practice: Facing New Procedural and Jurisdictional Questions,* 4 JIDS, 521, 537 (2013).

425 HERNANDEZ, *supra* note 10, at 137.

its 70th anniversary certainly provides an opportunity to reflect on the Court's long-term future, but the Court is and always will be 'the guardian of the legality for the international community as a whole, both within and without the United Nations'.[426]

15 April 2015

426 *Questions of Interpretation and Application of the 1971 Montreal Convention arising from the Aerial Incident at Lockerbie (Libyan Arab Jamahiriya v. United States of America), Provisional Measures, Order of 14 April 1992, I.C.J. Reports 1992*, p. 114, Separate Opinion of Judge Lachs at p. 138.

www.ingramcontent.com/pod-product-compliance
Lightning Source LLC
Chambersburg PA
CBHW061608180926
51615CB00006B/23
9789004271678